# OXFORD ENGLISH MONOGRAPHS

*General Editors*

NORMAN DAVIS      HELEN GARDNER

ALICE WALKER

# OXFORD ENGLISH MONOGRAPHS

Fulke Greville, Lord Brooke

# THE REMAINS

## BEING POEMS OF MONARCHY AND RELIGION

EDITED BY

G. A. WILKES

OXFORD UNIVERSITY PRESS

1965

*Oxford University Press, Amen House, London E.C.4*

GLASGOW  NEW YORK  TORONTO  MELBOURNE  WELLINGTON
BOMBAY  CALCUTTA  MADRAS  KARACHI  LAHORE  DACCA
CAPE TOWN  SALISBURY  NAIROBI  IBADAN  ACCRA
KUALA LUMPUR  HONG KONG

TO
MY FATHER AND
MOTHER

# PREFACE

THE purpose of this edition is to make available those poems of Greville's which cannot be read at present, unless one has access to the first edition of 1670, or to the text of Grosart (Fuller Worthies' Library, 4 vols., 1870). *A Treatise of Religion* had been meant to appear in the posthumous collection of Greville's poems, the *Certaine Learned and Elegant Workes* of 1633. But it was suppressed after the printing had begun, and in all known copies of the 1633 folio the text begins at page 23. The poem was eventually published as part of *The Remains of Sir Fulk Grevill Lord Brooke* (1670), sharing the volume with *A Treatise of Monarchy*. This treatise was the occasion of Richard Baxter's complaint in 1681, that 'Sir *Fulk Grevil*... hath a Poem lately Printed for Subjects Liberty, which I greatly wonder this Age would bear.'[1]

The most comprehensive modern edition of Greville, Geoffrey Bullough's *Poems and Dramas* (2 vols., Edinburgh, 1939), contains all the verse published in the 1633 folio. The present volume, containing all the verse excluded from it, makes the whole of Greville's poetry available in a critical edition. It is the first edition to be based on the Warwick MSS., which, for *A Treatise of Monarchy* and *A Treatise of Religion* at least, offer a superior text. The Warwick MSS. were not available to Grosart when he began his edition of Greville, though they had come to hand in time to be hastily and erratically collated in his fourth volume. The only other nineteenth-century editor of Greville—Robert Southey, as compiler of *Select Works of the British Poets* (1831)—had reprinted the 1670 text.

I am grateful to the Earl of Warwick for permission to use the manuscripts in his keeping, and to his agents, H. G. Godfrey-Payton & Son, and the officers of the Warwick County Record

---

[1] 'The Epistle to the Reader', in *Poetical Fragments* (1681).

Office (especially Mr. Colin Hughes) for assistance given. This edition of *The Remains* was first envisaged at Oxford in 1953–5, pursued subsequently at Sydney with help from the University research fund, and brought almost to completion during a sabbatical year spent in the United States in 1961 through the generosity of the Huntington Library, California and the Folger Shakespeare Library, Washington. I am indebted to those who have suggested corrections and modifications in the typescript, especially the late Professor F. P. Wilson and Miss Helen Gardner; the responsibility for any shortcomings that remain I reserve to myself.

G. A. W.

*University of Sydney*
*October 1964*

# CONTENTS

# REFERENCES AND ABBREVIATIONS

The following abbreviations and cue-titles have been adopted:

Bullough      *Poems and Dramas of Fulke Greville, First Lord Brooke*, ed. Geoffrey Bullough (2 vols., Edinburgh, 1939).

*Cal. S.P. Dom.*      *Calendar of State Papers Domestic.*

*DNB*      *Dictionary of National Biography.*

Grosart      *The Works in Verse and Prose Complete of . . . Fulke Greville, Lord Brooke*, ed. A. B. Grosart (Fuller Worthies' Library, 4 vols., 1870).

*Hist. MSS.*      *Reports of the Historical Manuscripts Commission.*

*HLQ*      *The Huntington Library Quarterly.*

*Life*      *Sir Fulke Greville's Life of Sir Philip Sidney*, ed. Nowell Smith (Tudor & Stuart Library, 1907).

*MLR*      *The Modern Language Review.*

*SP*      *Studies in Philology.*

# GENERAL INTRODUCTION

FULKE GREVILLE is still one of the more remote of the Elizabethans. Known as the friend and biographer of Sidney, he sometimes figures in discussions of the Elizabethan sonnet as the author of the *Caelica* series; from his less familiar Senecan plays, and his treatises, he has acquired a vague repute as a penetrating, inscrutable thinker; he is claimed from time to time as a neglected metaphysical. Greville's verse, whatever the problems of its interpretation, falls into three main divisions —lyrical, dramatic, and discursive—which correspond broadly to the stages of his development. The best way of introducing *A Treatise of Monarchy* and *A Treatise of Religion* is to show the place they occupy in Greville's poetry as a whole.

The claim on the title-page of the 1633 edition of his works, that they had been 'Written in his Youth, and familiar Exercise with *Sir Philip Sidney*', is probably true of only the earlier sonnets in *Caelica*. Greville (b. 1554) came of an old Warwickshire family, was educated with Sidney at Shrewsbury School, and entered Jesus College, Cambridge, in 1568. Sharing Sidney's ambition to distinguish himself in the service of the state, Greville became his companion at court, accompanying him on his mission to the emperor Rudolph in 1577, and also as one of the escort accompanying Anjou to the Netherlands in 1582. He had volunteered for service in the Low Countries in 1580, and rode in tournaments in 1580, 1581, and 1584.

While the *Caelica* sonnets cannot be certainly dated, they most probably belong to these years. Sidney, Greville, and Dyer are represented as 'Mates in Song' in the two pastorals introducing Davison's *A Poetical Rapsody* (1602), and Greville's regret that Sidney's death left him 'to play the ill poet in my own part'[1] confirms that the two had been writing contemporaneously.

[1] *Hist. MSS. Hatfield House*, iii. 189. See also *Life*, p. 150. A more

811710 B

In the love sonnet Greville discovered much of his individuality as a poet, but the form was not to prove finally congenial to his talent. One does not need to read very far into *Caelica* to find that Greville wears the Petrarchan and Anacreontic fashions with some discomfort. The obligatory themes—praise of the mistress, the pains of absence—are celebrated without fervour; the cynicism that enters the series in sonnets xix, xxi, and xxiii cannot afterwards be dislodged; and the 'prettiness' and hyperbole of sonnet convention are steadily worsted by Greville's more insistent colloquial manner. The theme that comes to engage him most powerfully, however, is the upheaval caused by love in 'the little world of man'. Love is seen as a rebel force usurping the sovereignty of reason, provoking the contention of Honour and Beauty, Wit and Affection, Patience and Desire, bringing a chaos to the mind. As in one sonnet after another Greville follows the interplay of these rival forces, *Caelica* becomes a first sketch for a possible *Treatie of Humane Love*, and a first treatment of that sense of human division and bewilderment that is to extend through his later work.

The impression left by the *Caelica* poems is that Greville's capacity is not for song, but for intellectual analysis; not for courtly compliment, but for the intricacies of debate and discussion. These are the talents developed in his three Senecan plays. They probably belong to the fifteen-nineties, as Greville explained that the lost play, *Antonie and Cleopatra*, was destroyed not as 'a contemptible younger brother to the rest', but lest it should be 'construed, or strained to a personating of vices in the present Governors, or government', his disquiet being caused by 'the Earle of *Essex* then falling'.[1] If the reference to *Antonie and Cleopatra* as 'younger brother to the rest' means that it was the most recently written, then *Mustapha* and *Alaham* must also have been in existence at the time of the Essex

comprehensive biographical account of Greville than is possible here may be found in G. Bullough, 'Fulk Greville, First Lord Brooke', *MLR*, xxviii (1933), 1–20. I have discussed the date and order of his poems in more detail in 'The Sequence of the Writings of Fulke Greville, Lord Brooke', *SP*, lvi (1959), 489–503.                                        [1] *Life*, pp. 155–6.

rebellion in December 1600. All three plays probably belong to the Senecan experiments of the Pembroke circle, in the last decade of the century.

As a dramatic poet Greville is still under Sidney's influence. In the first chapter of the *Life* he had commended Sidney's doctrine that the 'representing of vertues, vices, humours, counsells, and actions of men in feigned, and unscandalous Images, is an inabling of free-born spirits to the greatest affaires of States'.[1] *Mustapha* and *Alaham*, 'no Plaies for the Stage',[2] fall under this principle of 'delightfull teaching'. Their purpose, as formulated by Greville, is 'to trace out the high waies of ambitious Governours, and to shew in the practice, that the more audacity, advantage and good successe such Soveraignties have, the more they hasten to their owne desolation and ruine'.[3] The choice of subjects from oriental sources— a sign of Greville's circumspection—allows him to study political power in its more irresponsible and despotic forms.

He was now able to write from an increasing experience of public affairs. After an unsuccessful bid to enter the Commons in 1580, Greville sat for Heydon in Yorkshire in 1584, and then came to represent Warwickshire in 1586—and continued to do so in the parliaments of 1588, 1593, 1597, 1601, and 1621.[4] Through the influence of Sir Henry Sidney he had obtained the reversion of the office of Secretary for Wales in 1583, and by 1587 was secure in the goodwill of Essex, and advancing in favour at court. Greville's standing with the queen may be judged from his correspondence with Bacon in 1594 over the position of Solicitor General.[5] He achieved his first major state appointment, as Treasurer for Marine Causes, in 1598, and in 1600 his report on trading conditions in the East[6] contributed to the formation of the East India Company.

[1] Ibid., pp. 2–3.    [2] Ibid., p. 224.    [3] Ibid., p. 221.
[4] See Sir John Neale, *The Elizabethan House of Commons* (1949), pp. 52–53—correcting some confusions in the *DNB*.
[5] The letters are cited in Spedding's *Letters and Life* (1869), i. 298, 302.
[6] Given in John Bruce, *Annals of the Honorable East India Company* (1810), i. 121–6.

The transition from the sonnet to the Senecan play marks the first acknowledgment of graver purposes in Greville's writing, and the emergence in him of the political moralist. In *Mustapha* and *Alaham* he scrutinizes the stresses and disorders of the body politic, the discord in the state when the monarch is weak, the dangers of court intrigue, the lawfulness of sedition against a tyrant. To these problems Greville brings the strenuous, involuted style that has become recognized as one of his characteristics. Commending the women characters in the plays in his *Specimens*, Lamb stipulated that 'it requires a study equivalent to the learning of a new language to understand their meaning when they speak'.[1]

From the choruses to the plays, the verse-treatises developed. The treatises, which as Greville explains in the *Life of Sidney*, are 'no such strangers to the scope of the Tragedies, but that a favourable Reader might easily find some consanguinitie between them', were 'first intended to be for every Act a Chorus'.[2] As, during his work on the plays, certain choruses grew beyond dramatic requirements, they were detached and elaborated as separate poems. In this way was evolved *The Declination of Monarchy* (numbered among the treatises in the *Life*), which at its 'first birth' was 'divided into three parts, with intention of the Author, to be disposed amongst their fellows, into three diverse Acts of the Tragedies'.[3] Although the date of this movement from drama to treatise cannot be exactly determined, Daniel's reference to Greville in 1599 as holding the view that it does not 'ill beseeme the function of a *Poem*, to discourse',[4] suggests that it may have occurred at about the turn of the century.

Having once attained the treatise-form, Greville did not afterwards relinquish it. He continued to add short poems to *Caelica*, on subjects like politics and religion, but these are usually in the six-line treatise stanza, aptly described by Croll

[1] *Works* (ed. Hutchinson, 1940), i. 66.
[2] *Life*, pp. 150–1.
[3] Ibid., p. 152.
[4] *Musophilus* (1599), ll. 997–8, in *Poems*, ed. A. C. Sprague (1930).

as 'chips thrown off in the shaping of the longer works'.[1] *A Treatise of Monarchy* (apparently the earliest work in the form) was followed by *A Treatie of Warres, An Inquisition upon Fame and Honour, A Treatie of Humane Learning,* and *A Treatise of Religion.* As the Warwick MSS. show, Greville was persistent in revising his poems, and he employed scribes to copy them, but he intended that none should be published in his lifetime.[2] His exclusion from public life from 1604 to 1614,[3] still to be adequately explained, may have contributed to this decision. Although Greville was knighted at the coronation in 1603, in the next year he lost his appointment as Treasurer of the Navy, and was also in difficulties about his office in Wales. In the *Life of Sidney* there are a number of indications of his estrangement from Cecil, and his fortunes could not have been helped by contemporary rumours of his sympathy for Arbella Stuart.[4] Greville remained out of public life for ten years.

He was active in this interval in developing the properties he had been steadily accumulating since 1587 (when he had been granted the estates of the recusant Lord Paget), and particularly in restoring Warwick Castle, granted to him in 1604. The account of Greville's possessions and revenues in 1609 shows a total income for that year of over £13,200.[5] He was by this time well known as a patron of letters—Daniel, Camden, and Speed were among those assisted by him—and he was later to found a history lectureship at Cambridge, negotiating with the continental scholars Vossius and Dorislaus to occupy it.

On Salisbury's death in 1612 Greville sought the aid of Rochester in obtaining the Secretaryship, without success. In 1614, however, when Arbella Stuart was imprisoned and half insane in the Tower, he returned to public life as Chancellor of the Exchequer. Greville was prominent on a number of councils

---

[1] M. W. Croll, *The Works of Fulke Greville* (Philadelphia, 1903), p. 29.

[2] See *Life*, pp. 219–20.

[3] Although Greville signed the declared accounts of the treasurer of the Chamber every year from 1611–12 to 1616–17, the accounts for 1611–1612 were not completed for signature until 1614.

[4] See *Hist. MSS. Portland*, ix. 142, and P. M. Handover, *Arbella Stuart* (1957), p. 152.  [5] *Hist. MSS. Earl Cowper*, i. 69–70.

and committees under James, and in 1621 was raised to the
peerage as Lord Brooke. He continued to sit on the Privy
Council and, after the king's death in 1625, remained at court
under Charles. Greville was stabbed to death by his servant
Ralph Haywood on 1 September 1628, at the age of seventy-four.

Greville's progression from the sonnet sequence to the Senecan play, and from the chorus to the discursive poem, marks his
gradual realization of his identity as a reflective poet. The
tendency to probe, speculate, and discuss that could find only
an imperfect expression in *Caelica*, that had been encouraged,
and yet still held under constraint, by the movement to the
drama, found in the verse treatise its full scope and exercise. As
Greville devotes his poetry entirely to analysis and disquisition,
the treatise becomes the vehicle of his gravest and most mature
thinking. *A Treatise of Monarchy* represents his earliest work
in the genre, and *A Treatise of Religion* his latest.

The priority of *A Treatise of Monarchy* to the other treatises is
attested by its closeness in theme to the plays, and by Greville's
admission that one section of it, *The Declination of Monarchy*,
is a reshaping of three choruses from the tragedies. His account
of the changes undergone by this section shows that *A Treatise
of Monarchy*, in the form in which we now have it, is at some
distance from the form in which it may have existed at *c.* 1600.
Greville explains how the three choruses were detached from
the plays to be elaborated separately; how misgivings about 'the
tendernesse of that great subject' caused him to suspend work
for a time, then to dress the poem in 'richer garments' to conceal
its deformities, and next to 'take away all opinion of serious-
nesse' by making the treatment ironical, and finally to restore its
gravity again by introducing illustrations from the history of
Rome, Sparta and Greece.[1]

As *The Declination of Monarchy* is but one of fifteen discourses composing *A Treatise of Monarchy*, the earlier form of
the treatise, and the stages of its later evolution, are now beyond

---

[1] *Life*, pp. 152–4.

recovery. The occasional topical references indicate the period over which the composition and revision may have extended. In 'Of Commerce' (st. 406) the queen is referred to as no longer alive, and in 'Of Church' (st. 214) there is an allusion to the excommunication of Venice in 1606. While the mention of the new Dutch Republic in 'Of Weake Minded Tyrants' (st. 102) may not refer specifically to the truce of 1608, the allusion to France's 'late fowrth *Henrie*' in 'Of Croune Revenue' (st. 434) shows that Greville was still at work on that section after 1610.[1]

*A Treatise of Monarchy* remains the earliest of the treatises in inception, and it preserves a character of its own. This may be explained by defining its relationship to the plays more exactly. Greville's aim in the tragedies had been to 'trace out the high waies of ambitious Governours', and in *Mustapha* and *Alaham* his immediate concern had been to examine the dangers of excessive power, the evils of intrigue and aspiration, the problems of tyranny and sedition. In the course of pursuing these issues Greville became absorbed in a deeper one. The overriding impression one receives from the plays is a sense of man as a helpless, bewildered creature, at the mercy of competing forces within. It is the dilemma stated by the Chorus Sacerdotum in *Mustapha*:

> Oh wearisome Condition of Humanity!
> Borne under one Law, to another bound:
> Vainely begot, and yet forbidden vanity,
> Created sicke, commanded to be sound:
> What meaneth Nature by these diverse Lawes?
> Passion and Reason, selfe-division cause.

This sense of human incapacity and discord becomes the deeper theme of the plays, and a comparison of the earlier and later versions of *Mustapha* shows the preoccupation growing stronger with the passage of time.[2] Formulated in the Chorus

[1] See also st. 166, 280, 399, 441, and notes.

[2] The earlier versions of *Mustapha* are MS. ff. II. 35 in the Cambridge University Library, MS. V. b. 223 in the Folger Shakespeare Library, and the unauthorized quarto of 1609. The later versions are the Warwick MS. of the play, and the text of the 1633 folio.

Sacerdotum in terms of the conflict of passion and reason, the predicament comes to be seen more emphatically, in Greville's later work, as a consequence of the fall.

The advantage of distinguishing these two tendencies in the plays—the immediate concern with issues of statecraft, the deeper sense of man's inherent frailty in his fallen state—is that *A Treatise of Monarchy* may at once be identified as a development of the first (as the later treatises, especially *A Treatise of Religion*, are a development of the second). In *A Treatise of Monarchy* the metaphysical problems that had begun to engage Greville in the plays are held in abeyance: it is the most practical and realistic of his treatises, an essay on government by an Elizabethan statesman. Some of the claims made for the complexity of Greville's thinking, and for the 'tensions' existing between one part of his work and another, come from a failure to distinguish what the purpose of *A Treatise of Monarchy* really is, and how it is set apart from his other discursive poems. It is true that the assumption on which the treatise depends is that monarchy, like all other such institutions, is a product of human infirmity. But while this postulate is made, and from time to time recalled in the course of the discussion, the treatise itself is a study of monarchy as it is, and a statement of the policies required to maintain it. *A Treatise of Monarchy* is not a fundamental inquiry into the right by which a monarch rules, or into the grounds upon which his rule might legitimately be overthrown: it is dedicated to showing how his rule may be made effective.

The treatise falls loosely into three divisions, the first (sections I–V) being an examination of monarchy in general terms; the second (sections VI–XII) taking up particular aspects of government, like law and revenue; and the third (sections XIII–XV) comparing monarchy to other systems of rule. In the first division Greville establishes the premisses on which his treatment rests. He invokes the fiction of the golden age to present the ideal state before the rule of law, when princes and subjects lived in 'one republique, by united hearts'. The first kings were worshipped as gods after their death, and their subalterns were 'noe vayne favourites', but champions like Hercules, who laboured for the common good. Monarchy as we know it arose with the lapse of the world from this primal perfection. With the passing of the golden age, and the withdrawal of the gods from the earth, men resigned their liberties to kings, who in their turn were hungry for power, until the state was achieved

> Whence neither makers now, nor members held
> Men are; but blankes where pow'r doth write her lust,
> A sprightlesse masse, which for it cannot weld
> It self, at others pleasure languish must . . .  (st. 55)

By using this myth of the origin of states in 'Of the Beginning of Monarchy' and 'Declination of Monarchy to Violence', Greville presents kingship (by indirection) as something less than a divine office, and kings as sharing in the weaknesses that afflict their subjects. In the sections that follow, however, he is quick to throw his weight behind the cause of monarchic rule. As history shows (section III), to depose kings is to plunge the state into anarchy; weak rulers (section IV) must preserve order by wisely choosing their ministers, pitting one faction against another to dissipate their strengths in rivalry, and, by availing themselves of all 'Engines of powre' bequeathed by the past, retain the 'auntient formes' to which 'mans freedome is already sould'. On the other hand the strong ruler (section V) is urged to heed the examples in history of monarchs who overreached themselves, and to avoid all acts that could imperil his estate. If sovereign power should be misused, however, redress does not lie with man:

> But if pow're will exceed, then lett mankinde
> Receave oppression, as fruites of their error;
> Let them againe live in their duties shrinde,
> As their safe haven from the windes of terror,
> > Till hee that rais'd powre, to mowe mans synnes downe,
> > Please, for pow'rs owne synnes, to pluck of her Crowne.
> > > (st. 191)

The second general division of the treatise, moving from monarchy in general to an analysis of its various aspects, contains 'Of Church', 'Of Lawes', 'Of Nobilitie', 'Of Commerce', 'Of Croune Revenue', 'Of Peace', and 'Of Warr'. These are some of the topics that again fall under Greville's notice in *An Inquisition upon Fame and Honour*, *A Treatie of Warres*, and *A Treatise of Religion*, where the conflicting standpoints taken have fostered notions of the 'complexity' of Greville's thought. The view of laws, religion, and war taken in *A Treatise of Monarchy*, however, is consistent with Greville's limited purpose. He does not offer a complete theory 'Of Lawes' in the section under that title, for instance, but a discussion of law as an element in state policy. Religion likewise is treated from the standpoint of the responsibilities of the monarch, while the section 'Of Warr' (unlike the later *Treatie of Warres*) is a statement of effective military and naval policy. The treatment of each topic is appropriate to the place it occupies as a chapter in a statesman's manual.

Greville's attitude is also consistent from chapter to chapter. If the end of government is 'publique good', then only the rule of a monarch can ensure it. In each phase of state policy discussed the sovereign's interests are paramount. While religion must be the 'first foundation' of his reign, in state affairs the mitre is kept subordinate to the sceptre; while law may not be the servant of the king's will, he should use it to consolidate his power; to the nobles should be delegated enough authority to support his rule (keeping in place 'that tame wilde beast, People'), but not enough to contest it. The 'generall conventions' of the kingdom are upheld as a monarch's best means of allowing the ventilation of grievances, and parliament is approved as a means of taxing people with their own consent. 'What expect men for their lives and goods', Greville asks, 'but some poore feathers owt of their owne wings?'

The underlying concern of this division of the treatise is that the king's power is to be upheld, preserved from encroachment, and fostered by military, civil, and fiscal policies that will

ensure the state's well-being and security. The same concern
extends to the last and most theoretical phase of the argument,
a comparison of monarchy to other systems of rule. It was a
commonplace of Elizabethan political theory to examine the
merits of three forms of government—monarchy, aristocracy,
and democracy—and to prefer the first to the other two. Greville's treatment conforms to this tradition.[1] No arguments in
favour of aristocracy or democracy are advanced anywhere:
their disadvantages are set against the advantages of monarchy,
and examples are culled from history in support. The aristocratic
and democratic systems are finally dismissed as accidents thrown
up in the process of mutability, and mankind's inclination to
them as another token of human fickleness and corruption.
Greville upholds monarchy as the correspondence in the body
politic to the sovereignty of reason in the microcosm, and the
only bulwark against disorder:

> And as we doe in humane bodies see,
> Where reason raignes in cheife, not the affection,
> Order is greate, not wanton libertie,
> Man to himself, and others a direction;
>    Where if too much abstracted or let fall,
>    The tares of passion there runne over all:
>
> So when men fall away from *Monarchie*,
> Whether it be to States of few, or more,
> Change leades them nearer unto *Anarchie*
> By divers minutes, then they were before;
>    Since unitie divided into manie
>    Begetts confusion, never frende to anie.    (st. 657–8)

It may be the wry, astringent quality of Greville's observa-
tions that has brought into discussions of his political thought

[1] The pattern derives (in a simplified form) from the analysis of rival
constitutions in Plato and Aristotle, and analogues to Greville's discussion
may be pursued from such familiar handbooks as Mulcaster's *Positions*,
Castiglione's *The Courtier*, and Sir John Elyot's *The Governour*, to Thomas
Smith's *De Republica Anglorum* (1583), Jacques Hurault's *Politicke, Moral
and Martial Discourses* (tr. Golding, 1595), Bodin's *Six Bookes of a Commonweale* (tr. Knolles, 1606), even to nonentities like John Barston, author of
*The Safegarde of Societie* (1576).

the names of such 'progressive' thinkers as Buchanan, Machiavelli, and the author of the *Vindiciae contra Tyrannos*.[1] His conception of monarchy as the product of human infirmity (in which kings and subjects share alike) could well be provocative, were its implications pursued. (Richard Baxter's protest, that 'Sir *Fulk Grevil* . . . hath a Poem lately Printed for Subjects Liberty, which I greatly wonder this Age would bear', has already been noted.) But to pursue these implications was not Greville's concern: accepting monarchy as a fallible human institution, he writes to show how it may be sustained and improved. Whereas a theorist like John Poynet argued that a tyrant might be deposed, Greville holds that his tyranny must be endured (st. 191); practices that Machiavelli would have approved he spends a dozen stanzas (164–75) condemning; his opposition to the Church in politics makes him a foe of the Calvinist ideal of the theocratic state. The natural context of *A Treatise of Monarchy* is not the theories of Buchanan, Calvin, or Machiavelli, but rather the judicious realism of Greville's own parliamentary speeches, like his address to the Commons on precedents and the subsidy in 1593:

The poor are grieved by being overcharged; this must be helped by increasing our own Burthen; for otherwise the weak feet will complain of too heavy a body; that is to be feared. If the feet knew their strength as we know their oppression, they would not bear as they do. But to answer them, it sufficeth that the time requireth it. And in a Prince power will command. To satisfy them, they cannot think we overcharge them, when we charge our selves with them and above them: But if nothing will satisfy them, our doings are sufficient to bind them.[2]

---

[1] The growing comment on Greville's political thought includes N. Orsini, *Fulke Greville: Tra il Mondo e Dio* (Milan, 1941); H. W. Utz, *Die Anschauungen über Wissenschaft und Religion im Werke Fulke Grevilles* (Bern, 1948); Jean Jacquot, 'Religion et Raison d'État dans l'Œuvre de Fulke Greville', *Études Anglaises*, v (1952), 211–22; and Hugh N. Maclean, 'Fulke Greville: Kingship and Sovereignty', *HLQ*, xvi (1952–3), 237–71, and 'Fulke Greville on War', *HLQ*, xxi (1957–8), 95–109.

[2] Sir Simonds D'Ewes, *A Compleat Journal of the . . . House of Commons* (1693), p. 490.

In September 1615, speaking at a meeting of the Privy Council held to consider measures to relieve the king's debts (in the face of popular complaints against impositions), Greville said he 'would rather move some questions than deliver his advice'.

One question was whether their Lordships would hold it fit that everything that was vulgarly complained of were of necessity to be amended. All impositions were not unlawful; nor all monopolies: in all ages and in all states some of both kinds have been done and held warrantable. Another question was whether their Lordships would not think that many of those things which were moved for preparation were meet to be referred to Parliament and handled there. It was a pleasing thing and popular to ask a multitude's advice; besides, it argued trust, and trust begat trust; and such a mutual confidence might perhaps dispose their minds to a greater freedom towards the King.[1]

Where Greville is set apart from other political theorists of the time, it is for his candour and perception, for the realism that steadily prefers truth to comfort, rather than for the 'audacity' of his speculations. He writes with a mind quite free from illusion, seasoned by long experience of state affairs: but always he is of the king's party.

As the longest of Greville's verse-treatises, *A Treatise of Monarchy* affords the best opportunity for studying the literary problems of the form. It is a form that lies outside the orbit of the aesthetic doctrines that had guided Greville hitherto. He acknowledged in the *Life* that though Sidney's pen was dedicated to 'morall Images, and Examples', and never 'vanishing pleasure alone', yet he had always 'that dexterity, even with the dashes of his pen to beautifie the Margents of his works',[2] so that his teaching was made 'delightful'. Believing that 'no man that followes can ever reach, much lesse go beyond that excellent intended patterne of his', Greville chose a different course:

For my own part, I found my creeping Genius more fixed upon the Images of Life, than the Images of Wit, and therefore chose not to

[1] James Spedding, *Letters and Life of Bacon* (1868), v. 200–1.
[2] *Life*, p. 223.

write to them on whose foot the black Oxe had not already trod, as the Proverbe is, but to those only, that are weather-beaten in the Sea of this World, such as having lost the sight of their Gardens, and groves, study to saile on a right course among Rocks, and quicksands.[1]

Declining the appeal to the sympathies and feelings of the reader on which Sidney had insisted, Greville is more intent to declare than to persuade, addressing himself to those whose experience of the world has placed them beyond enchantment.

If his treatises cannot be accommodated to Sidney's theories, however, they do remain in an older tradition of *miscere utile dulci*. It is the tradition in which verse had long been recognized as an auxiliary to writing of an instructive or hortatory kind— exemplified in Walton's popular verse-rendering of Boethius (1410), Tusser's *Hundreth Good Pointes of Husbandrie* (1557), or Hunnis's verse translation of Genesis (1578)—and which Greville refers to in *A Treatie of Humane Learning*. Poetry and music, in Greville's later thinking, are 'things not pretious in their proper kind', but they are allowed a certain value

> as pleasing sauce to dainty food;
> Fine foyles for jewels, or enammels grace,
> Cast upon things which in themselves are good.
> (st. 112)

Even this tradition he defines very strictly, disdaining the pretty arts of rhetoric for words 'which doe most properly expresse the thought':

> For the true Art of *Eloquence* indeed
> Is not this craft of words, but formes of speech,
> Such as from living wisdomes doe proceed;
> Whose ends are not to flatter, or beseech,
>     Insinuate, or perswade, but to declare
>     What things in Nature good, or evill are.
> (st. 110)

This is an exacting standard, which in *A Treatise of Monarchy* meets its severest test. Setting aside the principle of 'delectation',

[1] *Life*, pp. 223–4.

Greville aims at the more austere poetic effect of sententious and preceptual verse, seeking to engage the mind directly. The norm of *A Treatise of Monarchy* is a style of disciplined exposition, sustained by the six-line stanza through its contests with Greville's syntax, and frequently shaping an idea to memorable statement. The difficulties of the enterprise are manfully resisted, if not always overcome. Precision and discipline are admitted poetic virtues, but they are apt to pall when sustained through a poem of almost seven hundred stanzas, and while it is enlightened to hold that there are no subjects unfit for poetry, some sections of 'Of Commerce' and 'Of Croune Revenue' fortify the suspicion that the draining of fens and the collection of taxes are not high on the scale. Even through these arid stretches Greville's tenacious mind—querying, discriminating, qualifying—keeps the argument pressing on, and his magisterial tone lends dignity to the whole. The more memorable passages come as he turns from the immediate and contingent to view his subject in a larger perspective, as at the conclusion to 'Of Weake Minded Tyrants' he contemplates tyranny, rebellion, order, and anarchy as part of the cycle of *vicissitudo rerum*, springing from its source in the imperfection of man:

> For vices soone to heights and periods rise,
> Have both their childehood, state, and declination;
> Are sometime currant, but at noe time wise,
> Like blasing starres, that burne their owne foundation,
>     Or shadowes, which the shew of bodies have,
>     And in self darknes, both a life and grave . . .
>
> Thus rose all states, thus grew they, thus they fall,
> From good to ill, and soe from ill, to worse;
> Tyme for her due vicissitudes doth call,
> Error still carrying in it self her Curse:
>     Yet lett this light out of these clowds breake forth:
>     That pow'r hath noe longe being, but in worth.

These are the chords sounded in *A Treatise of Religion*. In the later treatises the deeper issues which Greville had begun to explore in the dramas, then held in abeyance in *A Treatise of*

*Monarchy*, are finally confronted and resolved. The later treatises (all to be placed after 1610–12, as none of them is mentioned in Greville's account of his writings in the *Life*) are collected in one volume in the Warwick MSS., with a note in Greville's hand indicating that he considered *A Treatise of Religion* the most important:

> These treatises should be thus placed.
> 1. Religion.
> 2. Humane Learninge.
> 3. Fame & Honor.
> 4. Warre.

*A Treatise of Religion* was also intended to stand first in the *Certaine Learned and Elegant Workes* (1633), occupying the twenty-two pages that have been suppressed.[1]

Through *A Treatie of Warres*, *An Inquisition upon Fame and Honor*, and *A Treatie of Humane Learning* Greville had been working, through a reconsideration of his earlier themes, towards a new metaphysic. In *A Treatise of Religion* it receives its final statement. The problem to which he addresses himself is the one that had occupied him almost from *Caelica* onward, the problem of mortal imperfection and its cure. Seen earlier as a result of the warfare of passion and reason, it is seen now as a result of man's plight as a fallen creature: the situation is defined in such later poems in *Caelica* as 'Wrapt up, O Lord, in mans degeneration' and 'When as Mans life, the light of humane lust'. In *A Treatise of Religion* the dilemma is not merely defined, but also resolved. Greville now declares unequivocally how regeneration may come, in verse that has all the dignity and assurance of his later manner:

> What is the chaine which drawes us backe againe,
> And lifts man up unto his first Creation?
> Nothinge in him his owne hart can restraine,
> His reason lives a captive to temptation,
>     Example is corrupt, precepts are mixt:
>     All fleshlie knowledge frayle, and never fixt.

---

[1] See below, pp. 22–23.

It is a light, a guifte, a grace inspired,
A sparcke of power, a goodnesse of the good,
Desire in him, that never it desired,
An unitie where desolation stood;
　　In us, not of us; a spirit not of earth,
　　Fashioninge the mortall to immortall birth.
                                    (st. 2–3)

This is Greville's first statement of his theme. As the treatise progresses he reaffirms and extends it, so that the poem follows a wave pattern, as Greville moves out to censure alternative courses and to condemn the world that fails the test of his standards, then retires to declare again the truths to which he holds. From the position attained in this treatise, all the values he had entertained in the earlier ones are rejected. The benefits that knowledge might confer (already strictly defined in *A Treatie of Humane Learning*) are banished by the conviction that it is beyond man's power to raise himself unaided; the stoic ideal upheld in *A Letter to an Honorable Lady*, and the degree of virtue found in fame and honour (in the *Inquisition*), are alike dismissed as delusions; earlier counsel on the choice of bishops (*A Treatise of Monarchy*, st. 226–9) is countermanded by the feeling that the hierarchy should be dispensed with altogether.

The preoccupations of the statesman yield to the preoccupations of the moralist, and Greville's writing turns inward. Its focus becomes his conception of 'the elect'. The elect are not those predestined by God for salvation, but those who accept his calling, persevere in faith and works, and constitute themselves a 'Church invisible' where the 'sect and Schisme' of the outward church cannot intrude. From Greville's contemplation of man as 'lost in all thinges but Election' comes the emotional force of this treatise, and with it a vindication of his later ideals of style. Though in *A Treatise of Religion* Greville's purpose is still to instruct, he is not merely setting down precepts, but offering truths to which he is personally pledged: the ideas come to us as emotionally attested by the poet:

Then judge pore man! Gods Image once, 'tis true,
Though nowe the Devills, by thine owne defection,
Judge man, I say, to make this Image newe,
And clense thy fleshe from this deepe-dy'de infection,
What miracles must needes be wrought in you,
That thus stand lost in all thinges but Election?
  What livinge death, what strange illumination
  Must be inspir'd to this regeneration?

Must not the grace be supernaturall,
Which in forgivinge gives sanctification;
And from this second *Chaos* of his fall
Formes in mans litle world a newe Creation?
  And must not then this twice-borne child of heaven
  Bringe forth in life this newe perfection given?

                                        (st. 41–42)

Writing of this kind is distinct from the perplexed, agitated manner of the plays, and from the dispassionate commendation of ideas in *A Treatise of Monarchy*. It has an austerity which satisfies Greville's canons of style, and yet the ideas are so refracted in his feeling that its austerity becomes moving, its discipline eloquent.

While it was not by design that *A Treatise of Monarchy* and *A Treatise of Religion* were separated from the rest of Greville's work and issued together almost forty years afterwards, yet in some ways they properly form a volume of *Remains*. *A Treatise of Monarchy* is the kind of poem to be valued for completing the range of an author's work, and making possible the adequate study of his thought; *A Treatise of Religion* is the kind of unpublished work whose recovery adds to his achievement. The appearance of *The Remains* in 1670 confirmed Greville's reputation as an intimidating poet. Richard Flecknoe wrote commendatory verses in 1671:

          Food, for *strong minds*! whilst of your lighter stuff
          The weaker find in *other Books* enough,
          Whose *Master-strokes*, great wits do looke upon
          With reverence and admiration,

> While Novices, and those of meaner wit
> Are not grown up to th'admiring of them yet . . .[1]

The limited audience of undaunted readers which Flecknoe called for, Greville was to find in Lamb, in Swinburne (who linked Greville and Chapman as the two poets 'most genuinely obscure in style upon whose work I have ever adventured'),[2] and in T. S. Eliot, to whom it seemed in 1934 that 'Fulke Greville has never received quite his due'.[3] Perhaps none of these later readers was quite so perceptive of the singularity of Greville as Coleridge, whose 'Farewell to Love' was patterned on *Caelica*, lxxxiv, and who wrote three lines from Cowper in Lamb's copy of the *Certaine Learned and Elegant Workes*, as a 'Motto for the Whole Volume':

> A quarry of stout spurs and knotted fangs
> That, crook'd into a thousand whimsies, clasp
> The stubborn soil.[4]

---

[1] 'On the Works of *Fulk Grevil*, Lord *Brook*', in *Epigrams of all sorts* (1671), B5$^v$–B6$^r$.

[2] *Contemporaries of Shakespeare* (1919), p. 25.

[3] 'John Marston', in *Elizabethan Essays* (1934), p. 195.

[4] *Coleridge's Miscellaneous Criticism*, ed. T. M. Raysor (1936), p. 243.

# TEXTUAL INTRODUCTION

## The Texts

THE surviving texts of *A Treatise of Monarchy* and *A Treatise of Religion* are two: the manuscripts of each poem at Warwick Castle, and *The Remains of Sir Fulk Grevill Lord Brooke* (1670).

The Warwick MSS. are six volumes bound in vellum, marked on the spine A, B, C, D, E, and F. They were described by Bullough in his edition of Greville's *Poems and Dramas* (1939), i. 27–32; the following is a summary account of the two manuscripts relevant to an editor of *The Remains*.

A is a manuscript 9 by $13\frac{1}{2}$ inches, with 115 leaves written on both sides and gathered in eights, containing *A Treatise of Monarchy* alone. It is in the hand of the scribe designated *b* by Bullough, with corrections by another scribe, and some corrections by Greville himself. Though the stanzas are numbered from 1 to 664 in the margin, there is no general title to the treatise, only the successive titles 'Of the Beginning of Monarchy', 'Declination of Monarchy to Violence', and so on, each beginning a new page. The subheadings 'Sect. 1°:', 'Sect. 2°:' in their sequence are in different shade of ink, as though added later. The manuscript is carefully written, although the majuscule and minuscule forms of 'k' are sometimes hard to distinguish.

B is a manuscript 8 by $12\frac{1}{2}$ inches, with 90 leaves $(14+(16\times4)+12)$, containing *Of Humane Learning, Of Religion, An Inquisition upon Fame and Honor*, and *A Treatie of Warres*, in that order. *Of Religion* occupies 38 pages, and is copied in the hand of the scribe (designated *d* by Bullough) who made the revisions in A. (This scribe also copied the other poems included, except for *Of Humane Learning*, which is in the hand of the scribe of *A Treatise of Monarchy*. The corrections and revisions in *Of Religion* have all been made by the scribe responsible for it, though corrections in Greville's hand appear elsewhere in B. Again the text has been transcribed with care, although the majuscule and minuscule forms of 'd' are not readily distinguishable, and the majuscule 'l' is identifiable only by size. The erratic use of the capital 'c' is a feature of the manuscripts of both *A Treatise of Monarchy* and *A Treatise of Religion*.

*The Remains* was entered in the Stationers' Register on 2 December 1669, and published the next year. The title-page read as follows:

THE | REMAINS | OF | Sir *FULK GREVILL* | Lord Brooke: | BEING | POEMS | OF | MONARCHY | AND | RELIGION: || Never before Printed. || *LONDON*, | Printed by *T. N.* for *Henry Herringman* at the sign | of the *Blew Anchor* in the *Lower Walk* of the | *New Exchange* 1670.

Collation: 8°, A⁴ B–O⁸. 108 leaves paged from B1 (1) to O7 (205). 16 is misnumbered as 19 and 175 as 165; A1, A2ᵛ, O8, O8ᵛ are blank. A1ᵛ Imprimatur W. Morice. A2 Title. A3 An Advertisement. B1 A Treatise of Monarchy. N1 A Treatise of Religion.

Six copies of the text have been collated, those in the Dyce library, the University Library, Cambridge (two copies), the National Library of Scotland, and the Huntington and Folger Libraries. There are the usual number of variants where type has merely shifted, e.g. stanza 69 is numbered in one state as 6. Other typographical variants are the omission of the dashes that mark the missing line in stanza 169 and the closing up of the type to cover the blank line, and the placing of the page-numbers 65 and 73 in the inner margin instead of the outer. But of true textual variants affecting the readings of the text none has been noticed.

*The Remains* is carelessly printed; the only indication of the provenance of the printer's copy is given in the publisher's 'Advertisement', written almost forty years after Greville's death.

When he grew old he revised the Poems and Treatises he had writ long before, and at his death committed them to his friend Mr. *Michael Malet* an aged Gentleman in whom he most confided, who intended, what the Author purposed, to have had them Printed altogether; but by Copies of some parts of them which happened into other hands, some of them came first abroad, each of his Works having had their fate, as they singly merit particular esteem; so to come into the World at several times; he to whom they were first delivered being dead, the trust of these remaining pieces devolved on Sir *J. M.* who hath given me the Licensed Coppy of them.

Michael Mallett was one of the agents employed by Greville in the management of his estates, and he continued in the service of his heir, Robert Lord Brooke.[1] That he had charge of Greville's manuscripts and intended to print them is unlikely, since the responsibility for the 1633 edition appears to have lain rather with Greville's executor, Sir John Coke.[2] The identity of 'Sir J. M.' is a matter of conjecture. I have found no connexion between Sir John Mallet of Enmore, Somerset, and Michael Mallett; Sir John Mennes, who had published collections of verse with Herringman, styled himself 'Sir J. M.' on his title-pages, but his interest in such poetry as Greville's would have been faint.

*A Treatise of Religion* had been intended for publication in the *Certaine Learned and Elegant Workes* (1633), for the entry in Herbert's office-book reads:

Received from Henry Seyle for allowinge a booke of verses of my lord Brooks, entitled *Religion, Humane Learning, Warr*, and *Honor*, this 17 of October 1632, in mony, 1*l*. 0*s*. 0*d*. in books to the value of 1*l*. 4*s*. 0*d*.[3]

Although plainly included in the copy allowed by Herbert, *A Treatise of Religion* is absent from the volume as printed, where the signatures begin at 'd'. It seems safe to accept Greg's conclusion that the poem occupied the missing leaves.[4] Malone suggested that Laud may have been responsible for its

---

[1] *Hist. MSS. Earl Cowper*, i. 64–65, 70, 85, 231, 233–5, 449.
[2] Cf. John Verney's complaint to Coke about the inclusion of the letter *Of Travell* (Bullough, i. 26–27).
[3] *The Dramatic Records of Sir Henry Herbert*, ed. J. Q. Adams (New Haven, 1917), p. 41.
[4] *Bibliography of the English Drama*, iii (1957), 1068–9.

suppression,[1] and this is not unlikely in view of the anti-prelatical tenor of the treatise. In 1627 Laud had been informed of the unorthodox opinions of Dorislaus, the first appointee to Greville's history lectureship at Cambridge, and with the intervention of the bishops of Winchester and Durham the lectures had subsequently been suspended.[2]

## The Choice of Copy-Text

Of the two exemplars, *W* and *1670*, neither can be accounted for as a copy of the other. The *W* text has a number of revisions and corrections, all found incorporated in *1670*, except for four readings in *A Treatise of Religion*.

In stanza 10, line 5 of *A Treatise of Religion*, *W* reads:

> Duties to parent, child, time, men, and place

with '1' written under 'men' and '2' under 'time', indicating that the order is to be reversed. In *1670* the order is unchanged.

The line following in *W* (st. 10, l. 6) at first read:

> All knowne by nature, but observe by grace.

Then the 'e' of 'knowne' was blacked out and the 'n' altered to 'e', to give the reading 'knowe'. *1670* reads 'known', with 'observ'd' to correspond.

In stanza 64 of the *W* text of *A Treatise of Religion*, the first line originally read:

> They doe in prayinge, and still pray in doeinge

Then a long 's' was superimposed on the 'y' of 'They', and 'e' added, forming 'These'. *1670* reads 'They'.

In stanza 108 the original reading in line 4 was:

> Ore-rulinge him, from whom their lawes were given

Then 'lawes' was crossed through and 'rules' written above. *1670* gives the unrevised text.

---

[1] Edmond Malone, *Historical Account of . . . the English Stage*, in his *Shakespeare* (ed. Boswell, 1821), iii. 231 n. 6.

[2] See Wren to Laud, 16 December 1627, in *Cal. S. P. Dom.* (*1627–8*), p. 470; and Ward to Ussher, 16 May 1628, in Richard Parr's *The Life of James Usher* (1686), pp. 393–4.

These are all indications that *W*, as we now have it, presents a later stage in the revision than *1670*. As the scribe of *A Treatise of Religion* has also made corrections in the *W* text of *A Treatise of Monarchy* (copied by a different scribe), the *W* version of that poem may be placed at a similarly late stage. In this case, however, there is nothing to suggest that the copy for the *1670* text of *A Treatise of Monarchy* is not equally late. Indeed the textual superiority of *W* could not be very confidently maintained by these arguments alone. The four revisions in question are ones that a hasty compositor may have mistaken or overlooked; a more comprehensive view of *W* and *1670* tends to show that both present a late stage of the text; there is a handful of readings in *1670* (discussed presently) to suggest that it may contain sporadic revisions later than those found in *W*.

The general superiority of *W* does emerge positively, however, from an examination of the variants through the two texts as a whole. A comparison of *1670* with the manuscript reveals over two hundred instances of corruption, and it may help to indicate the textual authority of *1670* to distinguish the main categories into which these fall.

The most readily identified errors in *1670* are due to the misreadings of the compositor, or of the scribe on whom he depended.[1] Typical instances in *A Treatise of Monarchy* are 'weare' for 'weave' (34/5, 99/2), 'finely' for 'firmely' (150/3), 'Justice' for 'Justlie' (326/3), 'leave' for 'leade' (370/4), 'excel'd' for 'exil'de' (475/6), 'Feathers' for 'Fathers' (579/2), '*France*' for 'traunce' (590/2), and in *A Treatise of Religion* 'Since' for 'Sinne' (9/2), 'have' for 'hate' (30/5), 'shorned' for 'shortned' (59/2), 'fitteth' for 'filleth' (61/3), and 'Feare' for 'Seare' (69/3). Other instances of corruption due to carelessness are the omission of words (*M.* 185/5, 557/2, 593/6; *R.* 27/1, 47/5, 87/6); errors of attraction (*M.* 621/6, *R.* 84/2); and changes in word-order coming from the effort to hold too much in the head at a

---

[1] The fallibility of the compositor is indicated by the catchwords 'Neither' and 'Whom' at M4$^r$ and M4$^v$, where the first words in the text following are (erroneously) 'Nor' and 'Who' respectively.

time, as when 'well mixt and happy confluence' (*M.* 34/3) becomes 'well happy mixt, and confluence' (see also 12/5, 188/3, 462/2). There are over sixty errors of this class that substantially impair the text, and as many more small infidelities (e.g. *M.* 131/1, 355/4, 456/3, 519/5) that show the force or subtlety of what the poet wrote being dissipated in transmission.

A second easily recognized source of corruption is the tendency in *1670* to modernize and regularize the text. Thus in *A Treatise of Monarchy* 'checker' becomes 'Exchequer' (377/2, 398/1), 'imberge' becomes 'Imbargo' (408/4), 'mutine' becomes 'mutiny' (425/5, 497/6), 'thorough' becomes 'through' (*passim*), and 'statuas' becomes 'statues' (339/4, 479/5). As such changes frequently affect the number of syllables in the line, further sophistication sometimes occurs. In stanza 19, line 6 of *A Treatise of Religion*, for example, *W* reads:

> Men easlie change all what they easlie take.

In *1670* 'easlie' (occurring twice) becomes 'easily', and then an effort has been made to reduce the number of syllables in the line by leaving a word out:

> Men easily change all they easily take.

The old form of the present plural 'be' is replaced by the modern 'are' (*M.* 176/5, 530/4, 641/1), and archaisms like 'despair in' become 'despair of' (*M.* 608/1).

Some of these variants in *1670* suggest that an attempt is being made—sometimes officious, always imperceptive—to remove the awkwardness from Greville's style, and improve the text. Where he is in the habit of using 'man' as a collective, sometimes with plural verbs and pronouns (*M.* 31/2, 78/2, 368/5), *1670* will read 'men'. In *A Treatise of Religion* the substitution of 'So that' for 'So as' (13/5—cf. the usage at 86/2, 113/1) falls under the same principle, as does the alteration of 'other' (used as plural) to 'others' (*M.* 149/4, 170/3). Examples of the more officious alteration are *R.* 114/6, where the word inserted is plainly meant to help the meaning along, but shows a misunderstanding of it; and *M.* 427/4, where the

*1670* variant saves the rhyme, but destroys the sense. (This
failure to grasp the intention of the text is also reflected in the
punctuation of *1670*, as at *M*. 308/3, 478/2, or 540/3–6.) Other
sophistications may be suspected at *M*. 247/1 and *R*. 73/3. It
would be uncertain, however, whether such readings as
'*Cybele*' for '*Sybilla*' (*M*. 61/3), '*Seleucus*' for '*Zaleucus*' (243/3),
and 'shapes' for 'shrapes' (297/3) are intended to set the text
right, or come simply from a misreading of it.

The third class of variants is intermediate between these
deliberate changes and the unintentional miscopyings. It consists of the numerous readings in *1670* that make sense, but are
weaker than the readings in *W*. Instances in *A Treatise of
Monarchy* are 'dumb' for 'dymm' (40/1), 'times' for 'crymes'
(82/6), 'end' for 'bonde' (421/2), 'highly' for 'lightlie' (542/1),
and in *A Treatise of Religion* 'Fear' for 'beare' (28/1), 'stools' for
'Schooles' (78/2), and 'hopes' for 'scope' (92/5), where the context shows that *W* is to be preferred. Usually there is a similarity
in form to suggest how the variant arose (as in the instances
cited), or circumstances pointing to an error of attraction
(*M*. 117/3, 192/3, 479/3, 523/2, *R*. 58/4) or eye-slip (*M*. 68/1). In
other instances where the two texts offer alternative readings
it is characteristic of *1670* to present the one that is the more
obvious and expected (*M*. 13/6, 27/3, 100/1, 140/5, 259/6, 528/4;
*R*. 51/4, 61/1, 74/6).

The evidence that *1670* offers a less reliable text of *A Treatise
of Monarchy* and *A Treatise of Religion* than the Warwick MSS.
is too oppressive to be resisted. Nevertheless *1670* retains a
textual value in helping to detect occasional scribal errors in
*W*, and—more important—as containing one or two revisions
that *W* lacks. That they are the author's revisions is an assumption to which I can see no likely alternative. In stanza 295 of
*A Treatise of Monarchy*, for example, *W* reads:

> Conscience (I say) is to the people deere,
> And libertie they (like all creatures) love,
> What then neads any witty practise heere,
> Where men upon such fayre wheeles easely move?

That Greville wrote 'witty practise' (l. 3) I do not doubt, for he uses the identical phrase in a similar context in the *Life of Sidney* ('any nimble or witty practise, crafty shifting, or Imperious forcing humors'[1]). In *1670*, ll. 3–4 read:

> What then needs any force or practice here,
> Where men upon such fair wheels easily move?

The alteration to 'force or practice' is an improvement, bringing out more strongly the idea of compulsion, and the point that compulsion is needless where already 'men upon such fayre wheeles easely move'. It is too purposeful a change to be classed with the general run of *1670* variants, which come typically from misreading, misapprehension, or an editorial response to something apparently unsatisfactory or inelegant in the text.

A similar variant occurs in stanza 435 of *A Treatise of Monarchy*, where *W* reads:

> Againe, for wealth though theis faire grounds be laid,
> And treasure gotten by theis harmeless mynes;
> If order yet be not aswell obaid
> In the expence, wealth suddenlie declines;
>     And want growne from the mans faults, to the Crowne,
>     More fatallie pulls Kinge, and people downe.

For ll. 5–6, *1670* reads:

> And want pressing through mans faults, on the Crown,
> More fatallie pulls King and People down.

The change from the rather featureless phrase 'growne from the mans faults' to 'pressing through mans faults' is again one which no editor would have had any motive for making. It is quite against the general tendency of variants in *1670*, which is not to strengthen featureless lines, but to reduce any singularity to the level of the unexceptionable.

Greville's habits in revision may be studied in the various changes made in *W*, all recorded in the apparatus. Along with the obvious improvements there is a tendency to fidget with the text (e.g. *M.* 334/6, 424/4, 566/6, 589/6), making alterations

---

[1] *Life*, p. 176.

that no one but the author would immediately see the point of
making. Variants in *1670* that appear to be of this character are
*M.* 420/2 (discussed in the notes) and *M.* 653/2, while the readings at *M.* 465/5 and *R.* 63/4 seem to show an intention imper-
fectly realized in *W* being achieved in *1670*. Variants in this
class require particular scrutiny, in view of the general trend in
*1670* to 'improve' the text, and the apparatus contains a number
of variants of the type of *M.* 515/6 and *R.* 32/1, which have
been considered and rejected.

Except for the instances so far given, I have departed from
*W* only in cases of obvious scribal error (e.g. *M.* 323/1, 342/2,
405/5, 575/5). Any cases that might seem less than obvious are
treated in the notes (e.g. *M.* 410/1, 489/1, 543/4, *R.* 17/6). With
recurring variants like 'these' for 'those', and 'through' for
'thorough', I have not been able to assume that *W* is always
right: each decision is open to inspection in the apparatus.
Instances where both *W* and *1670* seem corrupt, and have
been emended, are *M.* 468/5 and 589 (marginal note).

### The Present Edition

An edition from manuscript of *A Treatise of Monarchy* and
*A Treatise of Religion* must inevitably reflect some of the irre-
gularities of Elizabethan scribal practice, and some of the
disparity between the systems followed by different scribes.
In the Warwick MSS., however, such peculiarities are not very
distracting, and there are other good reasons for preserving the
accidentals of the text. The manuscript of *A Treatise of Monarchy* has revisions by Greville himself, and *A Treatise of
Religion*, occurring in a volume also revised by him, has
corrections presumably made at his direction. They sometimes
show a meticulous care of detail, as where in *A Treatise of
Monarchy* the spelling 'culler' has been systematically altered
to 'color', and the spelling 'plaste' to 'plac'd'. While there would
be no warrant for assuming that every feature of these manuscripts has Greville's approval, his supervision of the text
is some ground for tolerating its occasional eccentricities.

Adherence to *W* also has the advantage of helping to remove the artificial division between these two treatises and the rest of Greville's verse, created by the 'Restoration' guise they assumed through being published in 1670.

Fidelity to the accidentals of the Warwick MSS. does not extend to reproducing scribal contractions, every detail of scribal pointing, or such conventions as the long 's', 'ff', and the interchange of 'i' and 'j', and 'u' and 'v'. These have all been assimilated to modern practice. The contraction 'cõn' at the end of a word has been regularly expanded to 'tion', to conform to the spelling most often occurring in *W* when the word is given in full. I have received much help from the punctuation of *W* (which in difficult passages is usually a better guide to the author's intentions than *1670*), though it has not been possible to follow it uniformly. I have thought it better to err by keeping too close to Elizabethan example than by deviating too far from it, and wherever in the text the pointing seems heavy, it reflects *W* or *1670*.

Punctuation aside, the apparatus records all variants in *1670* from the copy-text that are significant or representative (besides revisions in *W* itself where they occur). Spelling variants in *1670*, however, have been included only where there are special circumstances warranting it, as when they affect the number of syllables in the line (suffringes, sufferings), or show the modernizing tendency of *1670* (shreeve, sheriff), or on occasion suggest a different sense (synne, seen).

# THE REMAINS

# AN ADVERTISEMENT.

THE Author having dedicated all his Monuments to the Memory of Sir *Philip Sidney*, whose Life he did write as an intended Preface to these; it will not be fit to add any other then a brief Advertisement to acquaint the Reader, he was that Sir *Fulk Grevill* whose Noble Line by Matches with the Honourable Families of *Nevil, Beauchamp*, and *Willoughby* Lord *Brooke* make good the observation of Hereditary advantages, of Mind as well as Body, by Descents purely derived from Noble Ancestors; the Excellency of his Qualities rendring him an eminent Courtier in Queen *Elizabeths* Raign, and in King *James's* time, under whom he had the Honourable emploiments of Chancellour of the Exchequer and Privy Counceller, and was by Letters Patent of that King, in consideration of services done to the Crown, made Lord *Brooke*; to the Title of which Barony by Descent from *Willoughby* he had right: and having always lived a Batchelor (which was no small advantage to the freedom of his mind) He died in the Seventy fourth year of his Age, *Ann. Dom. 1628.* having been also Counsellor of State for about Three years to King CHARLES the First.

When he grew old he revised the Poems and Treatises he had writ long before, and at his death committed them to his friend Mr. *Michael Malet* an aged Gentleman in whom he most confided, who intended, what the Author purposed, to have had them Printed altogether; but by Copies of some parts of them which happened into other hands, some of them came first abroad, each of his Works having had their fate, as they singly merit particular esteem; so to come into the World at several times: he to whom they were first delivered being dead, the trust of these remaining pieces devolved on Sir *J. M.* who hath given me the Licensed Coppy of them: and that the Reader may be more fully informed of the Author and his Writings, and how they are related to each other, we must refer to that wherein, besides his friend *Sidneys* Life, he gives account of his own and of what he had written.

H. H.

# A TREATISE OF MONARCHY

## OF THE BEGINNING OF MONARCHY

### Section I

#### 1

There was a tyme before the tymes of story,
When nature raign'd, in stead of lawes or artes,
And mortall Goddes with men made upp the glory
Of one republique, by united hearts.
    Earth was the common seat, their conversation
    In saving love, and ours in adoration.


#### 2

For in those goulden dayes, with natures chaines
Both Kinge, and people seem'd conjoyn'd in one:
Both nurst alike with mutuall feeding vaynes,
Transcendency of either side unknowne,
    Princes with men usinge noe other artes,
    But by good dealing, to obtaine good hearts.


#### 3

Pow're then maynetayn'd it self even by those artes
By which it grewe, as justice, labour, love;
Reserved sweetnes did it self impart
Even unto slaves, yet kept it self above,
    And by a meeke descending to the least,
    Enviless sway'd, and govern'd all the rest.

A TREATISE OF MONARCHY: *title from 1670, which adds By Sir* FULK
GREVILL *Lord* BROOK.      Section I *Ed.*: Sect 1°: *W*, SECT. I. *1670*

4

Order there equall was, tyme Courts ordayn'd
To heare, to judge, to execute, and make
Fewe and good rules, for all greifs that complayn'd:
Such care did Princes of their people take,
    Before this art of power allay'd the trueth;
    Soe glorious of mans greatnes is the youth.

5

What wonder was it then, if these thrones found
Thankes as exorbitant, as was their meritt;
Witt to her highest tributes being bound,
And wound upp by a princely ruling spiritt
    To worshipp them for their Gods after death,
    Whoe in their life exceeded humane faith?

6

And shall it error, nay impiety
In heathen soules be thought, to recompence
The absent with immortall memory,
Goodnes with praise, and benifitts with sence?
    Or rather such a golden natur'd vayne,
    As in the world might golden dayes mayntayne?

7

For where should thanckfull ingenuity
Thinke the feare-thundringe Scepter fitt to rest
With knowledge, vertue, and felicity,
But in milde *Jupiters* well doing brest?
    Or where but in *Olympus* heav'n to be,
    Which was his dwelling place in *Thessalie?*

5/1 these] those *1670*    3 her] give *1670*    6/4 benifitts] Benefit *1670*

### 8

And if departed soules must rise againe,
Severely to become examined,
And byde the judgement of reward or payne,
What Chancelors seeme fitter for the dead
  Then *Radamanthus* and sterne *Minos* were,
  True types of justice while they lyved here?

### 9

Thus Kinges may see while greatnes did discend,
And care as farre spread, as authoritie,
Grace did restrayne, and disgrace did amend:
The vice was hatefull, and the Majesty
  Of justice held upp for a common good,
  A worke by kinges and men well understood.

### 10

Kinges creatures then were noe vayne favourites,
But guardians of the poore, eyes of the Crowne,
Least height of place should oversee the right,
And help the prowde to pull the humble downe:
  All lawes like Cobwebbs, catching little flies,
  But never great ones, without Princes eyes.

### 11

Under *Euristeus* that brave Prince of *Greece*,
Noe *Pallas*, noe *Narcissus* delicate
Were Minions, whose lustes did the people fleece,
Nor could sufficed be with *Midas* state,
  And whose effeminate unactivenes,
  To make themselves great, still made Scepters less.

  11/6 still made] *cancelling* did make

12

But *Hercules*, a brave laborious spiritt,
Whoe having freed *Greece* from home-tyrannie,
As borne of more then his owne soyle to meritt,
Was sent to purge the earthes iniquity:
   *Ægypt* of *Busire*, of *Diomedes Thrace*,
   *Italie* of *Cacus*, *Spaigne* of *Gerions* race.


13

Nor could a Goddess spite (which *Juno* vailes
Under imployments spetious pretences)
Change nature, or make true worth strike her sailes,
One God appeasing other Godds offences;
   Whence shee that by his labours sought his doome,
   There made his trophie, where shee ment his toomb.


14

Yet did hee raise noe *Pyramis* for payne,
But his republiques good, his maisters fame;
As thinckinge selfeness but a triviall gaine
To him, that buildes an universall frame:
   Noe trophies fitt for worth, but love and praise,
   Which shadowe-like still follow actyve rayes.


15

*Jason* againe (whoe serv'd *Thessalia's* kinge)
What els did hee affect from dangers past,
When hee the fleece of *Colchos* home did bringe,
Then in the rolles of large tyme to be plac't,
   For undertaking passages unknowen,
   Through which the wealth of many states have growen?

12/5 of *Diomedes Thrace*] *Diomedes* of *Thrace 1670*    13/5 Whence] When
*1670*    6 his trophie] him trophies *1670*

### 16

Now whil'st pow're did thus really proceed,
Not on advantage, humor, sleight, or will,
Her zeale with honour mixt, peas'd every deed,
Tyme did not yet encline to maske her ill;
    Wordes grewe in hearts, mens hearts were large and free,
    Bondage had then not brought in flatterie.

### 17

But by decree of fate this Corporation
Is altered since, and earthes faire globe miscarried,
Mans craft above these Gods in estimation,
And by it, wisdomes constant standerd varied:
    Whereby the sway of many yeares are gone,
    Since any Godhead rul'd an earthly throne.

### 18

Whether it was mans false *Pygmean* witt,
Captivinge envy, or the giants pride,
Which forc't these worthies to abandon it
I knowe not; but some disproportioned tyde
    Of times self humours hath that commerce drown'd,
    To which this image showes those tymes were bound.

### 19

And when these golden daies were once expired,
Tyme straight claym'd her succession in the brasse,
And to her ends new instruments inspired,
With narrow selfenes, stayning all that was:
    Power still affects more inequalitie,
    Which made mankinde more curiouse to be free.

18/1 was] were *1670*          19/1 these] those *1670*          4 stayning] *cancelling*
to stayne          5, 6 *cancelling* Stirring power upp to inequality, / And making
man as curious to be free.

### 20

Devided thus, kinges quitt that fathers hand
In government, which men did earst adore:
People againe by nomber sought to stand,
And scorn'd that power which erst they did implore;
   Goodnes goes from the earth, and greatnes too,
   In will, feare, craft, men forming all they doe.

### 21

Hence these Gods tyr'd with neighbourless deceipt,
Have rais'd their thrones above mortality,
And chang'd their sweet aspects with sower retreyt,
Whence all thinges blest before, since blasted be
   With tempests, earthquakes, fire, and thunders terrors,
   Shewing and threatning mans corrupting errors.

### 22

By which strange plagues these Gods did testify
Mankinde to be of such a mettall cast,
As neither fire can melt, ayre qualifie,
Water dissolve, or stroke of hammer wast:
   Noe native notion, lawe, or vyolence
   Fashion his hard heart to an humble sence.

### 23

But that hee still should grudge at government,
Scorne mercy, yet rebell at tyrannie,
Repine at discipline, rest discontent
Both with his equalls, and authority:
   As in whome power might without goodnes be,
   And base subjection without loyaltie.

20/1 that] their *1670*    21/4 since] now *1670*    22/1 did] do *1670*
23/1 still should] should still *1670*

### 24

In which confused state of declination
Left by these Gods, mankinde was forc't to trust
Those light thoughts, which were moulds of his privation,
And scorning equalls, raise a Soveraigne must:
  For frailty with it self growen discontent,
  Ward-like must lyve in others government.

### 25

Man then repyne not at these boundless kinges,
Since yow endure the fate of your forefathers,
To whome God did foretell, on humane winges
How inequality once rais'd, still gathers;
  Their choice offended him, please you it must,
  Whose dreggs still in you, on you make it just.

### 26

Princes againe ore'rack not your creation,
Least power returne to that whence it began;
But keepe upp scepters by that reputation
Which raised one, to rule this world of man:
  Order makes us the body, you the head,
  And by disorder anarchie is bred.

### 27

Let each then knowe by equall estimation,
That in this fraile freehold of flesh and blood,
Nature it self declines unto privation,
As mixt of reall ill and seeming good;
  And where mans best estate is such a strife,
  Can order there be permanent in life?

25/1 these] the *1670*     27/2 this] his *1670*    3 it self] her self *1670*

### 28

Now if considered simply man be such,
Cast him into a throne, or subjects mould,
The function cannot take away this tuch,
Since neither what hee ought, or can, or would;
   Both kinge and man perplexed are in state,
   Improve their ends, and sett noe other rate.


### 29

In which imperfect temper, expectation
Proves unto each a perverse enemy;
While pow'r with soveraigne partiall contemplation
Aymes at *Ideas* of Authority
   More absolute then God himself requires,
   Whoe of us onlie what hee gives, desires.


### 30

Againe, while people doe expect from kinges
Such a protecting popularity
As gives, forgives, intends noe other thinges
But in a Crowne, a common slave to be,
   This over-valuinge each estate too farr
   Makes both full of misprision, as they arr.


### 31

In judging other, then let either knowe,
As they are man, they are a meane creation
Betwixt the heaven above, and hell belowe,
Noe more deserving hate, then adoration;
   Equall in some thinges are the great'st, and least:
   One disproportion must not drowne the rest.

30/5 This] Thus *1670*    31/2 man] men *1670*

32

The odds to be examined then is place,
What that doth challenge, what againe it owes;
Not peasing these in daintie scales of grace,
Where pure simplicitie for wisdome goes;
  Or vayne *Ideas* formed in the ayre,
  To self imagination onlie fayre:

33

But in the world as thrones now mowlded are
By chance, choice, practise, birth, or martiall awe;
Where lawes and custome doe prescribe how farr
Either the Kinge, or subject ought to drawe
  These mutuall tyes of dutie, love or feare
  To such a straine, as every man may beare.

34

Which place what is it, but of reverence,
A throne rais'd on mans reason, and affection;
Where that well mixt and happy confluence
Of earthly and celestiall reflection
  Should weave the publique, in the private good,
  And to protect both, governe flesh and blood.

35

Yet since election did resigne to birth,
True worth to Chance, brave industry to blood,
Nature to art, and force comaund the earth,
That natyve Commerce which wrought mutuall good
  Twixt Crownes and men, was soone exil'd from hence,
  And wee like beasts, left noe rights but in sence.

33/4 Kinge] *cancelling* throne    34/3 well mixt and happy] well happy
mixt, and *1670*    5 weave] weare *1670*    35/1 did] doth *1670*    6 rights]
right *1670*

### 36

To fortify which confident rais'd throne,
And keepe mankinde with it in unitie,
The witt of pow'r cannot suffice alone,
Man is not stronge to bynde humanitie:
   Therefore above man, they that man would bound,
   Still sought some showes of everlasting ground.

### 37

Hence was powers *Zenith* raised upp, and fixt
Upon the base of superstitions rites,
Whose visions with the trueth and error mixt,
Make humane wisdomes yet seeme infinite,
   By giving vayne opinion (borne of sence)
   Falsely the sacred stile of conscience.

### 38

For as by optick repercussions here,
The light with shadowes mixt, makes sence mistake,
Whereby the less oft greater doth appeare,
Creating *Castor* God for *Pollux* sake;
   And as the Rainebow but a shadowe being,
   By shadowes, formes another to our seeing:

### 39

Soe from the mirrour of these visions move
Second reflections, which doe represent
Formes of the ill below, and good above,
As humane lawes, fame, honour, government:
   All shewing man (though in unperfect light)
   That thrones may seeme, but are not infinite.

36/5 man would] would man *1670*   37/2 superstitions rites] superstitious
rights *1670*   39/1 move] more *1670*

### 40

Now if from these dymm shadowes there breake out
Light, to shew thrones are not indefinite;
In true religions cleare beames, whoe can doubt
But that pow're bounded is with wrong and right:
    The infinite in wisdome drawing downe
    The will of tyrants to the lawes of Crowne.

### 41

Where in that other superstitious spheare,
Chance, and opinions nimble idolls raigne,
Racking upp tributes out of hope and feare,
By which weake mankinde loose, stronge scepters gaine:
    As where noe lymitts be to powre or will,
    Nor true distinction betwene good and ill.

### 42

Soe that when man beholds this boundles sea
Of will, and noe shoare left to show her streames,
Hee straight beleives thoughts may saile every way,
Till pow'rs contrary windes disperse these dreames;
    And make men see their freedome bound soe fast,
    As it of noe forbidden fruite dare tast.

### 43

Yet happily had man not thus bin bounded
With humane wrests, as well as moulds divine;
Hee in his passions must have bin confounded,
Desire in him is such an endless Myne:
    *Eve* would have *Adam* bin, man kinge, kinges more;
    Till such destruction fall, as fell before.

40/1 dymm] dumb *1670*      41/1 Where in] Wherein *1670*      42/1 that]
then *1670*      43/5 man kinge] Man Kings *1670*

### 44

Therefore if power within these scepter lynes
Could keepe, and give as it would be repaid,
These mutuall fedd, and mutuall feedinge Mynes
Would still enrich, could hardly be decay'd;
 For chance gives mutuall confidence a blisse,
 And God helpes those frames, which showe likest his.

### 45

Besides, this activenes it self mainetaynes,
And rather then live idle, can doe ill;
Those images it rayseth in our braynes
Having alliance not with truth, but will:
 And to confirme this, strives to pull all downe,
 That lymitt the excesses of a Crowne.

## DECLINATION OF
## MONARCHY TO VIOLENCE

### Section II

### 46

Now though the world on these excentricks be
Fashion'd to move, and ballance her owne waight,
Not much inclininge to obliquity;
Yet is her ruler man, thorough self conceipt,
 Violence of pride, fate of corruption,
 Apt to give all her best workes interruption.

---

*Title in 1670*: DECLINATION OF MONARCHY [*rule*] *To Violence.*
Section II *Ed.*: Sect. 2:° *W*, SECT. II. *1670*  46/1 these] the *1670*
3 thorough] through *1670*

### 47

For since religions name, not nature came
To rule, those auntient forming pow'rs gave place;
The stile of conscience overwaighing fame,
And reason yeilding upp her soveraigne Mace
   Unto those lively pictures, which produce
   Unactive apparitions of noe use.

### 48

Which change straight wrought, but was not straightwaies found,
Power was soe vaild with formall lawes and bayts,
Under which still the infinite lay bound,
And man bewitch't with witts confused sleights,
   To make pow'rs throne the idoll of his heart,
   Transforming zeale and nature into art.

### 49

Soe that without the guide of clowde or fire,
Man since sailes fatall straights of hope and feare,
In ebbs and floodes of travelling desire,
Where what wee have, to us is never deare:
   Pow'r making men vainely, by offering more,
   Hope to redeeme that state they had before.

### 50

Hence falls it out that sillie people loose
Still by these thynne webbs of authority;
Which they that spinne, yet therefore cannot use,
Because these thredds noe more inherent be
   Within themselves, but soe transcrib'd to Crownes,
   As they raise pow'r by pulling freedome downe.

49/3 desire] desires *1670*      5 offering] off'ring *1670*

51

Thus by a credulous obedience,
Mankinde gave might a ground to build upp more;
Cooling and kindling his desire with sence,
Even of such thinges as were his owne before:
   Disease and error meeting both in this,
   That many follow, where one rooted is.


52

For thus embas'd, wee since want pow'r to tye
Others to us, or us unto our owne;
Our many passions serve to bynde us by,
And our distractions kepe our strengths unknowen;
   One holdinge that, which others give away,
   The base whereon all tyrannie doth stay.


53

Hence came these false Monarchall Councells in,
And instruments of tyrants states apart,
Which to their private, from the publique wynn,
While man becomes the matter, pow'r the art;
   Making obedience too indefinite,
   As taxt with all the vanities of might.


54

The tenure chang'd, nature straight chang'd the use,
For all the actyve spiritts follow might;
Ignorance, basenes, negligence, abuse,
Inconstancie, disunion, oversight
   By Crownes to people soe intayl'd are they,
   As noe subjection can put these away.

### 55

Whence neither makers now, nor members held
Men are; but blankes where pow'r doth write her lust,
A sprightlesse masse, which for it cannot weld
It self, at others pleasure languish must;
   Resolve to suffer, and let power doe all;
   Weakenes in men, in children naturall.

### 56

From which cras'd wombe of frailtie was brought forth
A giant creature in excesse of might,
To worke in all with every pow'r but worth,
Whoe, to be sure that never shall have right,
   Takes not God as hee is, but makes him new,
   Lyke to his endes, large, narrow, false, or true.

### 57

Religion, honor, natures lawes, and nations,
All Moulds derived from that first transcendent,
These Monsters stampt, or gave disestimation,
As they did finde them theirs, or undependent;
   Left nothing certaine here on earth but will,
   And that yet never constant, for 'tis ill.

### 58

Instance prowd *Mahomet* when hee propos'd
The Empire of this world to his ambition;
Under Gods name were not his acts dispos'd
To change mans faith, and freedome of condition?
   The sacred dove whispring into his eare,
   That what his will impos'd, the world must beare.

57/2 first] gift *1670*    58/6 beare] fear *1670*

## 59

Unto *Cambyses* all his sages vow'd
That in their reading they of noe law wist
Which mariage with his sister had allow'd,
But that their Monarch might doe what hee list:
    *Licet, si Libet*; and what be these other
    Then hellish wordes of *Caracallas* mother?

## 60

And doth not our great *Capitolian* Lord
Use the same compasse in each course hee steers?
Arre not those acts which all estates discord,
As kinges assassinate, mutiny of peeres,
    Stirr'd up by him under pretence divine
    To force those scepters, hee cannot encline?

## 61

Nay, hath hee not a higher pitch attain'd,
A more compendious power of perswasion?
Having since *Phœbus* and *Sybilla* raign'd,
Made himself such a tripode by occasion,
    As may not be examin'd, or withstood,
    But with the Godhead equally made good.

## 62

Which errors (like the Hectick feavers) be
Easie to cure, while they are hard to knowe:
But when they once obtayne supremacy,
Then easily seene, but hard to overthrowe:
    Soe that where pow'r prevents not this excess,
    Mytars growe great, by making Scepters less.

60/3 Arre] *cancelling* And        61/3 *Sybilla*] *Cybele 1670*        6 the] a *1670*
62/6 Mytars growe] *cancelling* The Church growes

### 63

Therefore did these prowd Tyrants live awake,
Carefull to cancell all inferior rights,
And in Creations still keepe pow'r to make,
To fitt each instruments, and fashion spiritts:
 That as the heads *Ideas* rule the heart,
 Soe pow'r might print her will in every part.

### 64

For active rulers seldome faile of meanes,
Occasion, color, and advantage too,
To bynde by force, by witt, by customes chaines,
And make the oppressed soules content to woe:
 Feare suffringe much, for feare to suffer more,
 As still by smart made greater then before.

### 65

Knowinge that men alike touch't never were,
That divers sence workes diverslie in woe,
The nymblest witts being still kept downe by feare,
Dull witts not feeling neighbors overthrowe,
The wise mistrust the weake, and strive to beare,
Thrones being stronge, because men thinke them soe:
 Yet marke at length, how error runs in rounds,
 And ever what it raiseth upp, confounds.

### 66

For when this power transendent growes secure,
Flattering it self that all is made for one,
Then will, which nothing but it self indures,
And pow'r that thinkes it stands and works alone,
 With an unsatiate pride and wanton ease,
 Surfetts it self with other mens disease.

63/5 heads *Ideas*] Head Ideas *1670*  65/1 Knowinge] *cancelling* They
knowinge

67

Hence lawes grew tedious, and the very names
Of God and trueth, whose natures died before,
A heavy burthen to these racking frames,
That with a word would wrest upp all, and more:
    Assemblies of estates disparagements be,
    Taxe, Custome, feare, and labour only free.


68

Thus thrones grew idolls, man their sacrifice,
And from the earth, as to the sunne above,
Tributes of Dewes and exhalations rise,
Soe humane nature yeilds up all, but love:
    Hating this strange transcendencie of might,
    As child of noe meane vice, but infinite.


69

Whereby these strengths which did before concurre
To build, invent, examine, and conclude,
Now turne disease, bringe question, and demurr,
Oppose, dissolve, prevaricate, delude;
    And with opinions give the state unrest,
    To make the new, still undermine the best.


70

*Caesar* was slaine by those that objects were
Of grace, and engines of his tiranny.
*Brutus* and *Cassius* worke shall wittnes beare,
Even to the comfort of posterity,
    That prowd aspirers never had good end,
    Nor yet excess of might a constant frend.

67/1 grew] grow *1670*    5 estates] Estate *1670*    68/1 Thus] Hence *1670*
3 Dewes] Dew *1670*    5 Hating] Having *1670*

71

Soe that although this tyrant usurpation
Stood peas'd by humors from a present fall,
Thoughts being all forc't upp to adoration
Of witt and pow'r (which such thrones worke withall)
  Yet both the head and members finite are,
  And soe must still by miscreating marre.

72

The nature of all overacting might
Being to stirr offence in each estate,
And from the deepe impressions of despight
Enflame those restles instruments of fate,
  Which as noe frendes to dutie or devotion,
  Easily stirr upp incursion, and commotion.

73

Occasion for a forreigne enemy,
Or such Competitors as doe pretend
By any stile, or popularitie,
Faction or sect; all whose endeavors tend
  To shake the realme, or by assassinate,
  Into the people to lett fall the state.

74

In which excesse of tyrants violence,
If *Nero* lack a forreigne enemy,
*Nero* from *Vindex* shall receive offence;
Safe from his guard *Caligula* shall not be.
  Or if these tyrants finde none worse then they,
  *Otho* shall help to make himself away.

71/6 soe must still by] must still by their *1670*     72/5 to] of *1670*    6 and]
or *1670*

75

But graunt the world slept in her misery,
Yett greedy time, that good and ill devours,
To crosse this headlonge course of tyranny,
Takes from the throne these auntient daring powrs;
    And by succession of mans discontent,
    Carries mischance upon misgovernment.


76

Wherein observe the witt of former daies,
Which feign'd their Gods themselves (oft to prevent
Pow'rs inclination to oppressing waies)
Came downe, and gave offences punishement,
    Least man should thinke above mortalitie,
    Against injustice there were noe decree.


77

For proofe, when with *Lycaons* tyrrannie
Men durst not deale, then did *Jove* to reforme
Discend, and savage natur'd crueltie
Fittlie into the greedy woolf transforme:
    Soe was that tyrant *Tereus* nastie lust
    Chang'd into *Upupas* fowle-feeding dust.


78

Hence was *Megera* and her sisters tyed
By God, to attend the cryes of mans oppressions;
Whether *Orestes* were for parricide
To be distracted with his owne impressions,
    Or *Pentheus* for his prowd blaspheming scorne,
    In many peeces by his mother torne.

78/2 mans] Mens *1670*    oppressions *1670*: oppression *W*

### 79

Thus as wee see these guides of humane kinde
Changed from Gods and fathers to oppressors;
Soe see wee tirannyes excesse of minde
Against her owne estate become transgressor;
 And either by her subjects craft betray'd,
 Slayne by themselves, or by Gods judgements swayd.

## OF WEAKE MINDED TYRANTS

### Section III

### 80

*Olympus* kept her scepter without staine,
Till shee lett fall pow'rs tender reputation
By gracing *Venus* and her sonne to raigne,
Whoe with the first Gods had noe estimation:
 For when these faint thoughts came to rule above,
 Power lost at once both majesty and love.

### 81

A worke of *Saturne*, whoe with narrow spite
Mow'd downe the fatt, and lett the leane eares springe,
That after his sith nothing prosper might;
Tyme that begetts, and blasteth every thinge,
 To barley making wheat degenerate,
 As Eagles did into the kytes estate.

### 82

But let us grant, excesse of tirranny
Could scape the heavy hand of God, and man:
Yet by the naturall variety
Of frailties, raigning since the world began,
 Faint relaxations doubtlesse will ensue,
 And change force into crafte, old crymes to new.

79/6 judgements] Judgement *1670* swayd] *cancelling* payd **Section III**
*Ed.*: Sect. 3°: *W*, SECT. III. *1670* 82/6 crymes] times *1670*

### 83

Worth must decay, and height of power declyne,
Vices shall still, but not the same vyce raigne:
Error in mankinde is an endles Myne,
And to the worst, thinges ever doth constraine:
　　Unbound it would lyve, and delight by change
　　To make those formes still welcome, that be strange.

### 84

Hence like a ball, how hath this world bin tost
From hand to hand, betwixt the *Persians, Meades,*
*Romans* and *Greekes,* each name in other lost?
And while *Romes* pride her government misleades,
　　To scorne the *Asian, Grecian* armes, and worth,
　　Made slave shee was to those lords shee brought forth.

### 85

What marvell is it then, to see the earth
Thus chang'd from order unto anarchie?
When these *Ideas* of refined birth
Were thus transform'd from reasons Monarchy,
　　Into that false oligarchie of passion,
　　Where Princes must beare every bodies fashion?

### 86

And whereby man may really conclude,
That in it self tyme onlie doth not change,
Nature affecting like vicissitude;
Whence to see vice succeed worth is not strange,
　　Weakenes and strength, aswell as youth and age,
　　Having in each estate a various stage.

83/4 doth] did *1670*　　6 those *1670*: these *W*　　85/2 unto] into *1670*

### 87

Soe that out of this *Phoenix* fire there breed
Birdes, that doe weare noe feathers of their owne,
But borrow'd plumes, which imping ever need,
And such as are by divers colors knowne,
 Not of, or for themselves, to move or be,
 But under them, that guide their infancie.

### 88

Which changling weakenes, made to serve, not raigne,
Possessing all without a doinge lust,
To add more scorne to her fore-runners staine,
Dare neither cherish ill, nor goodnes trust:
 But slacks those engines which o're wound before,
 And soe gives people back their owne, and more.

### 89

Then man! marke by this change what thou hast wonne
That leav'st a torride for a frozen Zone,
And art by vice vicissitudes undone,
Whose state is ever fatall to her owne;
 The active tyrant scarce allowing breath,
 While this unactive threatens lingering death.

### 90

For where to power absolute such spiritts
Are raised upp, as unacquainted be
How to create, to censure faults or meritts,
Where to be bound, to binde, or to be free;
 Amidd'st the ocean of mans discontent,
 They want both Mapp, and scale of government.

87/1 fire] *cancelling* fall breed] bred *1670*  88/5 o're] are *1670* 6 owne]
own again *1670*  89/6 lingering] lingring *1670*

### 91

Since where the pease betwixt heart, witt, and might
Unequall is, and witt predominant;
Opinions shadowes must seeme infinite,
The passive Circles large, the active scant;
    All cleare zones dimly overcast with feare,
    And to those false mists mankinde forc't to sweare.

### 92

Whence from inferiors, visions fitted be,
Deceiving frailtie with her owne desire;
Ease is made greatnes, trust a liberty,
A point of craft for power to retire,
    To worke by others held a soveraigne state,
    Resting as God, whoe yet distributes fate.

### 93

Under which clowdes, while pow'r would shadow sloth,
And make the Crowne a spetious hive for drones,
Unactivenesse findes scorne, and ruyne both;
Vyce and misfortunes seldome come alone,
    Pow'r loosing it self, by distast of paine,
    Since they that labour will be sure to raigne.

### 94

For though like *Æolus* from the hills of might,
Thrones can lett windes out, to move earth and sea;
Yet neither can they calme, or guide them right
From blasting of that mountaine where they lay;
    Because these sprites joyne, part, warr, and agree,
    To robb weake mindes, of stronge authority.

91/1 might] Right *1670*    4 The passive] To *Passive 1670*        93/4 misfortunes seldome come] Misfortune seldom go *1670*     94/5 and] *1670 omits*

### 95

Thus did old *Galba* raigne in pupillage,
Under the tutorshipp of twoe, or three,
Whoe robb'd, built, spoil'd, upon the publique stage,
Cloth'd with the vaile of his authority.
  Thus *Claudius* in his Empire liv'd a thrall,
  Scorn'd by those slaves, rais'd by him to doe all.

### 96

Besides, what feavers then must raigne, when these
Base idle fantosmes, creatures of grace,
Impossible to temper, hard to please,
Shall have the pow're to raise upp, or deface?
  Since meane borne natures, artless fortune great,
  Hate them that meritt, scorne them that intreat.

### 97

Which blasting humors wound both men and thinges,
Downe goe the schooles, the pulpitt, and the barr,
States fall, where power flies with feeble winges,
To make a man, such kinges oft kingdomes marre.
  Nothing, and all, alike are currant there;
  Order springes upp and dyes, change noe shape beares.

### 98

Hence comes contempt of lawes, and bullions fall,
Riddles of state, which gett by doing harme,
Statutes for words, bondage un-naturall,
Offices, Customes, Cittadells in farme,
  Engaging Crownes, making pow'rs name a stile,
  To ruyne worth, which it cannot beguile.

98/1 comes] come *1670*

### 99

Yet marke how vice (that it self onlie frends)
In her owne webb, still weaves her owne disease;
By disproportion, compassing her ends,
And disproportion ruininge her waies:
   For they that rose by providence, care, payne,
   And over pow're which wanted these, did raigne;

### 100

Growe fondlie scornefull, idlie imperious,
Despisinge forme, and turning lawe to will,
Abridge our freedome, to lord over us,
Loosing the fruit of humors with the skill;
   Till by degrees insensiblie they fall,
   By leaving those arts, which they rose withall.

### 101

When instantly those undertaking powres,
Care, hazard, witt, misplaced industrie,
(Which help't to build their oligarchall tow'rs)
Flie from these downefalls of prosperitie;
   As spiritts that to governe were created,
   And cannot lower properly be rated.

### 102

The pride of such inferiors did constraine
The *Swise* against the *Austrians* cantonise;
*Duke of*    Soe were the *Belgians* likewise forc't againe
*Alva*      A new *Republique* finely to devise;
   In which that Monarch was compeld to treat
   As with states equall free, not equall great.

99/2 weaves] wears *1670*   5 they] those *1670*   100/1 idlie] idle, *1670*

### 103

For vices soone to heights and periods rise,
Have both their childehood, state, and declination;
Are sometime currant, but at noe time wise,
Like blasing starres, that burne their owne foundation,
   Or shadowes, which the shew of bodies have,
   And in self darknes, both a life and grave.

### 104

Whence it proceeds that all workes of error
Live not in state of health, but sicke, and cured;
Change carrying out excess, to bring in terror,
Never securing, nor to be secured:
   But phisick-like in new diseases bredd,
   Either subtracts, or adds, till all be dead.

### 105

Thus rose all states, thus grew they, thus they fall,
From good to ill, and soe from ill, to worse;
Tyme for her due vicissitudes doth call,
Error still carrying in it self her Curse:
   Yet lett this light out of these clowds breake forth:
   That pow'r hath noe longe being, but in worth.

## CAUTIONS AGAINST THESE WEAKE EXTREMITIES

### Section IV

### 106

How to prevent, or stay those declinations,
And desperate diseases of estate,
As hard is, as to change the inclinations
Of humane nature in her love, or hate,
   Which whosoever can make straight or true,
   As well is able to create her new.

104/1 all workes] all the works *1670*   error] *cancelling* the error
Section IV *Ed.*: Sect. 4°: *W*, SECT. IV: *1670*   106/1 How] Now *1670*
those] these *1670*

### 107

Hence falls it out, that as the wise phisitian,
When hee discovers death in the disease,
Reveales his patients dangerous condition,
And straight abandons, what hee cannot ease,
    Unto the ghostlie phisick of a might
    Above all second causes infinite:

### 108

Soe many grave and great men of estate,
In such despaired tymes, retire away,
And yeild the sterne of government to fate,
Foreseeing her remediless decay;
    Loth in confused torrents of oppression
    To perish, as if guilty of transgression.

### 109

Whoe then can wary *Seneca* reprove?
After hee had observ'd his pupills rage,
The brother poyson'd (strange bewitching love)
The mother slaine, of vice his patronage,
If hee from bloudie *Nero* did remove?
    And as the pilotts doe in tempests growne,
    To fate give over art, and all their owne.

### 110

But graunt such spiritts were to be excus'd,
As by oppression or necessitie
Disgraced lyve, restrayned, or not us'd,
As part themselves of publique miserie;
    Yet whoe are free, must labour and desire
    To carry water to this common fire.

109/6 growne] groan *1670*

### 111

Have not some by equalitie of minde,
Even in the crossest course of evill tymes,
With passyve goodnes woonne against the winde?
Soe *Priscus* pass'd *Domitians* torride clymes,
    And scap't from danger to the full of daies,
    Helping fraile *Rome*, with un-offending waies.

### 112

Was it true valour, or timiditie,
That made sterne *Cato* soe impatient
Of his owne life, and *Caesars* victorie?
Vanity it was, like smoake, not permanent,
    That wrought this weake worke of stronge destinie:
    Where while hee lost himself, and *Rome* a freind,
    Hee lost that glorie which hee made his end.

### 113

For since the most estates at first were founded
Upon the wavinge basis of confusion;
On what but feare can his discourse be grounded,
That in distress dispairs a good conclusion?
    With mysteries of which vicissitude,
    Fate oftentimes doth humane witt delude.

### 114

Againe, whoe marke tymes revolutions, finde
The constant health of Crownes doth not remaine
In pow'r of man, but in the powres divine,
Whoe fixe, change, ruyne, or build upp againe
    According to the period, wayne, or state
    Of good or evills seldome changing fate.

112/6 himself] his life *1670*    113/4 a] of *1670*    114/3 in the] of the
*1670*

### 115

First then let Tyrants (as they doe encline
By nature, either way unto excesse)
Conceave, though true perfection be divine,
And noe where ever brought to passe with less;
   Yet in the world, which they would governe well,
   Cures and diseases oft together dwell.

### 116

And though to lyve by rule prowd man be loth;
Yet rules to Kinges and subjects are such staies,
As crutches be to feeble ages sloth;
Or as the maine turmoyled mother seas
   Doe finde those bancks, which then confine their course,
   When rage blowne upp, would els make all thinges worse.

### 117

Let noe man then expect a constant ayre
Betwene the sense of men, and senseless might,
Where one mynde makes skies fowle, another faire;
In passive Orbes whoe lookes for other right,
   Childelike must breake all toyes, for losse of one,
   And by their fall, add honour to a throne.

### 118

Rather let people, as in ayres infected,
Not seeke to master, but avoyd disease,
By absence now, by homage now protected,
Not looking high for stumbling in their waies:
   Least as of old, curst with confused speech,
   They now finde noe word currant, but beseech.

115/6 oft] both *1670*    116/2 Kinges] *cancelling* thrones    5 their] her
*1670*    117/3 mynde] man *1670*

### 119

Againe let weake kinges keep their humour chast,
Not daringe violence; least overbuilt,
They help to lay their owne foundations wast,
And failing themselves, multiply their guilt;
   Since hearts as stronge as their estates must be,
   That can enlarge themselves by tyrannie.

### 120

For as in weake estates, soe in weake mindes
To injure or oppresse humanitie
Stirrs upp right, witt, and heart in divers kindes,
To shew how easily hazard makes men free;
   Which prospect must appeare to these weake kinges
   A signe, that ruyne flies with nymble winges.

### 121

This weaknes which I meane hath divers kindes,
Some waterlike, easie to take impression,
And like it, leave not any print behinde,
Which I omitt, as fitt for noe profession:
The other wax-lyke, take, and keepe a mynde,
   And may in strengths, they have not of their owne,
   Be helpt by common duties to a throne.

### 122

For as when birdes and beasts would have a kinge,
To furnish this faire creature for a guide,
Out of their owne they gave him everie thinge,
And by their guifts themselves more surely tyde;
   Eyes, voyces, winges, and of their natures skill,
 . To governe, rayse, or ruyne them at will:

---

119/1 kinges] *cancelling* thrones   3 foundations] foundation *1670*  6 tyrannie]
*cancelling* injury        120/5 Which] Where *1670*        121/6 strengths,
they have] strengths they have, *1670*    122/6 or] and *1670*

### 123

Soe may these fraile unactive kinde of spiritts
Be with the milke of many nurses fedd,
All strivinge to hold upp the scepter rights
With subjects strength by Crownes authorised;
  Whereby the feeble may againe be wombed,
  And there gett life, even where it was intombed.

### 124

Which outward help of others providence
Watcheth occasion, peaseth each intent,
Nor is Crowne wisdome any quintessence
Of abstract trueth, or art of government,
  More then sweet sympathie, or counterpease
  Of humours tempred happily to please.

### 125

But their best help indeed is happy choice
Of underministers in every kinde,
By whome discretely thrones may judge the voyce
Of Images projected to their minde:
  And soe by weake, but wakefull jealosie,
  The true or false scope of propounders see.

### 126

Whence marke, how that young unexperienc'd spiritt,
*Alexander* (whoe was after nam'd *Severe*),
Duringe his youth, did of his people meritt,
By help of Councell uncorrupt, to beare
  The practize of his publique government
  Under good lawes, which gave good men content.

123/3 scepter] Scepters *1670*   4 strength] strengths *1670*      125/2 in]
of *1670*

### 127

Now though pow're hardlie can fitt spiritts to place,
Which must want judgement, wanting industrie;
And soe as rarely well dispose of grace,
Having but chance, noe true abilitie:
  Yet kinlesse fame helpes weakenes what to judge,
  Till from an *Eccho*, shee become a drudge.

### 128

For as the painter (curious in his art)
Extreame ill features easily represent;
And by deformity in any part,
Expresse the life, and likenesse to content;
  As hee in natures good proportion showes,
  That in her pride art equall with her goes:

### 129

Soe fame this quintessence of humane spiritt,
Bringes unto light the divers states of men,
And seldome to unworthines gives meritt,
Or letts perfection languish in a Denne;
  But on her winges alike beares either forth,
  The one as good, the other nothing worth.

### 130

Thus may fames many eyes, heads, winges and heart,
Instruct weake power to kepe her state upright,
And as to rule these is a maisters art,
Soe to rule by these, is one way of might,
  Wherein the Crowne can feele noe great distress,
  And for the people, they must sure finde lesse.

127/4 abilitie] Nobility *1670*    128/2 represent] represents *1670*   3 any]
every *1670*    5 proportion] proportions *1670*       129/1 spiritt *1670*:
spiritts *W*    5 beares] brings *1670*

### 131

Besides which help of fame, weake thrones shall finde
The witt of tyme, and selfenes in mens hearts
Will teach, how one man many men may bynde,
And raise the head by counterpoize of parts;
  All having charge, and subalterne degree,
  To ease the Auditts of authority.

### 132

Where els weake handes in mightie workes must faile,
And all transform'd be to usurpers passion;
Thrones then reserve your selves, choice, and appeale,
Greatnes her way must with some labour fashion;
  With many eyes hee must see wronge and right,
  That finite being, will rule infinite.

### 133

Or if pow'rs tender thoughts will needes make pleasure
The end of Crownes, which God made publique good;
Yet give your seconds scope in such a measure,
As may for cheifs still make you understood;
  Which one poore privilege yow may reserve,
  By thinking more then one can well deserve.

### 134

For as in bodies lyving (though decayd)
If all parts equally chance to be stained,
The whole is by an *equilibrium* sway'd,
As where noe odds can easily be gayned;
  And soe mortalitie adjurn'd as farr
  Oft as in those, all whose parts sounder are:

131/1 which] the *1670*        132/6 will] would *1670*

### 135

Soe these weake powers (in whome states are diseas'd,
By equall disproportion in each part)
May scape great fitts, and happily be eas'd,
Keeping her tottering ballance upp by art;
   In making faction, which destroyes the stronge,
   By peasinge weake pow'rs, to preserve them longe.

### 136

What had become of *Romes* vast Monarchy,
When *Galienus* buried was in lust,
Sloth, ryott, and excesse of vanity,
Even while the *Barbars* swarm'd, like barren dust,
   Had not the thirty, ryvalls to each other,
   From one mans tyranny preserv'd their mother?

### 137

Let place then rule, let favour raigne, not meritt,
And each in his predicament be kinge;
Doe of a head use neither powre nor spiritt
To audit, question, or judge any thinge:
   Only let faction multiply her seed,
   Twoe bodies headles seldome danger breed.

### 138

For equalls soone each other will oppose,
And both in thrones as suddenly unite,
To it they pray, they travell, they disclose,
Creation onlie ballanceth their might;
   Reserve, distribute that in jealous measure,
   Then Crownes may stand, and kinges may take their pleasure.

### 139

These partiall witts (which faction works withall)
Though fatall Judges, yet good sisters be;
Which while they stryve each other to enthrall,
Cleere upp the dymme lights of authority,
    And showe weake Crownes, what waight of hope or feare
    The state, or mynde of every man can beare.

### 140

Besides, thrones have all moulds of their forefathers,
Safe underbuildinges of the wisdomes dead,
Exchequers that revenewes judge, and gather,
Courts that examine treason to the head,
    Parliaments, conscience seats, tripods of law,
    Engines of powre, to keep desire in awe.

### 141

For forreigne practise, they have spies of tyme
And place, to which intelligence is due:
For Church, inferior functions and sublime,
To teach men God, and take a spirituall view
    Of schisme in doctrine, and in life of synne,
    That neither sect, nor scandall enter in.

### 142

Only, let not weake powrs lay new foundations,
Whoe cannot judge how tyme works on the old;
But keepe the auntient formes in reputation,
To which mans freedome is alredy sould:
    Since order over worne, is yet a frame
    Wherein confusion rarely weaves her name.

140/5 conscience seats] Councel-seats *1670*

### 143

Thus much for weakenes in that royall part,
Which doth concerne justice, that is supreame;
Whose golden lincks (though forg'd by powers art)
Safe circles are to compasse every Realme,
  And keepe out all thoughts of irreverence,
  As bearing in it every mans defence.

### 144

Where frailtie els, ever unfortunate,
Wanting true skales betwene place, witt, and heart,
Scatters the strength and honor of a state,
By suffringe more to play one tyrants part;
  And blowes the people like clowdes, here and there,
  As (till exhausted) objects of their feare.

### 145

Lastly, if these milde cautions faile to stay
These frailties, which disease-like turne and tosse,
And soe for that change every where make way,
Which change unguided, still begetteth losse:
  Then hee whoe cannot take, must taken be,
  Such sharpe points hath frayle mans supremacie.

## STRONGE TYRANTS

### Section V

### 146

Now from the setting of this evening starr,
Ascends that morning planetts influence,
Which both in light and glory passeth farr
These Cometts of stronge powre in feeble sence,
  And whoe from inequalitie of state,
  Stryve to make all, for one, unfortunate.

144/4 suffringe] suffering *1670*      STRONGE TYRANTS] Of strong
Tyrants *1670*      Section V *Ed.*: Sect. 5°. *W*, SECT. V. *1670*

## 147

I meane such confident imperious spiritts,
As over-act with restles scepter-witt,
Thincking the world inferior to their meritts,
And brooke noe other bounds or lawes in it,
 Then to make all their owne thoughts, words, and deeds
 Receav'd of people not as rules, but creedes.

## 148

Which soules thus overswolne with windie vyce,
Must wisely both allay'd, and moulded be,
Least torrentlike, they with the prejudice
Of people, wast their owne transcendency;
 And by their cutting reall groundes too thinne,
 Have their ambitions ever to begin.

## 149

For though throne-vyce be publique, like her state,
(And therefore must of force wound many wayes)
Yet some move scorne, some faults men wonder at,
Other harme not soe many as they please:
 Ill chosen vyces vanish in dispaire,
 Well chosen still leave something after faire.

## 150

*Vitellius* vertuelesse in life and raigne,
Yet by a gluttons familiaritie,
The *German* armies did soe firmely gaine,
As against *Otho* hee had victorie;
Brake the pretorian forces; and in vaine
*Vespasian* had aspir'd his Monarchie,
 But that each vice fitts not all times and states,
 For what one age affects, another hates.

### 151

*Pertinax* againe, in whome predominant
Fewe vyces were, yet narrownes of heart
Made him the fortune of great Armyes want;
Where *Caesar* mixt of vyces, worth, and art,
    Had with the people for his death such moane,
    As if in him *Rome* had bin overthrowne.

### 152

In him, that first did spoyle her treasurie,
Ravage her provinces, and tirrannize;
While as bewitch't with prodigalitie,
They sell themselves, for what in their powre lies:
    Thus pleasing vices sometimes raise a Crowne,
    As austeere vertues often pull it downe.

### 153

Power therefore must those womanish slight errors,
Which publish to the world self love, or feare,
Carefully shunne, as crafty peoples myrrours,
To show both what the kinge, and Crowne can beare;
    And teach mankinde, on humours to take hold,
    That other wise with thrones durst not be bold.

### 154

From hence the *Macedonians* did gett heart,
To dally with that tendernes they found
In their great kinge, and finely frame an art
To keepe the Monarch with his owne thoughts bound;
    For when *Hephestion* died, hee did aspire
    Through him to make a God of his desire.

151/4 of] with *1670*

### 155

Unto which God, some straight did altars build,
Some sacrific'd, others sware by his name,
Some told their dreames, others were vision-fild,
All which inspirings from *Hephestion* came;
   As grace or disgrace did in *Nero's* dayes,
   To those that did his singing scorne, or prayse.

### 156

Aspirers therefore on corruption founded,
Should use their vyce, as merchants doe their ware;
Not choake the markett, least their vents be bounded,
But marshall these thinges which excesses are,
   Soe as by vyce made slaves, they may not be,
   But rather vyce made arts of tyrannie.

### 157

For majesty then sinckes, when private vice
Is not kept servant to the publique state;
But rather Crownes with comon prejudice
Subjected basely to their vices fate;
   Because of consequence, then power must
   Serve them in all thinges, that observe their lust.

### 158

Wise *Salomon* was taken in this nett,
When those strange woemen which bewitch't his mynde,
By it a powrefull government did gett,
To wave his owne faith, and seduce mankinde;
   For which vyce, if his heires did loose the throne,
   It proves disorder never goes alone.

155/4 *Hephestion*] *Hephestion's 1670*

### 159

Againe as Tyrants are ecclips'd by this,
Soe falls the scepter, when it banckrupt growes
In common fame, which natures trumpet is,
Defect for ever findinge scorne below;
 For reputation airye though it be,
 Yet is the beauty of authoritie.


### 160

Which to improve, stronge princes must despise
All arts that blemish birth, place, courage, worth;
For Tyrants unto men then sacrifice
Their thrones, when inward errors they show forth;
 Which curiouslie the wise have ever us'd
 To keepe conceal'd, well ballanc'd, or excus'd.


### 161

Such are extortions, crueltie, oppression,
Covetousnes, endlesse anger, or displeasure,
Neglect, or scorne of person, or profession,
Pryde, basenes, rudenes, vayne expence of treasure:
 All which like nomber multipli'd by place,
 Doe in the man the monarchy disgrace:


### 162

Dissolving due respect and reverence,
Which gentle raynes in actyve princes handes
Give such restraint or latitude to sence,
As with the end of government best stands;
 And whoe letts fall these pleasing inward tyes,
 Must either fall in state, or tyrannize.

### 163

Let *Rehoboham* then in all his waies
Avoyd younge Councells, which enflame the hearts,
And soe on ruyne, pow'rs foundation layes,
In which light youth hath still the cheifest parts:
   Their witt is force, the old mans force is witt,
   And then for thrones, let man judge which is fitt.

### 164

But above all, such actions as may bringe
His faith in doubt, a stronge prince must eschew,
Because it doth concerne a boundless kinge
To keepe his wordes, and contracts, steddy, true,
   His graunts entire, graces not undermyn'd,
   As if both trueth, and power, had but one mynde.

### 165

What did it profitt that great *Charles* the fifte,
To trafficque with the prowd simplicitie
Of *German* princes, by unprincely shift,
Mis-letterd writts, a conclave subtilty?
   Since ill fate then, and ever will befall
   That broken faith aspirers worke withall.

### 166

The precept of *Lysander*, to beguile
Children with toyes, and men with perfidie,
Records himself by this infamous wyle,
To be their tutor in malignitie,
   Whoe since conclude that perjury noe synne,
   Which by equivocation enters in.

---

163/2 Councells] Council *1670*   6 let man judge which is fitt] let no man
judge what's fit *1670*   165/5 will] did *1670*   166/1 precept] precepts *1670*

### 167

A vice soe hatefull never, as when it
Borrowes the vayle of justice, for deceipt:
Hollow *Tiberius* playes not with his witt,
But to give his false practise better waight:
    Hence sacred virgins are to be defilde
    By hangmen first, to have the law beguil'd.

### 168

The poetts showe, what creditt with these Gods
Truth had, by sacred oath of *Stygian* lake,
The heavy doomes, and still tormenting rodds,
Which they reserv'd for them that sware, and brake;
    And freed from paine if these pow'rs could not be,
    What shall wee thinke of tyrants blasphemy?

### 169

Did *Tantalus*, belov'd of *Jupiter*,
With his owne *nectar*, and *ambrosia* nurst;
Or *Battus* painelesse in perjuring err?

    When *Tantalus* in hell sees store, and starves,
    While sencelesse *Battus* for a touchstone serves?

### 170

Thus see wee how all tymes, all sorts of faith,
Some by the clowd of fayned transformation,
Other by humane censure unto death,
And some by heavy doome of discreation,
    To keepe truth sacred, carefully have sought,
    Without which noe society is ought.

169/5 While] Which *1670*    170/3 Other] Others *1670*

### 171

Therefore let powre in her deliberations,
Take time, and care, before shee undertake;
That shee an equall princely calculation
Of wealth, strength, titles, feare, and hope may make:
   Because if Tyrants there pease all things right,
    To doe, or to forbeare, it gives them light.

### 172

The payne no more, or rather not soe much
To shunne the sickness, as to seeke the cure;
And yet in gaine, and honor farre more rich
It is, within her strength to rest secure,
   Then peece, vayle, yeild when shee hath done amisse;
   Since great discent in scepters fatall is.

### 173

Powre make your leagues, guifts, contracts therefore just,
Since wronge prescribes not Crownes, by tyme or deed;
Thrones never wanting meanes, occasion, lust,
To try by hazard, how their right shall speed,
   In whose uncerten Orbe yet Princes shall
   Oft finde mischance upon misdoinges fall.

### 174

For howsoever to the partiall throne
Of mighty power, the acts of truthles witt
May currant goe, like brasse, amongst their owne;
Yet when the world shall come to judge of it,
   Nature, that in her wisdome never lies,
   Will shew deceipt, and wronge, are never wise.

171/4 feare] fears *1670*    172/1 payne] pain's *1670*    173/6 mis-
doinges] misdoing *1670*

### 175

But grant this honour unto faithlessnes,
That sometimes it may prosper with occasion,
And make true wisdome in apparance less,
Yet what gaines powre by losse of reputation?
   Since everie blossome which ill doinge beares,
    Blasteth the fruite of good success, with feares?

### 176

Againe, as Tyrants ought to soare above
This reach of humours, soe ought they to beare
A rulers hand, and every spiritt move,
That under them shall governe, hope, or feare:
   Since by whose wisdome states be governed,
    They, of the same states, are reputed head.

### 177

Yet must not this supremacie discend
Of sect, or faction to become a part:
Since all is theirs, all must on them depend,
And to make use of each side, is their art:
   Els like kinges forc't for refuge to one towne,
    They in that one, cast dice for all their Crowne.

### 178

Rather must they by providence unite
All parties soe, as none may gage their state,
Or to their private ends, withdrawe from might,
But give their greatest, such a yeilding rate,
   As like the earth plough'd upp, they may not groane,
    Though greedy power exhaust more then her owne.

176/4 governe,] govern *1670*    5 wisdome . . . be] wisdomes . . . are *1670*
178/3 to] in *1670*    5 may] must *1670*    6 her] their *1670*

### 179

For faction els lurcking in hopes and feares,
When it awakes by oportunitie,
Straight *Hidra*-lyke in many foreheades beares
Horror, division, multiplicitie;
   Nor safe unto it self, nor to those kinges
   That unto meane birdes, will lend Eagles winges.

### 180

Therefore should this well masked Cockatrice
Be carefully even in the egg supprest,
Before the venome of her poisoninge vice
Against the prince, and kingdome be addrest;
   It being not safe for stronge witted might
   To give subjection any regall right.

### 181

For as wee see in deepe corrupted ayres,
Each petty sicknes turnes to pestilence,
And by infection, common ruyne beares:
Soe, in the orbe of kinges omnipotence,
   Faction oft makes each private discontent
   Swell above law, to plague the government.

### 182

For to make bodies stronge, proves heads are weake,
And soe twoe sects prepared in one Realme,
Which doth the beautie of obedience breake,
By tempting discontented myndes to gleane;
   And soe force thrones to one side for protection,
   Whose being is to keepe both in subjection.

### 183

Nor holds one rule alyke with weake, and stronge,
Since weake kinges raigne doth verie seldome raise
Such spiritts, as dare shufle right and wronge,
At least what breeds them, breeds their counterpease;
   Corruptions weake-births therefore yeilding many,
   Least liberty should be ingross'd by any.

### 184

Whereas this other princely stirring stuffe,
Oft by example gives new lawes to kinges,
With danger to Soveraigntie enough,
By those new fashions which they give to thinges:
   Therefore are factions here to be supprest,
   Which in mylde tymes support weake princes best.

### 185

Now how powre soe should ballance thinges and myndes,
As all dissentions may in her unite,
Or from what place, powre arguments should finde,
To make the crooked undergoe the right,
   How it should peirce the tender skynne of passion,
   And yet to these wounds instantly give fashion,

### 186

Stronge hearts learne out of practicke wisdome must,
Which knowinge how to paie each with his owne,
By mixing good and ill, with feare and lust,
Reape among thornes, seedes by them never sowne;
   And make the people yeild upp their estate,
   To add more still to government they hate:

183/1 one] our *1670*    2 raigne doth] raigns do *1670*    5 weake-births] weak
birth *1670*    184/3 Soveraigntie] Soveraignity *1670*    185/5 tender] *1670*
*omits*    6 to] in *1670*

187

Which artificiall stirrage of affection,
Having but small affinitie with good,
Noe essence, but an essence like reflection,
Will best by opposites be understood,
  The fowle excess of ill being onlie that,
  Which to avoyd in powre I levell at.


188

Therefore, as litle bridles to restrayne
Mans clyming minde in princes boundless might,
Let tyrants thinke that all their acts remayne
Spread like *Apollo's* beames, in each mans sight:
  Which by the divers fate of good or ill,
  Either produce scorne, malice, or good will.


189

Lastly, this tyrant powre (vayle of the man)
In peoples eyes must not assiduous be;
What hath respect, appeares but now and than:
Reservednes, that art of tyrannie,
  Equally graceth both paine and reward;
  Demission works remission, not regard.


190

Thus much in breif to temper headstronge vyce,
Which thorough princes, often wounds the Crowne;
To shunne which daungerous racking prejudice,
Tyrants should all signes of their selfenes drowne;
  And yet by odds of place worke every man
  To serve them with the best, and worst they can.

188/3 thinke that] that think *1670*    190/3 prejudice] precipice *1670*

191

But if pow're will exceed, then lett mankinde
Receave oppression, as fruites of their error;
Let them againe live in their duties shrinde,
As their safe haven from the windes of terror,
    Till hee that rais'd powre, to mowe mans synnes downe,
    Please, for pow'rs owne synnes, to pluck of her Crowne.

## OF CHURCH

### Section VI

192

Thus having in few Images exprest
The effect which each extremity bringes forth,
Within mans nature, to disturbe kinges rest;
What enemies againe they be to worth,
    As either guyves, which freedome doe restraine,
    Or *Jubilees* which lett confusion raigne;

193

There rests to show, what these degrees of vyce
Worke, when they fixte be to the Moulds of might;
As what relation to the prejudice,
Or help they yeild of universall right;
    Vyce getting forces farre above her owne,
    When it spreads from a person to a throne.

194

For as in princes natures, if there be
An auditt taken, what each kinde of passion
Workes, and by what usurp't authority,
Order, and reasons peace they doe disfashion;
    Within mans litle world it proves the same,
    Which of pow'rs great world doth confound the frame.

191/1 then lett] then, then let *1670*     Section VI *Ed.*: Sect. 6° *W*, SECT.
VI. *1670*     192/3 kinges] mans *1670*     6 raigne; *Ed.*: raigne *W*, *1670*

### 195

Whence spread kinges self love into Church or law,
Pulpitt and barr straight feele corrupted might,
Which bounded will not be, much lesse in awe
Of heavenly censure, or of earthly right:
   Besides creation, and each other part
   Withers, when powre turnes nature into art.

### 196

For as betwene the object, and our sence,
Looke where the *Mediums* doe prove dymme or cleere,
Mens myndes receave formes of intelligence,
Which make thinges either faire, or fowle appeare:
   Soe betwene powrs lust, and the peoples right,
   The *Mediums* helpe to cleere, or dazell light.

### 197

Therefore to lett downe these high pillard thrones
To lower orbes, where prince and people mixe,
As Church, lawes, Commerce, rights well temperd zones,
Where neither part extremity can fixe,
   Either to bynde transcendence by constraint,
   Or spoile mankinde of all rights, but complaint:

### 198

And where by this well ballancinge of might,
Regalities of Crownes stand undeclyn'd,
Whose beinges are not to be infinite,
And soe of greater price then all mankinde;
   But in desire and function tempered soe,
   As they may currant with their people goe.

196/4 make] makes *1670*   5 the] *1670 omits*   197/3 rights *Ed.*: rights,
*W*: Rights *1670*: *see note*

### 199

When *Theopompus, Lacedemons* kinge
Had rays'd upp a plebean magistrate,
(Lyke *Roman* tribunes) which the soaringe winge
Of Soveraigne excesses might abate;
   Hee therein saw, although hee bounde his childe,
   Yet in a lesse roome hee did surer build.

### 200

For infinite ambition to extend
The boundes of powre (which finite pow'rs must weld)
As vayne is, as desire to comprehend,
And plant eternity in natures feild;
   Whereby the idle, and the overdoing
   Alike runn on, their owne destruction woeing.

### 201

Active then, yet without excesse of spirritt,
Stronge princes must be in their government,
Their influence in every thinge of meritt,
Not with an idle, glorious name content;
   But quicke in nimble use, and change of wombes,
   Which els prove peoples snares, and princes tombes.

### 202

Placing the first foundation of their Raignes
Upon that frame, which all frames els exceeds,
*Religion*, by whose name the Scepter gaines
More of the world, and greater reverence breeds
   In Forrayners, and homeborne subjects too,
   Then much expence of bloud or wealth can doe.

202/5 Forrayners] Forrainer *1670*   homeborne] home-bred *1670*   6 or]
and *1670*

### 203

For with what force Gods true religion spreads
Is by her shadowe superstition knowne;
Whence *Mydas* having over *Phrigia* shedd
Seedes of this ceremony, till then unknowne,
  Made *Asia* safer by that empty word,
  Than his forefathers had done by the sword.

### 204

And is not *Mahometts* forg'd *alchoran*
Both with the heathen in authority,
And to the Christians mis-ledd Miter throne,
Become a verie racke of tirranny?
  Their spirits united, eating men like food,
  And making ill ends with stronge armies good.

### 205

Religions faire name by insinuation
Secretly seizeth all powers of the minde,
In understanding raiseth admiration,
Worshipp in will, which natyve sweet lincks bynde
  The soule of man, and having gott possession,
  Give powrefull will an ordinate progression:

### 206

Forminge in conscience lynes of equitie,
To temper lawes, and without force infuse
A homeborne practise of civilitie,
Currant with that which all the world doth use,
  Whereby divided kingdomes may unite,
  If not in truth, at least in outward rite.

206/6 rite] *cancelling* right

### 207

Therefore I say powr should be provident,
In guidinge this cheif strength of tirranny
With caution, that the clergie government
Give not the Miter, Crowne-supremacie:
    Making the *Sultan* and the *Caliph* one,
    To tyranize both *Cair*, and *Babylon*.

*These 2 were
the places of
residence of
the Caliphes*

### 208

The Churches proper armes be teares and prayer,
*Peters* true keys to open earth, and skye,
Which if the high preist out of prides despaire
Will into *Tibris* cast, and *Paulls* sword trye,
    Gods sacred word, hee therein doth abandon,
    And runns with fleshlie confidence at randome.

### 209

Milde people therefore honour you your kinge,
Reverence your preists, but never under one
Fraile creature both your soule and bodie bringe,
But keepe the better part to God alone;
    The soule his image is, and only hee
    Knowes what it is, and what it ought to be.

### 210

Least els by some idolatrous conceipt
You give them, that at synne can cast noe stone,
Meanes to pluck downe the Godhead, by deceipt,
And upon mans inventions raise a throne:
    Besides, where swords and Cannons doe unite,
    The peoples bondage there proves infinite.

207/2 guidinge] judging *1670*    *Marginal note 1670 omits '2'*    208/1 prayer]
prayers *1670*    3 the high preist . . . prides] the Priest . . . his prides *1670*
209/1 kinge *1670*: kinges *W*    210/5 swords] sword *1670*

### 211

Princes againe wake, and be well advis'd,
How suddenly in man kinges powre is drown'd;
The Myter rais'd, the Scepter prejudic'd,
If you leave all rights superstition bound:
    For then as soules more deare, then bodies are,
    Soe these church visions may strayne nature farr.

### 212

Kinges therefore that feare superstitions might,
Must crosse her courses in their infancie,
By which the *Druides* with their shadowed light,
Gott goodes from them that tooke their words, to be
    Treble rewarded in the life to come;
    And works not paradice the same for *Rome*?

### 213

For with like mysticall dexterity,
Rackinge the living soules through rage of synne,
And dying soules with horrors mystery,
Did not the Myter from the scepter wynne
    The third part of our world, till *Luther* came,
    Whoe shak't the doctrine of that double frame?

### 214

Lye not *France, Poland, Italie* and *Spaigne*
Still as the snow doth, when it threatens more,
Lyke engynes, fitted to drawe back againe
Those that the true light severed before?
    And was not *Venice* excommunicate,
    For curbing such false purchasers of late?

---

211/6 nature] *cancelling* dutie    212/1 superstitions] superstitious *1670*
2 her] their *1670*    213/1 like] such *1670*  2 through *1670*: thorough *W*
5 our] the *1670*    214/6 purchasers] purchases *1670*

### 215

Which endles thirst of sacred avarice,
If in the infancie it be not bounded,
Will hardlie by prosperity growe wise;
For as this church is on apparance founded,
  Soe besides schooles, and Cells which vayle her shame,
  Hath shee not armies, to extend her name?


### 216

Power for a pensile, conscience for a table,
To write opinion in of any fashion,
With witts distinctions, ever merchantable,
Betwene a princes throne, and peoples passion?
  Upon which texts shee raiseth, or pulls downe
  All, but those objects, which advance her Crowne.


### 217

Pow'r therefore be shee needie, or ambitious;
Dispos'd to peace, or unto warr enclyn'd;
Whether religious in her life, or vitious;
Must not to Myters soe enthrall mankinde,
  As above truth and force Moncks may prevayle,
  On their false visions, Crowne rights to entaile.


### 218

Againe, let not her Clarkes by *Symons* waies,
Lay wast endowments of devoted spiritts,
And soe pull downe, what their forefathers raise,
With honour in their actions, if not meritt;
  Least as by pryde they once gott upp too high,
  Their basenes feele the next extremity.

216/6 those *1670*: these *W*          217/4 mankinde] *cancelling* her mynde
218/3 raise] raisd *1670*

### 219

For first, besides the scandall and contempt
Which these base courses on their doctrine cast;
The stately monuments are not exempt,
Because without meanes, noe tyme-workes can last:
    And from high pompe a desperate discent
    Showes both in state, and Church, misgovernment.

### 220

Whereof let her take heed, since when estates
From such a greatnes doe begin to fall,
Discent is unto them precipitate:
For as one gangren'd member ruynes all,
    Soe what the modestie of one tyme leaves,
    The time succeeding certenly bereaves.

### 221

Therefore must thrones (as Godds of formes exterior)
Cast upp this earthlie mettall in good mould;
And when men to professions prove superior,
Restrayne prowd thoughts, from doing what they would;
    Guydinge the weake, and stronge, to such extension,
    As may to order, sacrifise invention.

### 222

And hereby worke that formall unitie,
Which brookes no new, or irreligious sects,
To nurse upp faction or impietie,
Change ever teaching people to neglect;
    But raise the painefull, learned, and devout,
    To plant obeying conscience thorough out.

219/2 these]|those *1670*

### 223

Vaylinge her doctrine with antiquity,
Whence, and where although contradicting sects
Stryve to derive, and prove their pedigree,
As safest humane levells to direct
   Into what mould opinion should be cast,
    To make her true, at least like truth to last.

### 224

Or if their times will not permitt a truce,
In wranglinge questions, which breake natures peace,
And therein offer God and man abuse;
Let powre yet wisely make their practise cease,
   In Church, or Courts, and bynde them to the schooles,
    As busines for idle, wittie fooles.

### 225

Ordering, that people from the pulpitt heare
Nothing, but that which seemes mans life to mend;
As shadowes of eternall hope and feare,
Which doe contract the ill, and good extend;
   Not idle theoricke, to tickle witt,
    Empty of goodnes, much more nyce then fitt.

### 226

To which refininge end, it may seeme just,
That in the Church the supreame magistrates
Should antient be, ere they be put in trust,
Since aged witt best tempers, and abates
   These heady and exorbitant affections,
    Which are of blinde, prowd youth the imperfections.

### 227

The *Romane* lawes for magistrates admitt
None, that had not pass'd the meridian lyne
Of youth, and humours incident to it;
And shall it not in functions Divine
   Be more absurd, to let that youth appeare,
    And teach, which wise men thinke scarce fitt to heare?

### 228

Besides, chast life yeares easelyer may observe,
Which temper in cathedrall dignitie,
Though wyves be lawfull, yet doth well deserve,
As to their functions leaving them more free:
   Instance, their learned works that liv'd alone,
   Where married Bishopps left us few, or none.

### 229

And if men shall object that this restraint
Of lawfull mariage, will increase the sinne
And soe the beautie of the church attaint,
By bringinge scandall through mans frailtie in;
   I say mans fall is synnes, not Churches shame,
   Ordain'd by censure to enlarge her fame.

### 230

Censure, the life of discipline, which beares
Pow'rs spirituall standard, fitt to governe all
Opinions, actions, humours, hopes, or feares,
Spread knowledge, make obedience generall;
   Whence man instructed well, and kept in awe,
   If not the inward, keepes the outward law.

227/6 which] what *1670*      229/4 through *1670*: thorough *W*     230/3 or]
and *1670*    6 keepes the] yet keeps *1670*

### 231

Which forme is all that tyrranny expects,
I meane to wynne, to change, and yet unite,
Where a true kinge in his estate affects
Soe from within man, to worke out the right,
As his will neede not lymitt, or allay
The liberties of Gods immortall way.

### 232

Where tyrants discipline is never free,
But ballanced, proportioned, and bounded
Soe with the temporall endes of tyrannie,
And waies whereon powrs greatnesses are founded;
As in creation, fame, life, death, or warr,
Or any other heads that Soveraigne are.

### 233

Powre may not be opposed, or confounded,
But each inferior Orbe, commaund or serve,
With proper latitudes distinctly bounded,
To censure all states that presume to swerve;
Whereby the common people, and the throne
May mutually protected be in one.

### 234

Not rent asunder by sophistication
Of one fraile synner, whose supremacie
Stands by prophane, or undervaluation
Of Gods anoynted Soveraignitie;
And by deviding subjects from their kinges,
Soares above those thrones, which first gave him wings.

234/6 him] them *1670*

### 235

Affecting such irrevocable might
With us, as to their *Muftie Turkes* lyv'd under;
Or rather sacriledge more infinite,
From *Jove* to wrest away the fearefull thunder:
   *Salmoneus* pride, as if the truth then fell,
   When hee alone rul'd not earth, heav'n, and hell.

### 236

*Salmoneus*, whoe while hee his Carroach drave
Over the brasen bridge of *Elis* streame,
And did with artificiall thunder brave
*Jove*, till hee peirc't him with a lightning beame:
   From which example, whoe will an Idoll be,
   Must rest assured to feele a deitie.

### 237

Thus much to showe the outward Churches use,
In framing upp the superstitious spheare,
Subject alike to order, or abuse,
Chain'd with immortall seeming hopes, and feare;
   Which shadow-like their beings yet bereave,
   By trusting to be, when their bodies leave.

### 238

Where if this outward worke which power pretends,
Were life indeed, not fraile hypocricy,
Monarkes should need noe other lawes to frend,
Conscience being base of their authoritie:
   By whose want, frailty flashing out mans error,
   Makes thrones enwall themselves with lawes of terror.

236/5 will an] *cancelling* would     238/1 this] that *1670*

## OF LAWES

### Section VII

#### 239

Hence when these antient frending Godds foresaw,
Schisme and devision would creepe into nations,
By this subjecting subtilty of law,
Which yet did yeild their makers reputation;
    They, out of grace, sent downe their progenie,
    To keepe men, as they were created, free.

#### 240

Were not to this end *Ceres* well fram'd lawes
As proper for mankinde, as was her corne?
Unto which cleer-ey'd nature gives applause,
As mutuall duties to which man is borne;
    And from which noe soule can deliverd be,
    By tyme, discretion, or authoritie.

#### 241

Which lawes were not engrav'd in stones, or brasse,
Because these mettalls must corrupt with tyme,
Mans understanding that impression was,
Which did contayne these Images Divine;
    Where conscience seal'd with horror plagueth those,
    That against these borne-duties doe oppose.

#### 242

But after mankinds hard, and thanckles heart
Had banisht mylde *Astrea* from the earth,
Then came this sophistrie of humane arts,
Pictures, not life of that celestiall byrth;
    Falling from lawes of heav'n-like harmony,
    To mans lawes, which but corrupt reason be.

Section VII *Ed.*: Sect. 7°. *W*, SECT. VII. *1670*      240/4 As] By *1670*

### 243

Of this kynde *Solon* was in *Athens* one;
*Lycurgus* cobwebbs over *Sparta* spread;
The *Locrians* by *Zaleucus* netts were knowne;
By *Zoroastres Bactria* was misledd;
 *Numa* was hee, that first enthralled *Rome*,
 And natures freedome under legall doome.

### 244

After which change, men have lyv'd more devided
By lawes, then they at first by language were;
For whoe before by reasons light were guided,
Since fondlie worshipp to such idolls beare,
 As these new maisters stirr upp in mans heart,
 Whoe seldome finde truth in the weaker part.

### 245

A Maister peece of powre which hath extinct
That former light of nature men lyv'd in,
Holding the world to Crowne opinions linck't,
Whoe simply prize not good, nor punish synne:
 But whatsoever doth withstand their will,
 That barr, as if by nature it were ill.

### 246

Yet in mans darknes since Church rites alone
Cannot guard all the parts of government,
Least by disorder states be overthrowne,
Powre must use lawes, as her best instrument;
 Lawes bring Mappes, and Councellors that doe
 Shewe forth diseases, and redresse them too.

243/3 *Zaleucus*] *Seleucus 1670*  244/1 devided] divide *1670* 5 these]
those *1670*

### 247

And though perchance at first sight lawes appeare
Like prisons, unto tyrants Soveraigne might;
Yet are they secretts, which powre should hold deere,
Since envilesse they make her infinite:
 And sett soe faire a glosse upon her will,
 As under this vayle powre cannot doe ill.

### 248

After *Augustus* had by civill sword,
Made that large empire thrall to his ambition,
Men yet retayn'd their priviledge in wordes,
And freelie censur'd everie mans condition;
 Till by the lawes of wounded majestie,
 Nor wordes, nor lookes, nor thoughts were left them free.

### 249

For then was this reproof of publique vice,
And censure of their Emperors misdeeds
Made treason, and mainetayn'd with prejudice
Of men enforc't to nurse destroying weeds,
 I meane that vice which tyranny protected,
 And by example all the earth infected.

### 250

Hence was it not a trespasse capitall
For men to say vayne *Nero* sange not well?
In nature then what latitude at all
If o're mans freedome tyranny thus swell?
 Whether by law men roote or ruyne take,
 Sure am I scepters it doth sacred make.

247/1 And though perchance] For though perhaps *1670*

H

251

Besides, lawes fixe the bents of peoples mindes
From pryinge upp, while selfenes doth intend
Other mens faults, and therein heedless bynds
That common freedome, which they would extend;
   Laying an impost upon everie vice,
   To spread the Crowne by peoples prejudice.


252

This was that apple fatallie cast downe
By *Momus*, to sett Goddesses at warre,
Which er'st too busie were with *Joves* high Crowne
And Cabinet, where all doomes fixed arre,
   Judg'd by a shepeard, for it was thought due
   That to inferiors they submitt that sue.


253

Old *Rome* againe was never out of strife
Betwene the people, and the magistrates,
Till *Appius* brought from *Athens* rules of life,
Which are calld lawes in everie other state;
   Whetting their edges soe against their owne,
   As none found leasure to restrayne a throne.


254

Since then by lawes the best, and worst affections
Of pride-borne tyrants formd and disform'd be,
To give for them some generall directions,
As stayes against confounding liberty,
   I thincke were fitt; aswell to showe th'abuse
   In making, as their good effects in use.

251/2 intend] *cancelling* extend    254/5 th'abuse] the abuse *1670*  6 effects]
effect *1670*

### 255

Therefore though sometimes powre doe lawes applie
To humours, or occasions, tyme, or place,
Yet those are found of most equalitie,
Which beare a carefull universall face:
   Whereas particuler, and present lawes
   Diseases oft in tymes succeeding cause.

### 256

Againe those lawes which universall be,
And therbie freelie currant everie where,
Doe with the groundes of nature best agree,
And so with man most reputation beare;
   As reason cast in frames to mowld his passion,
   Which kept in boundes, keapes all his acts in fashion.

### 257

But the true grounde indeed of humane lawes,
Ought to be that lawe, which is ever true,
His lighte that is of everie beinge cause,
Beyond whose providence what can be new?
   Therefore as meanes betwixt these two extreames,
   Lawes should take light at least from those sweete beames.

### 258

Yet by the vyolence of superiors passion,
And wandring visions of inferior spiritts,
Powre to make up it selfe strives to disfashion,
Creatinge errors new as well as meritts,
   In hope to forme mans outward vyce by lawes,
   Whose power can never reach the inward cause.

255/1 though] if *1670*    6 tymes] time *1670*    257/1 indeed of] of all
our *1670*   5 these *1670*: those *W*    258/4 errors] error *1670*

### 259

Yett doe these lawes make spiritts of their profession,
Or such as unto them subject their state,
Publiquely wiser, warier of transgression,
Fitter to traffique, or negotiate;
    Both in all other Countries, and their owne,
    Farr more respected, and much sooner knowne.

### 260

For as the man that meanes to write, or drawe,
If hee unperfect be in hand, or head,
Makes his straight lynes unto himself a law,
By which his after workes are governed;
    Soe be these lynes of life in everie Realme,
    To weigh mens acts, a well contenting beame.

### 261

Hence must their aphorismes which doe comprise
The summe of law be published, and stil'd
In such a common language as is prisd
And us'd abroad, not from the world exil'd;
    Least being both in text, and language thrall,
    They prove noe coynes for traffique generall.

### 262

For is it meete that lawes which ought to be
Rules unto all men, showld rest knowne to few?
Since then how can pow'rs soveraignitie
Of universall justice beare a shew,
    Reforme the judge, correcte the advocate,
    Who knowinge law alone commaunds the state?

259/6 sooner] better *1670*    261/6 noe] not *1670*    262/6 commaunds]
command *1670*

### 263

After the infancie of glorious *Rome*,
Lawes were with Church rites secreatlie enshrinde,
Poore people knowinge nothinge of their doome,
But that all rights were in the Judges mynde;
   *Flavius* revealed this snaringe mysterie,
   Greate men repind, but *Rome* it self grew free.

### 264

So with the craftie preisthood was the yeere
Made short or longe, by their intercalation:
Sellinge the tyme to publicans more deere,
Till *Caesar* did reforme this computation,
   And brake these thredds of avarice they spunne,
   Measuringe swifte time by due coorse of the sunne.

### 265

Hard therfore is it for men to decree,
Whether it better were to have no law,
Or lawes kept onlie as a mysterie,
In their brest, that revenewe from it draw;
   Whether to barr all mandates be not one,
   With spreading them in dialects unknowne.

### 266

For as when leiturgies are published
In forraigne tounges, and poore sowles forc'd to pray;
The tounge is trusted without hart, or head,
To tell the lorde they knowe not what they say;
   But onlie that this preist obedience,
   Twixt grace and reason, damms th'intelligence:

264/2 longe] large *1670*        265/1 therfore is it] is it therefore *1670*
3 lawes] Law *1670*   4 brest] breasts *1670*   266/6 damms] damns *1670*

### 267

So when our law the beames of life and light,
Under a clowde or bushell shall burne owt,
The forraine accents, which are infinite,
Obscuringe sence, and multiplienge dowbte;
    Wee blinded in our wayes by this ecclipse,
    Must needes apologize for many slipps.

### 268

Againe, lawes ordered must be, and sett downe
So cleerlie as each man may understand,
Wherin for him, and wherin for the Crowne,
Their rigor or equalitie doth stand:
    For rocks, not sea-markes els they prove to be,
    Fearfull to men, noe frends to Tyrannie:

### 269

As makinge Judges, and not Princes greate,
Because that dowbtfull sence, which they expound,
Raiseth them upp above the Princes seate,
By offringe strength, forme, matter, and a ground
    To fashion all degrees unto their end,
    Through mens desires which covett law to frend.

### 270

And as the papists doe, by exposition
Of dowbtfull sences in Gods testament,
Claime to their chaire a soveraigne condition;
So will these legists in their elemente
    Gett above truth, and thrones; raisinge the barr
    As high as those unerringe prowd chaires arr.

270/1 And] For *1670*    2 dowbtfull] double *1670*

### 271

All which just ballancing of Judge and law,
Bee worckes of wise and understandinge mighte;
As it is under orders lynes, to draw
These coorts supreame, which manage wronge and right;
  Well auditinge all Counsells of estate,
  And geevinge each degree his proper rate:

### 272

Prohibitinge these lawless marts of place,
Which by permission of a careless Crowne,
Corrupte, and geeve the magistrate disgrace,
With servile purchase of a sellinge gowne;
  And so rate justice at as vyle a price,
  As if her state were peoples prejudice.

### 273

Againe, the length and strange varietie
Of processes and trialls, Princes must
Reforme; for whether their excesses be
Founded uppon the judge, or pleaders lust,
  The effect of eyther ever proveth one,
  Unto the humble subject overthrowne.

### 274

In course of law besides powre must advise,
Whether for triall of mens pryvate righte,
It will be founde just, equall, fitt, or wise,
To give the judges any other lighte,
  Then in mens titles by cleere evidence,
  In case of cryme by testimonie of sence.

271/2 worckes] matks *1670*   5 all] ill *1670*     272/1 these] those *1670*
273/4 the judge, or pleaders] Judges or Pleaders *1670*   6 subject] Subjects
*1670*

### 275

Againe, if common justice of the Kinge
Delayd, dishonor'd, or corrupted be,
And so the subjecte rackt in everie thinge
By these wordmongers, and their libertie;
    Whether Gods governement amongst his owne,
    Was not more wise, which advocates had none?

### 276

The warlike *Lacedemon* suffered not
In her republique any advocate,
The learned *Athens* neither used lott,
Nor plea; but partie, and their magistrate;
    As if these courts would never staineles be,
    Which did allow that gayninge mysterie.

### 277

Because their end, being meerely avarice,
Windes up their witts to such a nimble strayne,
As helpes to blinde the judge, not give him eyes,
And when successivelie these come to raigne,
    Their old acquainted traffique makes them see,
    Wronge hath more clyents, then sinceritie.

### 278

Hence these new judges made, sometimes adhere
Unto the plaine wordes, sometimes sence of law,
Then againe binde it to the makers chaire,
And now the whole text into one parte draw;
    So that from home, who shall but fowre yeeres be,
    Will thincke lawes travelld have, as well as he.

278/3 Then bind it to the Makers of their chair *1670*

### 279

Moreover, to give justice readie eyes,
Kinges heere and there in provinces remote
Should to establish proper coorts devise,
That their poore subjects might not lyve by rote;
  Nor yet by charge of cares farr fetched right,
  Give more advantage to oppressinge might.

### 280

Such be those seaven sinews misticall,
In the French monarchie sent from the braine,
To spread both sence and motion thorough all,
And over sence, opinion, custome raigne:
  *Paris, Grenoble, Toulous, Burdeaux, Rone,*
  *Dion,* and *Aix,* seaven pillars of a throne.

### 281

Which were they not ofte subjecte to infection
From noysom mistes beyonde the *Alpes* arisinge,
Would keape the health of that state in perfection,
As well from fallinge, as from tyranisinge;
  But fate leaves noe man longer quiet heere,
  Then blessed peace is to his neighboure deere.

### 282

Powre then stretch noe grounds for grace, spleene, or gaine,
But leave the subject to the subjects law;
Since equalls, over equalls glad to raigne,
Will by advantage more advantage drawe;
  For throne examples are but seldome lost,
  And followd ever at the publique cost.

279/4 rote] vote *1670*

283

People by nature love not to obay,
By force and use yet grow their humours mixt,
Now softe like wax, now hardened like the clay,
And so to make, or marr, soone mov'd, or fixt,
  As theis two moderators witt and might,
  To their ends wave, or lett them stand upright.

284

Crafte though unpunished in majestie,
Yet never governs, but worcks by deceipt,
Base instrument of humane frailtie,
Which auditts not by standerd, number, waight;
  But with false lights makes tyrranie descend
  To doe, and hide, by which stayres none ascend.

285

Crownes therefore keape your othes of coronation,
Succession frees noe tyrranie from those,
Faith is the ballance of powrs reputation,
That circkle broken, where can man repose?
  Since scepter pledges, which should be sincere,
  By one false act growe banckrupt every where.

286

Make not mens conscience, wealth, and libertie
Servile without booke to unbounded will;
*Procrustes*-like he racks humanitie,
That in powrs owne mould casts their good, and ill;
  And slaves men must be by the sway of time,
  Where tyrranie continews thus sublime.

283/2 By force and use *1670*: By force, and use; *W*    3 hardened] hardned
*1670*    284/2 never governs] *cancelling* shifte commaunds not    285/6 false
act growe] *cancelling* act will growe       286/4 good, and ill] good will *1670*

### 287

Observe in greatnes this one abstract notion,
That odds of place, possest by speritts inferior,
Must finde strange hills and dales in every motion,
Nature and chance growing by turnes superior;
   Whence inward weakeness never shalbe able
   To keape her owtward borroughed glories stable:

### 288

Yet above all theis, tyrants must have care,
To cherish those assemblies of estate,
Which in greate monarchies true glasses are,
To shew mens greifes, excesses to abate;
   Brave mowlds for lawes, a *medium* that in one
   Joynes with content a people to a throne.

### 289

Besides a safe wrest for theis boundles kinges
To get supplie, or enviles reforme,
Those overstretched, or relaxed strings,
Of many members which might els deforme,
   Still frend to thrones, who (as lords of the choise)
   Gyve life or death to all acts by their voyce.

### 290

For as in man this little worlde of ours,
All objects which affect him diverslie
With payne, or pleasure, under feelinge pow'rs
Of common sence, are summon'd presentlie,
   And there diminisht, judged, or approv'd,
   A *Crisis* made, some changed, some remov'd:

287/6 her] the *1670*    288/6 a throne] the Throne *1670*    289/1
for] of *1670*   5 frend] friends *1670*

### 291

So in the kingdoms generall conventions,
By confluence of all states doth appeare,
Who nurseth peace, who multiplies contentions,
What is to people, what to greate men deere;
   Whereby soveraignitie still keepes above,
   And from her center makes these circkles move.

### 292

Againe since parliaments assembled be,
Not for the end of one state, but of all;
Practise of noe side can be counted free,
Anger of greatnes there is short-breath'd fall,
   Altring, displacing, raysing, pullinge downe,
   Offends the burroughs, adds not to the Crowne.

### 293

People like sheepe and streames goe all one way,
Bounded with conscience, names, and libertie;
All other arts enhance, doe not allay
The headlonge passions they are govern'd by:
   Crafte teacheth Crafte, practise goes not alone,
   But ecchoes self witt back uppon a throne.

### 294

Small punishments faile not to multiplie
These *Hydra* heads, and gives them glorie cheape;
Blood weere too much, greate bodies cannot dye;
Powre that sows truth, may wealth and honour reape;
   Men joy in warr for conscience, and can dye,
   Givinge their wealth, to save their libertie.

291/4 is to] to the *1670*

### 295

Conscience (I say) is to the people deere,
And libertie they (like all creatures) love,
What then neads any force or practise heere,
Where men upon such fayre wheeles easely move?
    It may stirr Jelowsie, but cannot frend
    That which both kinge and men should make their end.

### 296

Pow're therfore bringe all wayes degenerate
Back to their old foundations, whence they grew,
And suffer not theis pillars of estate
By private selfnes, to become still new;
    Of private orbes th'orrisons are not greate,
    Must they not then diminish, where they treate?

### 297

The large tymes, strength-lyke, kept ellections free,
Shreeves us'd noe selfe art in their County dayes,
Greate men forbore those shrapes of majestie,
Which gave the people freedome in their wayes,
    And what can scepters loose by this free choise,
    Where they reserve the Royaltie of voyce?

### 298

At their will either to dispence with law,
When they are made as prisons of creation,
Or legall yokes which still more bondage draw,
By bringing penalties in reputation;
    Mylde people of the throne desiringe leave
    More spetious nets on all estates to weave.

---

295/3 force or practise *1670*: witty practise *W*     296/5 private] *cancelling*
present     297/2 Shreeves] Sheriff's *1670*     3 shrapes] shapes *1670*
6 the Royaltie] *cancelling* regalitie

### 299

Freedome of speech ecchoes the peoples trust,
That credit never doth the soveraigne harme:
Kinges wynne the people by the people must,
Wherin the scepters is the cheifest charme:
    People (lyke infants) joy in little thinges,
    Which ever draws their councells under Kinges.

### 300

Hence power often in her largest dayes
Hath chosen free and actyve instruments,
From subject faith, that in the subject wayes
Humblie to suffer have bin well content;
    And since man is no more then what he knowes,
    Ought he not pay that dutie which he owes?

### 301

And what expect men for their lives and goods,
But some poore feathers owt of their owne wings?
Pardons (I meane) from those law catching moods
Which they before had begged of their Kings:
    Let them speake freelie then, that freelie pay;
    Each creature hath some kynde of sabboth day.

### 302

Lastlie when princes most doe neede their owne,
People soone spye false lights of libertie;
Taxes there vanisht, impositions gone,
Yet doth the parliamentall subsidie
    Releive Kings wants at home with peoples wealth,
    And showes the world, that both states are in health.

299/4 scepters] Scepter *1670*    5 (lyke infants)] *1670 omits brackets*    300/3
subject . . . subject] Subjects . . . subjects *1670*    301/5 freelie then,
that] freely, then they *1670*    302/2 soone] do *1670*

303

From theis sweete mountaines therfore let us veiwe
The former greate estates which govern'd all,
And by the use of many people knewe
Which way to frame things for the generall;
Yet kept their soveraignitie above,
By usinge councells not of feare, but love.

304

The *Romane* state, for all free states a glass,
In her deliberations of waight,
When she did stryve to shunne, or bringe to pass
Her reall councells, or well maskt deceipt,
Had to her fyve and thirtie trybes recoorse;
Assemblinge many, to keape all from worse:

305

By them determininge in *Mars* his feilde,
The deninzinge of realmes, magistrates creation,
When *Rome* was barren, what did over yeelde,
When peace or warr, and whie had reputation;
Peasing the senates pryde, the peoples rage,
Leaste the excesse of one should all engage.

306

And by this equall ballance kepte uprighte
Her farr extended governemente and law,
Till warr, by over addinge unto mighte
The scale uneven did on her side draw;
And by a martiall mutinous election
Of Emperors, brought empire to defection.

307

Farr differente is the coorse of tyranie,
Where mans felicitie is not the end;
But selfe-contractinge soveraignitie,
Neither to scepter, nor to people frend;
The mysterie of iniquitie being there,
Not to assemble parliament for feare.

308

Instance the present brutishe rapsodie
Of mankynde under *Ottomans* base lyne;
Where if in one, man should assembled be,
Of their well beings freelie to define;
What were it but a liberall commission,
For them to cast of bondage by sedition?

309

The trew unitinge *Grecian* policie,
Of course frequented twise in everie yeere,
Theire auntient *Amphiction Synodie*,
A parliamente for many causes deere,
As well at home to curbe mens divers mindes,
As all encrochinge forrainers to bynde.

310

For actyve powre must not her bounds enlarge
By stretchinge Crowne rights (which by law descend)
To tax, impose, monopolize, or charge,
As if both God, and mans law had no end;
But to enhance prerogatives as farr,
By arts of peace, as they by conquest arr.

308/3 one, man] one Man *1670*    310/6 conquest] Conquests *1670*

### 311

Els when this crowne assumed libertie
Hath shuffled all distinct imperiall rests,
To give confus'd will soveraignitie,
Order thus shakte in thrones, in subjects brests
   Makes dutie nothinge els but servile feares,
   Where fruite alike for both, occasion beares.

### 312

And as theis lawes, which bynde mans birth to thrones,
Have therfore under wise Kinges governement
Never byn creatures of their wills alone,
But like man-yokes made by mankindes consent;
   So tax againe to one, from many paid,
   Is not by one voyce well, but many laid.

### 313

Much lesse ought pulpitt doctryne stylde above,
Thorough cathedrall cheires, or scepter mighte,
Short, or beyond the almighties tenure move,
Varienge her shape, as humours varie lighte;
   Least when men see God shrinde in humane law,
   Thrones finde the 'immortall chang'd to mortall awe.

### 314

And to descende from visions of the best,
Both place and persons from her shadows must
Bee so upheld, as all may subject rest
To powre supreame, not absolute in trust;
   So to raise fees beyond rewarde or meritt,
   As if they might both tax, and disinheritt.

311/6 fruite] fruits *1670*     312/6 by] from *1670*     313/3 the
almighties] th'Almighties *1670*   6 the 'immortall] the immortal *1670*
314/2 persons] person *1670*
811710             I

### 315

Which to avoyde as pow'rs cheife mysterie,
Birth, education may give Princes lighte,
Yea in each art the master peeces be
Helpes to selecte amonge the infinite;
    Noe worcke of chance, as from *Pandoras* tonne,
    But happie choice, by fames cleere eyesight wonne.

### 316

Againe though use of taking from mans youth,
Be but a dowbtfull way of discipline,
To worcke a habite in the love of truth,
Though instrumentall practise doe refine
    The servinge, not the judginge powers of witt,
    And for uprightnes, so the more unfitt:

### 317

Yet in the libertie of advocates,
Which are of judges now the nurserie,
Fame is a glasse, where governors of states
May see what good or ill proportions be
    In everie harte fram'd to doe wronge or righte,
    Against temptations both of gaine and mighte.

### 318

Nor ends this worcke, when men are chosen well;
Since place corrupts them, as it shows them forth,
Some humors rays'd, some humbled doe excell,
Securitie is noe true nurse of worth;
    Therfore that speritt of fame, which made the choice,
    Must still in eares of Princes keepe a voice.

315/4 Helpes] Help *1670*     317/3 states *Ed.*: states, *1670*: state, *W*

### 319

And whence hath powre more safe intelligence?
Since fame doth serve them at her proper coste,
And is not thrall to grace, or to offence;
Though sometyme clowded, verie seldome loste,
   And where she lyes by evill information,
   She thinkes retraite noe losse of reputation.

### 320

Now since theis rules for lawes, doe even like lawes
Equallie serve the tyrante, and the Kinge;
This, to good uses for the publique cause,
That, all mens freedome under will to bringe;
   One spider like, the other like the bee,
   Drawinge to helpe, or hurte humanitie:

### 321

If I without distinction doo sett downe
Theis humble precepts, in a common style,
Their difference beinge not plac'd in the Crowne,
But crafte or truth to governe, or beguile;
   Let him that reads in this, and in the rest,
   Each cruditie to his fayre ends disgest.

## OF NOBILITIE

### Section VIII

### 322

When wise *Prometheus* had his fine clay drest
To fashion man, he nothing more did shunne
Then natures uniformities in beasts,
Of which by arte, there can be nothinge wonne;
   Whence in theis creatures frame he did comprise
   Many both stronge and strange varieties,

321/6 ends] end *1670*    Section VIII *Ed.*: Sect. 8°. *W*, SECT. VIII. *1670*
322/3 uniformities] uniformity *1670*

### 323

That as there divers kindes be of complections,
So in them there might be preheminence,
Divers of sperit, vigor, and affections;
To keepe upp which degrees of difference,
    *Reason*, of life the guardian was ordaind,
    As conscience to religion was enchaind.

### 324

And to confirme this inequalitie,
Have not theis feigned Gods, in orbes above,
Gloriouslie plac'd that spetious hierarchie,
Whose influence doth inferior speritts move,
    And in slacke, or swift coorses, high or lowe,
    The divers honors of each beinge showe?

### 325

So that of force he must a stranger be
To their republique, that will not confess
The supreame synodes of this deitie
To be compos'd of differinge noblenes;
    And partiallie who can be placed there,
    Where they that cleerest shine, most honor beare?

### 326

By birth and worth, that *Hercules* high priz'd,
Shines he not over *Cassiopea's* head?
Justlie, she beinge onlie canoniz'd
For *Perseus* sake, who did her daughter wedd,
    And he that for annothers sake doth rise,
    His meritt not in worth, but favor lies.

323/1 there *1670*: their *W*    6 enchaind] chain'd *1670*    324/2 theis] the *1670*    326/1 priz'd] *cancelling* prays'd    3 Justlie] Justice *1670*

### 327

Woulde it not be an auckwarde consequence
To see that virgine fraile *Erigone*,
Who by compassion gott preheminence,
Adored by our mariners to be,
    Farr above those two brothers savinge lighte,
    Whose twynne-lyke glorie makes the *Zodiack* brighte?

### 328

Doth not *Orion* worthilie deserve
A higher place, even for the constant love
Wherwith he did the chaste *Diana* serve,
Then frayle *Bootes*, who was plac'd above,
    Onlie because the Gods did els foresee,
    He should the murtherer of his mother bee?

### 329

Let noe man therfore mutine, when they see
Powre borrough paternes of creating art,
Owt of theis thrones wherin the majestie
Of nature is maintaind, thorough everie part,
    By theis well laid distinctions of degree,
    Which grow confus'd againe by paritie.

### 330

For as the harmonie, which sence admires
Of discords (yet concordinge) is compounded;
And as each creature reallie aspires
Unto that unitie, which all things founded;
    So must the throne and people both affecte
    Discording tones, united with respecte.

327/1 an *1670*: of *W*    329/1 Let noe man therfore] Let therefore no man *1670*  4 thorough] through *1670*  5 theis] their *1670*    330/2 concordinge] according *1670*

### 331

By which consent of disagreing movers,
There will springe up aspects of reverence,
Equalls and betters quarrelling lyke lovers,
Yet all confessinge one omnipotence;
   And therin each estate to be noe more,
   Then instruments owt of their makers store.

### 332

From whence nobilitie doth of creation
A secreate prove to kings and Tyrannie;
For as the stampe gives bullion valuation,
So theis faire shadowes of authoritie
   Are marckes, for people to looke upp unto,
   And see what Princes with our earth can doe.

### 333

In whom it is greate wisdome to rewarde
Unequall worth with inequallitie;
Since it doth breede a prosperous regarde
As well to princes as to Tyrannie,
   When people shall see those men sett above,
   That more with worth, then fortune seeme in love.

### 334

Yet must this brave magnificence be us'd,
Not reallie to dispossess the Crowne
Either of powre or wealth, but so infus'd
As it may rather rayse then pull it downe;
   Which frugall majestie in growing *Rome*
   Gave her above all States a lastinge doome.

331/1 of disagreing] *cancelling* yet of discordinge   332/2 *cancelling* A pretious secreate prove in Tyrannie   333/4 princes] *cancelling* Tyrants
334/6 Gave her above all States] *cancelling* Over all states gave her

### 335

For she discern'd although her wealth were vaste,
Yet people, and desire did farr exceede yt;
So as what spred too farr, could never last,
And for a state to give away, and neade yt,
   Shadowes, for bodies, she saw were to choose;
   Which must both strength and reputation loose.

### 336

The way she therfore did observe to prise
Well doinge subjects, and incourage meritt
Were titles, trophes, which she did devise,
Costles, and yet of force to quicken speritts;
   Thus unto *Affricanus Scipio's* name,
   *Haniballs* and *Carthage* eccho'd were by fame.

### 337

His brothers surname *Asiaticus*,
The storie was of *Asia* subdued;
*Perseus* captyv'd by *Macedonicus*,
To *Jugurth* straight *Numidicus* ensued;
   By which coorse as each conquest brought forth more,
   So they by giving, still increas'd their store.

### 338

Besides, prowd Princes must in their creations
Of forme, worth, nomber, keape a providence;
For if too manie, that waynes reputation,
Bought worth, or none, letts fall their reverence,
   With men that thincke habilitie to doe,
   The scope creatinge powre is bounde unto.

### 339

For farewell publique styles, and dignitie,
When *Neros* darcke thoughts shall comunicate,
Unto his fellow minstrells levitie,
Tryumphall statuas, offices of state;
   Or honor to such sprightes, as though in age,
   Never serv'd *Mars*, nor *Muse*, but on a stage.

### 340

Nor must this spetious bodie rise so high
As it shorte shadowes may on people cast;
Or by reflection dymme the Princes eye,
Who creatures over greatnes cannot tast;
   But lyve like clowdes in middle regions blowne,
   Which rise and fall, to make their mover knowne.

### 341

Slaves with the *Romanes* were not justice-free,
If all but nobles should stand so confinde,
What wretched state were our humanitie?
As if stepmother-lyke, nature combynd
   With powre, not onlie to make most men slaves,
   But in a few lordes to prepare them graves.

### 342

Such lawes in *Poland* sett so easie rates
On meane mens lyves, rate greate mens lyves so high,
As they may murther all inferior states,
Yet subject to noe other justice lye
   Then (as for doggs) a senceles money-fine,
   As if men were not images divyne.

339/4 statuas] statues *1670*    342/2 rate *1670*: rates *W*

### 343

Against this can it strange, or wonder be,
Where creatures their creator overgrowe,
If Princes hould their Crownes by curtesie?
*Poland* and *Germanie* are ballanc't so,
   As scepters glorie is in both those lost,
   And nothing left Kinges, but a name to boast.

### 344

Faire *Albion* when she swelld with subjects worth,
And by her Princes meritts gatherd fame,
Examples then did to the worlde bringe forth,
That overgreatnes often sways greate frames;
   Instance her actyve Barons marshall pryde,
   Which helpte the royall issue to devyde.

### 345

Lykewise, while glorious *Naples* did enjoy
Of home borne Princes the felicitie,
Yet even then, peere-greatness did anoy
That dainty scepter with strange mutenie,
   As ofte as to the Pope it seemed good,
   To serve his turne by hott aspiringe blood.

### 346

Till at the length this waving course of theirs
Under a greate Lorde wrought their servitude;
Who now curbes all their mutinie with feares,
And yet that feare againe with hope deludes;
   Keepinge men like reedes, to his selfe ends bente,
   By makinge new *Rome*, with her owne content.

343/2 creator] Creators *1670*   5 those] these *1670*

### 347

Kinges therfore that woulde not degenerate
Their scepters arts to artles anarchie,
To many, few, or any other state
Must wiselie bounde their owne nobilitie,
 Not raising men by charge, but spetious show,
 Nor yet so high as they may overgrow.


### 348

In *Scotland* their hereditarie sheriffes,
Each as a viceroy in his natyve shere,
Add ofte to Princes dangers, peoples greifes;
Justice so lyke to faction lookinge there,
 As men are sometimes forc'te to fall from Kinges,
 For shadowe under subalterned winges.


### 349

Princes then knowe it to be ominous
For you, to spread, or to participate
That powre creatinge, which doth governe us,
Eyther to baseness, still unfortunate,
 Or els to such a strengthened corporation,
 As easilie cannot wave her reputation.


### 350

The luster wherin powre is magnified
Being onlie to commaund that tame wilde beast,
People I meane, who ofte prove dangerous tydes,
And love equalitie undistinguisht best;
 Against whose rage there is no better sence,
 Then well advised pow're may have from hence.

347/2 scepters] Scepter *1670*     348/2 (Each is a Vice-roy in his native
shire;) *1670*     3 greifes] grief *1670*     6 subalterned] subalternate *1670*
349/5 strengthened] strengthned *1670*

### 351

Where els, while both nobilitie and Kinges
So poise themselves, as neither can be greate,
The people pullinge feathers from both winges,
Will first like equalls, and not like subjects treate
    Of all prerogatives; and then aspire
    To be the doome, or standard of desire.

### 352

Wherfore this greate, and little corporation
Should so be tempered, as they both may give
Unto their head a strengtheninge reputation,
And thence that freedome take in which they live;
    People not rackt, exhausted, or made prowde,
    But to be kepte straight, evermore kepte bowd.

### 353

For soveraigne pow're, which cannot stand alone,
Must by her subalternes supported be;
Keeping a distance betweene everie one,
To shunne contempte, even in authoritie,
    Whose little springs unto that mother sea,
    Whence they derived are, must tribute pay.

### 354

Nor were these humane Gods so prodigall
Of given Honours, but they did reserve
A powre to curbe their Cittizens withall;
*Phœbus* well did his banishmente deserve,
    By offringe to theis thunder-worckers wronge,
    *Cyclops*, which to his father did belonge.

---

352/2 so be tempered] be so temper'd *1670*   3 strengtheninge] streng-
thning *1670*   353/2 subalternes] subalternness *1670*   354/5
offringe] offering *1670*

### 355

Now when theis ebbinge, or still flowing states,
Thrones wiselie have with bounds established;
Then that this frame prove not unfortunate,
Foe to it selfe, and dowbtfull to her head;
  Powre must with constant sterne of governemente,
  Suppress devidinge humorous discontent.

### 356

Espetiallie that brutish ostentation
Of private courage, which setts life and sowle
Not onlie at a triviall valuation,
But lifts a subject farr above his rowle,
  Into the princelie orbe of making lawes;
  As judge, and partie in his private cause.

### 357

Which confident assuminges, if they be
Suffred, doe much allay the soveraignes righte,
Since all the moulds of fame and infamie,
Powre of mans life, and death, be acts of mighte,
  And must be form'd by Majestie alone,
  As royalties inherent to a throne.

### 358

Whose delicate complexion is such
That if in any member it be wounded,
It gangrens all; nay when man doth but touch
Her mysteries, then is her state confounded;
  Besides, who as a Kinge dare kill a man?
  As man againe will kill Kinges, if he can.

355/4 her] the *1670*    357/2 soveraignes] Soveraign *1670*

### 359

Lastlie where many states become united
Under one throne, though not one governemente,
Civill dissentions easilie are invited,
And in mans nature (ever discontent)
　　Under the color of a private feowde,
　　More mischeife stirrd up is, then understood.

### 360

Thus absolute powrs that will respected lyve,
Must governe greatnes, with a greater mynde,
And care their actions may noe scandall give,
As unto change or littlenes inclin'd;
　　But with a constant universall care,
　　Make them good subjects, that ill people are.

## OF COMMERCE
### Section IX

### 361

When theis Gods saw mankinds simplicitie
Wander with beasts, as fellowes in creation,
To both their thirsts alike the water free,
Acornes their food, earth bed and habitation,
　　They tooke compassion, and from heaven sent
　　Their spiritts, who did handiecraftes invent.

### 362

Which misteries the slowness of mans witt,
In manie yeeres, could els not have attaind,
That as men grewe, so they might learne to fitt
Nature with arte, to be by them maintaind;
　　And on the earth finde hearbs for foode and health,
　　As well as underneath it, mynes for wealth.

Section IX *Ed.*: Sect. 9°. *W*, SECT. IX. *1670*          361/1 mankinds] *cancelling* mans    5 tooke] take *1670*

### 363

To which end *Ceres* downe to *Sicill* came
And spredd that fruitefull art of sowinge grayne;
As *Bacchus* taught the *Naxians* how to frame
The grape for wyne; and *Pallas* showd the veyne
Of planting olives, which doe beare her name,
  A goddess motherless, borne of his brayne,
  That over all the other Gods did raigne.

### 364

Which wisdome likewise first taught men to hide
Their naked skynne, that beares noe natyve wooll;
And by chaste *Pallas* did reveale beside,
How from the worme, of silken riches full,
  The peoples hands might worcke choice robes for Kinges,
  Which since the pride of man in common bringes.

### 365

Againe when mankinde was thus finelie taught
To use the earth, with all that on it grewe,
Instantlie *Vulcan* thorough her bowells sought
For pretious mettalls, then to people new;
  Helping this common dame of ours, the earth,
  By manie midwyves, unto many births.

### 366

Lastlie, least one clyme should abound, and burst,
Starving the rest which of her store had neede,
This active *Pallas* likewise was the firste
That founde, and gave theis movinge bridges speed,
  As well to importe, as to carrie forth,
  From zone to zone all richesses of worth.

363/2 that] her *1670*    5 her] *cancelling* the    365/3 thorough] through
*1670*        366/2 her] their *1670*

### 367

And of her lovinge father did obtaine
*Castor* and *Pollux*, as two savinge lights,
To calme the stormes, which hidden doe remayne
In furrows of the *Oceans* face, who spights
    To have his deepe complexion without leave
    Ploughd upp by those, that venture to deceave.

### 368

Thus did theis Gods, o're greate to dowbte the mighte
Of all the worlde, though pride and wealth they knew
Apte to conspire against the wayes of righte,
In hope to make soveraignitie still new;
    Yet suffer man to growe in wealth and pride,
    As helpes not to unite them, but devide.

### 369

Whence in the worlde they publisht that each Zone
Created needefull was of neighboure clymes;
And (for they must corrupte, that needed none)
God made them subject both to want, and tymes,
    That art, and nature changing each with other,
    Might nurse all nations, like a common mother.

### 370

For longe ere *Jove* slye *Mercurie* enjoynd,
By the advantage of his goulden tounge,
To fashion grounds, from whence arts might be coyn'd
To leade the weake, and qualifie the stronge,
    With an attentive sweete obedience,
    Helpinge his reason, to commaund his sense:

367/4 who spights *1670*: (who spights) *W*        368/5 man] men *1670*
369/1 that each ] *cancelling* every   3 And (for . . . none) *1670*: And for, . . .
none, *W*    370/4 leade] leave *1670*

### 371

Longe, as I said, ere this felicitie
Did theis ingenious Goddesses descend;
And in that goulden tymes simplicitie,
As unto neede, and not excesses frend,
   So finelie arte, and nature mix in one,
   As made powre rich with more then was her owne.

### 372

Thus see wee in this natyve imag'de lighte,
Noe lack where art and nature joyned be;
Who therfore will in idlenes delighte,
And make not doing his felicitie,
   As earth by him turnes wildernes againe,
   So nature in him rusts for lack of payne.

### 373

Labor and care then must familiar bee,
Thorough the vigor of mens education,
To give mankinde against necessitie
Protection, in some honest occupation;
   And all growe undertakers, not a drone,
   Both ignorance and idlenes unknowne.

### 374

To which end pow're must nurseries erect,
And those trades cherish, that use many hands;
Yet such as more by paynes, then skill effect,
And so by spiritts, more then vigor stand;
   Wherebie each creature may it selfe sustaine,
   And who excell, add honor to their gaine.

372/1 imag'de lighte] Image-light *1670*     374/2 that] which *1670*
3 skill] skill'd *1670*

### 375

For traffique is a quintessence, confected
Of mixte complection, in all lyving creatures:
The mirackles of which may be collected
Owt of those fine webbs, which on natures features
   Art worckes to make men rich, that are not good;
   A base, whereon all governements have stood.

### 376

*Venice* that famous merchant common wealth,
Raised her rich magnificence by trade,
Of Coasts, Townes, Creekes, erst refuges for stealth,
Alonge the midland sea the subburbs made;
   Spices of Egypte, Barbaries fine gould,
   All worcks of *Syria*, her marts bought and sould.

### 377

A Cittie, till the *Indian* trade was knowne,
That did like *Europes* checker fill, and spred,
Adding more provinces unto her owne,
By mynes of money which her trafficke fedd,
   Then marshall *Philipp* had subdued in *Greece*,
   Or he whose arte brought home that goulden fleece.

### 378

Wherfore with curious prospect theis prowde Kings
Ought to survey the commerce of their lande;
New trades, and staples still establishinge,
So to improve the worcke of everie hand,
   As each may thrive, and by exchange, the throne
   Growe rich indeede, because not rich alone.

375/2 complection] complexions *1670*    377/2 checker] Exchequer *1670*
4 which] with *1670*   6 that] the *1670*
811710       K

### 379

Whose mysteries, though term'd mechanicall,
Yet feede powres triumphes, nurse necessitie
By venting, changing, raysinge, letting fall,
Framinge worckes both for use and vanitie,
    In mutuall traffique, which while marts stand fayre,
    Makes natures wealth, as free as is her ayre.

### 380

To ballance theis by equall weights or measure,
The audyt of our owne must be the guide;
As what for use, for honor, gayne or pleasure,
At home or is, or els might be supplied;
    The rest so by exchange to rise or fall,
    As while none loose, wee yet may gaine by all.

### 381

For as in leagues of states, when eyther might
Advantages of tyme, wordes, humors, witt,
Unequallie have lost, or gotten righte,
This surfett ever brings disease with it,
    Which (lyke a torrent) failes not to breake owt,
    Leavinge with losse of faith, both states in dowbte:

### 382

So when theis little lymms of greate estates
By crafte become on either side opprest;
Can witt bynde pow're with her deceaving rates,
Or hatche her Cuckoes in the Eagles neast?
    Noe; marts and trades which natures standerds be,
    Straight finde, and breake this inequalitie.

379/6 Makes] Make *1670*    380/4 or is] now is *1670*    381/2 tyme]
times *1670*

### 383

Thus did the *Hanses* sometimes tyrranise
The Northern Princes, in their infancie
Of trade and commerce, till with tyme growne wise,
Kinges saw how Crownes deceav'd by homage be;
　Which once discern'd, theis Contracts wonne by stealth,
　Can never stand to harme a common wealth.

### 384

Now under merchant, myner, clothier, plough,
Are all theis arts and mysteries containd,
Which owt of earth, doe teach our Princes how
Their pompe in warr, and peace may be maintain'd;
　As in whose choice, use, governemente and measure,
　Though bullion wants, yet states recover treasure.

### 385

All which rich mynes made for the good of all,
Are yet abus'd, by shorte breath'd witts, that will
The price and true incouragemente lett fall
Of industrie, and excellence in skyll:
　Hopinge thorough ignorance, deceipte, and stealth,
　While they loose art and creditt, to gett wealth.

### 386

The cure of which contagious disease
Rests onlie in the powre of governemente,
That must with reall arts her people raise,
Not marr her marketts, to give frawde a vente,
　And can almost as well make flesh and blood,
　As artizans, that shall be true, and good.

383/4 by] with *1670*　384/3 earth] each *1670*　5 use, *1670*: use *W*
385/3 incouragemente] encouragements *1670*　5 thorough] through *1670*

### 387

For though each vice brings forth her occupation,
Wherin earth yeeldes the matter, art the forme,
To make gaine infinite, by transmutation,
Since formes redowbled triple gaines retorne;
   It being fatall to refyned synne,
   By stayninge manners to bringe proffit in;

### 388

Yet must there be a kynde of faith preserv'd,
Even in the commerce of the vanitie,
That with true arts their marketts may be serv'd,
And creditt kepte to keape them greate, and free·
   Weight, number, measure trulie joyn'd in one,
   By trade with all states, to inrich our owne.

### 389

Amounge which masse of arts, if one too much
Draw upp, then traffique stands, and realmes grow poore,
Whereas in states well tempered to be rich,
Arts be the men's, and men the Prince's are;
   Forme, matter, trade so worckinge everie where,
   As governement may finde her riches there.

### 390

Then must this supreame powre, this wakefull spirit
Observe proportion in her industrie,
Never her owne from traffique disinherite,
But keape exchange in due equalitie;
   Not bringing home more, then she carries forth,
   Nor buyeinge toyes, with things of staple worth.

387/1 forth] for *1670*    389/3 tempered] temper'd *1670*    4 Prince's]
Princes *1670*    390/1 this supreame] the supreame *1670*

### 391

But worcke her matter with her home borne hands,
And to that use fetch forraine matters too,
Buyeinge for toyes the wealth of other landes,
To gaine by all the good or ill they doe,
　Keepe upp the bullion, for it doth entise,
　Yet not transport it, for tys prejudice.

### 392

Wherein wise Princes ought to imitate
The *Saracens* enrichinge industrie,
Who *Egypts* wealth brought to their barren state,
Entisinge vyce by farr fetcht vanitie,
　And for their ostridge feathers, toys of pride,
　Gett staple wealth from all the worlde beside.

### 393

Which as a watchword, shows powre may impose
With lesse hurt on the commerce of delighte;
For there by deereness, what can creditt loose,
Where fancies value is so infinite,
　As wealth and reason judge not, but devise
　To serve her both with objects and with eyes?

### 394

Thus the *Sabeans* heapte upp masse of treasure,
By venting incense unto everie nation,
As well for superstition as for pleasure;
Thus *Syria* gott by *Balsam* estimation,
　And millions brought by custome to the Jewe,
　Wealth kepte for him, that their state overthrewe.

393/2 With lesse hurt on] *cancelling* Safelie uppon

### 395

Hence trayns the *Hollander* his little Childe,
To worcke toyes for the vanitie of us,
And in exchange our cloth to them wee yeelde,
Wyse men and fooles even serve each other thus;
    The standerd of the whole world beinge synne,
    To furnish hers, by carrienge owt and in.

### 396

Now though wise Kinges doe by advantage play
With other states, in setting tax on toys,
Which if leagues doe permitt, they justlie may,
As punishments for that vyce which destroys;
    Of reall things yet must they carefull be,
    Heere and abroade to keepe them custome free.

### 397

Provyding cloth and foode noe burthen beare,
Then equallie distributinge of trade,
So as noe one rule, what wee eate and weare,
Or any towne the gulf of all be made:
    For though from few wealth soone be had, and knowne,
    And still the rich kepte servile by their owne;

### 398

Yet no one Cittie rich, or Checker-full
Gives states such credit, strength, or reputation,
As that foreseeinge longe breath'd wisdome will,
Which by a well disposinge of creation,
    Breeds universall wealth, gives all content,
    Is both the myne, and skale of governement.

395/5 synne] seen *1670*    6 carrienge] carriage *1670*    396/2 in] by *1670*
4 punishments] punishment *1670*    397/3 and] or *1670*    398/1 Checker-
full] Exchequer full *1670*

### 399

Admitt againe the *Holland* industrie
Lay tax on victuall, spare their merchandize,
Yet is it noe grounde for a monarchie
To viewe his owne frame with *Democrate* eyes;
   Since soveraigne pow're in one, and many plac'd,
   From divers lights, must divers shadows cast.

### 400

Doe wee not see the fertile soyles decayd,
And Easterne Citties, by the tyrranie
Of that greate lorde, who his vaste wealth allaid
By bringinge all theis Citties into three?
   Which three prove greedy ill disgesting wombes,
   Not treasuries of wealth, but rather toombes.

*Constanti-
nople. Cayro.
Aleppo.*

### 401

And while theis forraine gulfes I thus describe,
My wish is that I may not seeme to stayne
Some oreswolne Cittie of the *Albion* trybe,
Which starvinge manie, smothered doth remayne,
   And yet will not be cured of this greife,
   By yeeldinge other neighbour townes releife.

### 402

Moreover, fix and marshall in such wise
Powre commerce must of strangers, with her owne,
As neyther may the other tyrranise,
But live like twynns owt of one bodie growne;
   The strangers shipps not banisht, nor their ware,
   Which double customes bringe, and gages are.

399/3 noe] not *1670*    400/4 theis] those *1670*    401/1 theis] the
*1670*  6 other] to the *1670*    402/6 customes bringe] Custome brings
*1670*

### 403

Noe monopolies suffred in the lande,
All interlopinge practises withstood,
In merchant laws a constant gentle hand,
Imposinge paraleld with letting blood;
    The bullion not enhanced, nor embased,
    The forainer not dandled, nor disgraced.

### 404

Lastlie, she labor must to draw her marts
Within her ports, and so the strangers wealth,
Framing such lawes and rates for forraine parts,
As publique Commerce may be kepte in health;
    Their goods as pawnes, their industrie as vents,
    To multiplie our traffique, shippinge, rents.

### 405

Which may be donne in any greate estate,
Whose natyve riches others doe exceede
In reall worth, and thereby may give rate,
And drawe home forraine states by gaine or neede;
    But where this wants, there treatie must supplie,
    Farminge our neighbours wares to worcke this by.

### 406

*Queene*
*Elizabeth*

So had that worthie, greate, and maiden Queene,
If she had lyv'd, brought home that staple wealth
Of the *Muscovian* Empire to have beene
Conjoyn'd with hers, for eyther Cuntries health;
    He selling his heere deerer, then els where,
    She fixinge by them both a staple heere.

403/1 suffred] suffered *1670*   2 interlopinge] interpoling *1670*   6 forainer]
Forrainers *1670*    405/5 there *1670*: their *W*

### 407

And when theis had byn stapled heere together,
The silkes and riches of all other parts
Must needes have followed theis greate standerds hither,
With such as lyve by Commerce, or by arts;
  A worcke alreadie by experience knowne,
  Trade having staid, or chang'd with ours alone.

### 408

And though the stranger rarelie will commytt
His shipp and ware to Island Princes states,
Yet if he wealth or freedome finde with it,
Feare of imberge it easilie abates;
  Since by the present gaine, if evill come,
  He hath to buy, or beare owt heavie doome.

### 409

Therfore lett Thrones, whose states have seas to frende,
Studie by trade to make their Navies greate,
As glorious engines, when they will offende,
Magnificent theaters, when they treate,
  Bridges that will transport, and moving towrs,
  To carrie in and owt triumphinge pow'rs.

### 410

Under which safe, yet moving policie,
Did finite *Athens* make the infinite
Forces of *Zerxes* owt of *Greece* to flie;
*Lepanto* likewise proves the Christian might,
  Able by sea to shake the Turkish powre,
  Where his lande armies all the worlde devoure.

408/4 imberge] Imbargo *1670*    409/2 their] her *1670*    410/1 moving
*1670*: wavinge *W*    4 Christian] Christians *1670*

### 411

*England*, this little, yet much envied *Ile*,
By spreading fame and powre many wayes,
Admitt the worlde at her land conquests smile,
Yet is her greatnes reverenc'd by Seas,
    The *Ocean* beinge to her both a wall,
    And engine to revenge her wronges withall.

### 412

To which end Kinges must strive, to add a spiritt
Unto the mariner; in warr and peace,
A minister of use, and dowble meritt,
Trainde without charge, to travell without cease;
    Powre hath no nobler, nor yet surer way,
    Then that by which both save, and gett they may.

### 413

Now though this course of trafficke may appeare
To multiplie strange shippinge, not our owne,
Yet in the practice all states finde it cleere,
That still by traffique mariners have growne;
    As shipps by manufactures multiplie,
    And where good shipps be us'd, vents cannot dye.

### 414

Instance of both the *Netherlanders* be,
Who have increast their shipping, with their marts,
Adding to each, by that faire industrie
Of manufactures many forminge arts,
    By wealth, and concourse of all other nations,
    Even in warr, growne rich with reputation.

412/2 mariner;] Mariner, *1670*

### 415

And though of staple riches they have none
By nature in their natyve Countrie bred,
To sway or to induce more then their owne,
Yet are they by theis arts established;
   Merchant and *Mars* his well mixt policie,
   Of all exchanges growne the nurserie.

### 416

Wherbie they want no bullion, cloth, nor foode,
But with the surpluss, when neede is supplied,
Enrich themselves, raise custom, yet doe good
To all their lymmes, amongst whome they devyde,
   Heere law, there Courts, heere one trade, there another,
   Least any should ingrosse, to hurt their mother.

### 417

Againe Thrones must, by regall providence,
Governe that much us'd unknowne mysterie,
And costless modell of intelligence,
Exchange, the type of merchants polecie,
   Wherby he rayseth or letts fall all thinges;
   And though inferior, byndes or looseth Kinges.

### 418

By which large providence of governement,
Both over natyve, and the forraine wealth,
None shall be overstraind or discontent,
But from the harte each lymme receave his health;
   The Crowne releev'd, without constraint or cravinge,
   By tributes for our safetie of our savinge.

415/5 *Mars* his] *cancelling Marses*    416/1 nor] or *1670*    2 is] is, *1670*
417/6 or] and *1670*    418/5 constraint] restraint *1670*

### 419

In all which faire perticulers recited,
Powre shall concurrence and assistance finde
From everie subject, with selfe ends invited,
To'improve arts, earth, men in everie kynde,
    Makinge the harvest greate, the labor small,
    By doinge all thinges, with the helpe of all.


### 420

Now, if against theis noble mynes of wealth,
Any from forrain straynes of tyrannie,
With Color to keepe all degrees in health,
Woulde bynde, or lymitt this prosperitie,
    As nursinge pride, and luxurie in one,
    Vyces that easelie clyme upp to a Throne:


### 421

And owt of theis false groundes make powre conceave
Povertie to be the best bonde of subjection,
Let him, to judge how much theis mists deceave,
Firste put himselfe in poverties protection;
    And he shall finde all wisdomes that suppress,
    Still by misforminge, make their owne formes less.


### 422

For everie open harte knowes riches be
The safest gages, to keepe men in peace,
Whose natures cannot rest in miserie,
Noe more then flesh can, till her anguish cease;
    So that who over slaves doe tyrranise
    By choice, are neither trulie greate, nor wise.

419/4 To'improve] To improve *1670*      420/2 forrain *1670*: over *W*
421/2 bonde] end *1670*

### 423

Therfore prowde Princes ever must propound
That royall, or ingenious designe,
Of makinge all men rich, not minute bounde,
And to the same end, studie to refine
  Nurseries of trafficke, mysteries, and art,
  To furnish equall wealth in everie part.

### 424

For poore then, tell me, how can scepters be,
When all their subjects shall in wealth abound?
Or how, not greate in fame and majestie,
When strangers helpe to frame our traffique sound?
  And so make people strengths unto their Kinge,
  Who, without theis mowldes, charge or danger bringe.

### 425

Besides, severelie heere may laws proceede
Against the drone, the vagrant man, or theife,
Where occupations doe supplie mens neede,
And labor give each familie releife;
  Lastlie, how can mens spiritts mutine heere,
  Where each mans private to him selfe is deere?

## OF CROUNE REVENUE

### Section X

### 426

The antient sages tooke our earth to be
A simple elemente, of one complexion,

423/2 or] and *1670*    5 of] for *1670*    424/4 frame] *cancelling* make
6 or] and *1670*    425/2 vagrant man, or theife] vagrant, or the thief *1670*
5 mutine] mutiny *1670*    Section X *Ed.*: Sect. 10°. *W*, SECT. X. *1670*

Differinge onlie by varietie
Of heates and colde from heavenlie reflection:
But nature which can never be confinde
To narrow contemplations of one mynde,

### 427

This abstract dreame of former tyme confutes:
For in the circuite of one clyme, her wombe
Compos'd as various is, as are her fruites:
Heere gould for lifes use, marble for our tombes,
Heere vaynes of silver, there quick mercurie,
Heere *Pales*, there *Pomona* fruitefull be.

### 428

Which sweete varietie doth not proceede
From influence, or temper by the sunne;
But from the first diversitie of seede,
Which did through her created vessells runne,
And to the heate (as tributes) pay their springes,
Which unto ripeness *Phœbus* after bringes.

### 429

Colde *Germanie* thus yeelds, from her deepe mynes
Under the earth, a lastinge springe of treasure,
Thus *Hungarie*, where *Phœbus* nearer shines,
Above the earth yeelds natyve wealth and pleasure;
As in her Center she besides containes
Of gould and silver many hidden vaynes.

426/3 by] in *1670*        427/4 our tombes] her Tomb *1670*    5 mercurie]
*Mercury 1670*

430

Hence againe *France*, though ever marshall bent,
Was by her late fowrth *Henries* policie,
Knowne for a paradice-like continent,
Who out of that discernd fertilitie,
  Both multiplied the Crowne, and peoples parte,
  By natures emulation with his arte.


431

From both which mynes, in and above the earth,
Nature excludes the sloth of each degree,
Offringe the riches of her many birthes,
Onlie where she her self gives industrie;
  As if both man and thinges must there consent,
  Where wealth is multiplied to ornament.


432

For as rich nature is the moulde of plentie,
So art againe is natures consumation;
Againe as *Phœbus* throne in stuffs was deintie,
And yet the worcke of farr more estimation:
  So under Kinges, not earth, or creatures dumbe,
  But art of men it is, that yeelds the summe.


433

Powre therfore, that theis pillars of estate
Church, lawes, trade, honour have established,
Must then take care as equallie to rate
Rents, and expence, that by those to the head,
  Wealth synnow-lyke may give a strength to move,
  And breede respect, by mixing feare with love.

432/3 stuffs] stuff *1670*    6 men] man *1670*

## 434

First, because forraine states beare reverence
Where they finde wealth in soveraignitie,
As they with neede keepe no intelligence;
Besides the'example of frugalitie,
    By cuttinge of excess, that els consumes,
    Tempers prowde vyce, which otherwayes presumes.

## 435

Againe, for wealth though theis faire grounds be laid,
And treasure gotten by theis harmeless mynes;
If order yet be not aswell obaid
In the expence, wealth suddenlie declines;
    And want pressing through mans faults, on the Crowne,
    More fatallie pulls Kinge, and people downe.

## 436

Therfore ought monarckes to be providente,
In weighing thinges, which though they triviall seeme,
Yet are of consequence in governemente,
As difference of dyet, custome, clyme;
    Since high rais'd *Athens*, and *Pireum* port,
    Had manners, and askt lawes of divers sort.

## 437

Whence I conclude that Northern Princes must
Cherish the staple rent of their demeasnes,
And to their owne inheritances trust,
Which to the Crowne of old did appertaine,
At least by Parliaments supplie their lust:
    Els shall theis Kinges be easelie overthrowne,
    That tax, and give the peoples with their owne.

434/3 with] which *1670*    4 the'example] the example *1670*    6 otherwayes]
otherwise *1670*    435/5 pressing through mans faults, on *1670*: growne
from the mans faults, to *W*    436/6 divers] different *1670*

## 438

And though the finer heates skorne theis safe steyes
Of Crowne Revenewes, as if powre and witt
From peoples wealth, might endles proffitt raise;
Yet in the practise, who observeth it,
   Shall finde those taxes, which the Sowth brookes well,
   Doe often make the colder clymes rebell.

## 439

Besides, who well observes a monarchie,
Shall finde disorder there a fatall thinge,
The head beinge both of unprosperitie,
Good fortune, fame, or infamie the springe:
   So that oppression, which makes both sides poore,
   Ought to have entrance at a narrowe doore.

## 440

Againe in taxes, differences be;
Some from the Crownes prerogative alone,
Pleadinge an overrackinge petigre,
Others, by Parliaments so mix the throne
   With common peoples good, as, but excess,
   Nothing can thence rise, to make scepters less.

## 441

*France* then! thow large extended monarchie,
Keepe to thie selfe thy change of Crowne demeasne,
For bleedinge taxes which breed miserie
In men, and so reflecte on Crownes againe,
   By forcinge them to sell tribunall seates,
   Which makes thy justice vyle, thy Judges greate.

441/2 thy change] the charge *1670*   6 makes] make *1670*

### 442

*Lewis* th'eleaventh of crafte, not majestie
The perfecte type, beinge asked what the Crowne
Revenewes might in *France* amounte to be,
Said *France* a meadowe was, which mow it downe
   As ofte as neede, or pleasure did require,
   Woulde yet growe up againe, to feede desire.

### 443

Where majestie indeed is kepte above
By true magnificence, rais'd of her owne,
Ryot a steepe is, whence states hedlong move;
The age of powre is by low stooping knowne,
   For as, but myters, few by stewes doe gett,
   So who, but *Negars*, tax on breathing sett?

### 444

Kinges then who would have their magnificence
To be maintaind by springes which should not faile,
Must with that Councell keepe intelligence,
Wherwith the dyinge farmer did prevayle,
   To make his Children digg his vyne for gould,
   Who founde it not in mettall, but in mould.

### 445

This vineyard in a Kinge is his demeasne,
Joyn'd with that art of arts, which man improves,
And enviless makes actyve monarckes raigne,
Rich both in peoples treasures, and their loves:
   What *Mydas* wish, what dreames of alchemie,
   Can with theis true Crowne mynes compared be?

442/3 in] of *1670*    443/3 whence] where *1670*    4 age] rage *1670*
444/1 who] that *1670*

### 446

Againe, prerogatives in governemente,
Which priviledg'd pow're at first to take, then prise
What might her true necessitie content,
Kinges should not multiplie, to prejudice
    That infancie, where men, by what they gave,
    The rest intended for their use to save.

### 447

But where success of tymes make powre exceede
This safe equalitie of olde foundations,
Rather with temperance qualifie that neede,
Then straine olde wordes to moderne intimation,
    And therby rack men, to provide for more
    Excess, then all those ages knewe before.

### 448

Of which excesse, whether the roote proceede
From humors naturallie unsatiate,
Or casuallie made vyolent by neede,
Odious those cures are which equivocate,
    As did *Caligula* when by quirckes of law,
    *Sibi* and *suis* he to sonns did draw.

### 449

And though it for a wisdome of estate
Enrowld be, in the senate howse of *Rome*,
When they with *Carthage* did capitulate,
That she must from her olde sea nurses come,
    Inferringe (Cittie) signified noe wall,
    But lawes, which men obey and rule withall:

446/6 save] have *1670*    447/1 success . . . make] excess . . . makes *1670*

### 450

Wherby although more gott were then was mente,
And by advantage evill acts made good;
Yet what this adds to any governemente,
Is in dishonor ever understood:
    Since craftie webbs which ofte serve present turne,
    To warne tymes cominge, doe lyke beacons burne.

### 451

Besides, if pompe of Princes must exceede,
In those kindes rather let their ryott be,
Whose natures though they leave a Crowne in neede,
And so embase the state of majestie;
    Yet keepe the bullion still within the lande,
    To goe, and growe, lyke fame, from hand to hande.

### 452

Yet as a springe for ever feede the Crowne,
By makinge people able to releeve,
Where ryotts that transport, pull scepters downe,
Give Kinges, and people, mutuall cause to greeve,
    At that extreame and fatall consequente
    Of coyne transported by misgovernemente.

### 453

Amonge whose manie heads, though not as cheife,
Is that most idle and unmeasured charge
Of leager agents, sent to take a breife,
How forraine Princes alter, or enlarge
    Alliance, Councells, undertakings, trade;
    Provisions to defend, or to invade.

450/1 were] was *1670*     451/3 a] the *1670*     452/5 consequente] consequence *1670*     453/1 not as] of the *1670*

### 454

Which undigested pompe was never knowne
Nor us'd of olde, but in the factorage
Of Merchants states, to pass away their owne,
By makinge Princes martes their proper stage:
    Whereby exchange, want, follie, or desire,
      To selfe endes they let fall, or raise thinges higher.

### 455

Els springes it from improper imitation
Of that longe breath'd incrochinge Courte of *Rome*,
Which to give her staind wares deere valuation,
And governe all by superstitious doome,
    From her false arcke theis cormorants sends forth,
      To pray on everie thinge they finde of worth.

### 456

And to that end retayneth everie where
A spie, promoter, treasurer, and mynte;
Whose charge those humbled Provinces must beare,
That are besides exhausted without stinte,
    By Preistes, who cherish for their pride and gayne
      Those synnes, the verie heathen did restraine.

### 457

The narrow center of which Cloister witt,
As it seekes to contract the deitie
In finite frames of arts contryvd by it;
So are the large acts of humanitie
    Shutt up in dungeons, by their muddie sence,
      That, except error, nothinge comes from thence.

454/1 undigested] indigested *1670*    456/3 humbled] humble *1670*

### 458

Now what affinitie can other Kinges
Assume with this, that onlie spend to knowe
Which feathers sore in forraine Eagles winges?
From whence there can noe other proffitt growe,
But vainelie by expence of wealth, to buy
The vitious formes of forraine tyrranie.


### 459

And so, by theis mistrained instruments
Bringe faction home amonge the liberall arts,
With her unequall mouldes of governemente,
To traffique, and distract the peoples harts;
Fre denizinge that practicall deceipte,
By which not small, but greate states gather weighte.


### 460

Out of the insight of which error, manie
Wise Kinges this moderne course have altered,
And rarelie either sent, or taken anie,
Unless for present good ocasioned,
To treate of mariage, commerce, peace, or warr,
In which returnes the expences answered arr.


### 461

Againe since as of duties, so expence,
There is a divers nature, and degree;
Kinges in the choice of their magnificence,
Though absolute they seeme, yet cannot be;
But bounde amoungst the manie heads of charge,
Cheifely their fame or empire to inlarge.

459/4 and] or *1670*        460/2 altered] alter'd *1670*

### 462

Nay, even in theis expences, which be founded
Uppon the lawes of honor, nature, state;
Wise Princes with their fortunes must be bounded,
Since all excesses be infortunate;
   And doe not onlie prejudice a throne,
   But leave noe creature master of his owne.

### 463

Of this kinde charge of Children, buildings be,
Howskeepinge, furnitures, guiftes, and rewardes,
All lively shadowes of authoritie,
To multiplie obedience, and regarde;
   Wherin yet Kinges should therfore keepe a measure,
   As in things fram'd to lyve, and dye with treasure.

### 464

Whence I conclude it for a monarchie
Wisdome, in her expences and creations,
To use a spare discreete frugalitie,
Which gives the worcke and worckman reputation;
   And so againe by all ingenious wayes
   Descendinge rents, not impositions raise.

### 465

And when with theis faire cautions Princes have
Forraine revenewes, and their natyve rents,
Disposed thus both to begett, and save,
They may with costles grace or disgrace vent
   Mens thoughts, and frame their dew obedience,
   More then can be wrought in them by expence.

462/2 honor, nature] Nature, Honor *1670*    4 infortunate] unfortunate *1670*
464/4 worckman] workmen *1670*        465/5 their *1670*: of *W*

### 466

For Kinges are types of heavenlie excellence,
Howbeit drawne in finite colors mixte,
With powre, and witt, both earthlie influence,
Yet were but theis arts in our Princes fixte,
　　How to be stronge by others love, and mighte,
　　Their states would soone clyme farr above their righte.

## OF PEACE

### Section XI

### 467

*Peace* is the next in order, first in end;
As the most perfect state of governemente,
Where arte and nature each to other frende,
Enlarge the Crowne, by givinge men content;
　　And what by lawes within, and leagues without,
　　Leaves nothinge but prosperitie to dowbte.

### 468

So that in her orbe there is lefte for Kinges
Greate undertakings, farr beyond the flighte
Or pitch, of any lower fethered winges,
The charge, care, Councell beinge infinite,
　　As undertakinge range of tyme, and seas,
　　Which tyrant like, to ruyne els findes ways.

### 469

Orderinge of boates, and bridges to be placed
Uppon advantage, for the trade of men;
Rebuildinge monuments, or townes defaced;
Clensinge of havens; drayninge dry of fenns;
　　Fittinge owt brookes, and meares for navigation;
　　All worckes of Princelie art, charge, reputation.

Section XI *Ed.*: Sect. 11. *W*, SECT. XI. *1670*　　468/5 range *Ed.*: rage *W, 1670*

470

Such was the clensinge of the *Egyptian* sluces,
Which got *Augustus* ornamente and foode,
For his pretorian bandes, and peoples uses;
In this kynde prov'd their *Appian* highway good;
  Those publique worckes, which active states bringe forth,
  Showing the stranger mapps of wealth and worth.

471

Therfore Kinges Providence should still adorne
Natures producements, by the pow're of arte;
But to subverte her frames proves scepters scorne;
Through *Athos* who yet sailes in any parte?
Is *Corinths Isthmus* from the mayne land torne?
  *Cæsars* vaine dreames, as if falne flatteringe *Rome*
  Over the free made elements, had doome.

472

The base of greate worckes, and the majestie,
Is when the worckers pow're and wisdom show
Both in the use, and possibilitie;
So over *Ister Trajans* bridge did goe:
  *Amasis* and *Cheops* how can time forgive,
  Who in their useless *Pyramids* would lyve?

473

Next, and of more refined policie,
The foundinge is of theis sweete nurseries,
Where knowledge, and obedience multiplie
The fame, and sinewes of greate monarchies;
  As schooles, which finelie doe betweene the sense,
  And natures large formes, frame intelligence.

470/4 their] the *1670*

### 474

Unto which end *Achaia, Athens, Creete,*
*Rhodes, Lacedemon,* and more were erecte;
Illustrious states, and pedagogies meete,
By reason and example to protecte
    The cominge ages, from that barbarisme
    Which first breeds ignorance, and after schisme.

### 475

Whence againe *Rome* in all her colonies,
Even while her Eagles marcht, had yet a care,
To plant the muses in the souldiers eyes,
Such meanes to move or qualifie they are;
    Where in the *Turcks* excess of tyrranie,
    Theis daintie Nymphes exil'de for ever be.

### 476

And to give more faith to this sympathie,
Which betweene *Mars* and *Muses* ought to rest,
The poetts in *Ideas* farr more free,
Then any other arts of mortall brest,
    Have in their fables ever show'd them mixte,
    As if devided, neither coulde be fixte.

### 477

Hence faine they, when *Jove* sent his daughters nyne
To polish *Greece,* he would not have them pass
Alone, expos'd to every savage myne,
Or rage, wherin the earth abundant was;
    But gave them *Hercules* for such defence,
    As actyve vertue is to innocence.

474/1 *Achaia*] in *Achai 1670*    475/6 exil'de] excel'd *1670*

### 478

Have not againe theis muses, when they singe
The *Io Pean* of their thundringe father,
*Apollo*, with his shaftes nock't in his stringe,
For consorte of their quire, or master rather;
   To shew where truth cheines not men by the eare,
   There savage nature must be rulde by feare.

### 479

Whence amoungst all the famous victories,
Which old *Rome* from the East did triumph on,
Even that of *Fulvius* well deserv'd the prise,
Who for a trophe of pow're overthrowne,
   Brought home the statuas of theis sisters nyne,
   And that of *Hercules*, alike devyne.

### 480

For which the Cittie did a temple builde,
As spoiles that their God *Mars* did better fitt,
Then all those dainties which fine *Asia* yeelde,
Or curious cobwebbs of *Egyptian* witt,
   Plenties of *Nylus*, wealth of *Macedone*;
   Which helpe not to raise up, but weyne a throne.

### 481

Hard by which temple *Rome* builte upp two more,
The one to worth, the other unto fame:
From worth, to fame there was an open dore,
From fame, to worth she did noe passage frame.
   The mynde of which brave nation was in this
   To shew that fame, but vertues shadow is.

478/2 thundringe father,] thundering Father *1670*     3 his stringe] the
string *1670*     479/3 well deserv'd] did deserve *1670*     4 trophe] Trophy
*1670*     5 statuas] Statues *1670*

### 482

Now though it rarelie be to be expected,
That all Kinges perfect should, lyke *Cæsar* be,
Who in himselfe both *Muse* and *Mars* erected;
At least with *Trajans* ingenuitie
   Let them that doe in either branch excell,
   Still in the other, cherish doinge well.

### 483

And as the Elephant, who not created
To swimme, yet loves and haunts the waters shore;
So let wise pow're in mightie empires stated,
Though boast they cannot in the muses store;
   Yet honor spiritts of *Parnassus* free,
   As knowinge best what fitts humanitie.

### 484

Nor is the buildinge of the Muses Cell
Powrs cheife worcke, but to manage everie spirit,
And frame each science so to doinge well,
As states and men may multiplie by meritt;
   All arts preferred by odds of practicke use,
   The meere contemplative scorn'd as abuse.

### 485

Cheiflie, this Cell-art of the wranglinge mouncks,
Captivinge both mans reason and his sence,
In dreames of yesterday, wherwith theis trunckes
Strive to corrupte divine intelligence;
   Their nominall and reall pedigrees,
   Beinge but discents of curious vanities.

### 486

And hence it is, the acts of peace and warr,
Never recorded heere so bravelie were,
As when theis abstracte witts lyv'd not to marr,
By makinge their fonde visions characts beare
    Of theis mens deeds, who, what by sword they wan,
    By pen as lively registred to man.

### 487

For as that actyve worth was then admir'd,
The effects it wrought being of a large extent;
So in those tymes less actyvelie inspired,
The styles of that tyme seeme magnificent:
    As if God made them trumpetts fitt for fame,
    Who by their deeds deserv'd to beare her name.

### 488

Meaning, that when tymes iron days should blast
That manlie discipline of doing well,
The art of writing should no longer last,
Lyke natures twynns that must together dwell;
    Doinge and writinge being to each other,
    As bodies be of their owne shadowes mother.

### 489

This was the forme, the birth, the education,
And art of that age, which did traine her owne,
To keepe upp greate estates in reputation,
Making them stand by worth, as they had growne,
    And drawing men from visions of abuse,
    To arts, wherof both warr and peace finde use.

487/2 a large] large *1670*        488/5 to each other] each to other *1670*
489/1 the birth, the education *1670*: the birth right, education *W*

### 490

In which accompte of objects still are life,
Speach, manners, scepter, spheare, earth, sheild and sea,
All reasons Children, by the sence his wife,
Fram'd to guide nature in an actyve way;
    Whether she would be rich, or serve her neede,
    Raising noe trophees for her, but by deede.

### 491

Now when of monarchies the mother seate
On theis cheife pillars thus shall setled be;
Then active Princes may growe rich, and greate,
By strivinge, under one selfe policie,
    Their provinces devided to unite,
    As worths addition unto natyve righte.

### 492

Which union must all divers things attone,
As Councells, laws, Church, Commerce, language, Coyne,
Degrees, and forces, so that in the throne,
As in one head, they may like members joyne,
    Intirelie, without any reservation;
    Which union is all els but combination.

### 493

A state, lyke unto coates with manie seames,
Subjecte to all the rents of tyme and chance,
As flotinge high uppon occasions streames,
Which one, by harminge others, doth advance,
    The wittie selfness of each humor hidinge
    That, which in common traffique proves devidinge.

491/3 active Princes] *cancelling* Princes actyve

### 494

Wheras that firste, and well united frame,
With head and members joyned to one end,
Can bringe forth nothinge to devyde the same,
Each in the whole, to it selfe being frend;
   Wherbie no inward storme can easelie rise,
   Nor outward forces doe it prejudice.

### 495

And though of theis the rights devided be,
Some into hands of people, some of Kinges;
Yet must not scepters by transcendencie
Drawe home their owne right with imperiall stringes,
   But by applause, to make upp this new chaine,
   Rather perswade the people, then constraine.

### 496

More tenderlie of force ought thrones to deale
With those, where men prescribe by righte or use,
For common likinge must to common weale
Be wonne, or man his proffitt will refuse,
   And turne his waxen mettall into steele,
   Which harming others, selfe harme cannot feele.

### 497

And when unto a true equalitie
All inequalities powre hath reduced,
Leaving her subjects noe regalitie,
Least divers myndes should easelie be seduced;
   They that enjoy them to restraine a throne,
   And they againe to mutine that have none;

496/3 common likinge] *cancelling* commonly Kinges: *see note*          497/6
mutine] mutiny *1670*          none; *Ed.*: none. *W, 1670*

### 498

Then yet all wandringe titles of succession
Wise Princes must with providence unite,
Els will theis Crowne rights leave a deepe impression,
That no sett course can longe continue righte;
    Since when the one lyne shall become extincte,
    All union builte on that base, lyes unlincte.

### 499

Moreover realmes of naturall discent,
When they with those which chance, or conquest wynne
Shall be united in one governemente,
Then scepters may more famous worckes begin;
    Plantinge new colonies in savage parts,
    There to spread wisdome, powre, laws, worth, and arts.

### 500

Followinge for guide of this establishmente,
Either the common standard of mans reason,
Or els that second lighte of governmente,
Which stories yeelde, and noe tyme can diseason,
    Drawne from those monarchies which overran
    In little tyme, all this knowne worlde of man.

### 501

Whose bent ambition still to conquere more,
Compell'd them wiselie to dispose their owne,
And by that discipline they us'd before,
Worcke nations conquer'd neare as soone as knowne,
    To lyve in order, and by trade gett wealth,
    With equall justice, keepinge both in health.

500/3 that] the *1670*   5 those *1670*: theis *W*

### 502

By which milde wisdome they grew lordes of fame,
As well as Crownes; and rather wanted men,
Then stages, meanes, or modells how to frame
Ruynes, mishapps to better forme againe;
  Building upon the barborous conquered,
  The uttermost of ill, well governed.

### 503

See wee not even amoung the brutish nations,
If men to them transport Civilitie,
Those colonies are deere in estimation,
And soone linckt with them in affinitie?
  Their comings construed not to spoile, or take,
  But as come from their dwellings for their sake.

### 504

So *Athens* with *Ionian* colonies
Did people *Asia*, *Lacedemon* spred
Her *Dorian* tribes thorough fertile *Italie*

And so by her that *Euxin* barbarous sea
Made hospitable is unto this day.

### 505

This the cheife pillar is of policie,
That ever by the *Romanes* was invented,
Enviless to uphold their monarchie,
And make the stranger with their yoke contented;
  Prodigall of *Rome* they to their neighbors were,
  Wherby her owne wombe did her empire beare.

503/3 estimation] reputation *1670*      505/6 her empire] the Empire *1670*
811710                                   M

### 506

For by this longe breath'd course it came to pass,
That all states did not onlie stand in awe
Of *Rome* as mistress, but the whole worlde was
Lincked with her in traffick, league, and law,
    And did so much adore the *Romans* fame,
      As they forsooke their owne, to beare her name.

### 507

Where in this craftie worlds declyning age,
Those large spred rootes, are withered, or dead,
All spiritts of worth to present powre ingage,
And there so mastered, dulld, or measured,
    As while men feare their little toyes to loose,
      Worth they choose rather to suppress, then use.

### 508

From whence it is, that wee finde of erectinge
Decayd estates, or Colonies derivinge,
Or proper lawes, the present tyme directinge,
Examples few; but many Princes strivinge
    Thorough feare of change, and fatall hate of paynes,
      With publique loss, to bringe in private gaynes.

### 509

Which privatenes forgetts tymes glorie past,
And useth tyme to come but to despise;
Her narrow ends, being on the present plac'd,
And so in narrow selfenes onlie wise;
    Noe undertakinge empire to extend,
      To purchase fame, or any noble end:

506/1 this] the *1670*    3 the whole] all the whole *1670*    4 with] unto *1670*
508/5 thorough] through *1670*

### 510

But selfelie to roote out our enemies,
Deface faire monuments, spoyle civill places,
Dispeople realmes of men, and earth of trees,
Spoilinge, to varnish tyrannies disgraces,
   And bringe the world to those dayes back againe,
   Where power did over beasts, not people raigne.

### 511

Againe, this arte of tyrant Cittadell,
Not sufferinge free Citizens but slaves;
What is it but a Councell owt of hell,
Makinge the Princes tryumphes, peoples graves?
   And sorts it not well with that *Sultans* worde,
  Who vaunts, grasse grows not, where his horse hath stood?

### 512

This is the cause the holie prophet spake
And wrote, but of fowre monarchies alone,
As if the rest theis lights did rather take,
To be on slaves a stricte dominion;
   Noe empire but a craftie vyolence,
   Whose ruynes never raise magnificence.

### 513

For that indeede is not true monarchie,
Which makes Kinges more then men, men less then beasts;
But that which worcks a perfect unitie,
Wheare Kinges as heads, and men as members rest,
   With mutuall ends lyke twynns, each helpinge other,
   In service of the common wealth, their mother.

511/5 that] the *1670*    512/5 Noe] Not *1670*    513/1 not] no
*1670*

### 514

Thus unto Kinges their Provinces remote,
(Which ofte els grudge at subalterne subjection)
May with good governement be kepte devote;
Men doe ascribe so much unto protection,
    And ofte adore most, what they least doe knowe,
    Lyke spetious thinges which farr of fairest showe.

### 515

And as mans harte, though in one place confinde,
Yet to remote lymms sends forth vitall pow'rs,
With ease or disease to affect the mynde,
Accordinge to her good, or evill howres,
    Whence sometymes armes have of her pulse more sence,
    Then other members, not so farr from thence:

### 516

Even so that providence of heavenlie love,
Which houlds the opposing elements in awe,
Though in her Throne advanced farr above
The finite reach of any mortall law,
    Yet never rests confinde to any seate;
    But by farr spreadinge, proves her owne powre greate.

### 517

Therfore since wisdome worckes both farr and nigh,
As boundless, not restraind to tyme or place,
Ador'de when absent, honor'd in our eye,
The more assiduous, still the more in grace,
    Repressinge mans ambition with his feare,
    A ballance Kinges must use, and people beare:

515/6 not so farr] less far off *1670*

### 518

On theis states what true judgment can wee lay
Which by the arts of craftie tyrranie,
So to their ends, doe peoples humours sway,
As throne-rights grow a kinde of mysterie?
  Whence *Mahomet* himself an *Idoll* makes,
  And draws mankynde to *Mecha* for his sake.

### 519

Thus did the *Caliph* of greate *Babilon*,
In former tymes, bewitch the barbarous nations,
With sighte of rich robes, shadows of his throne;
Reserv'd magnificence gives such reputation,
  Addinge to arts of powre, which still seemes more,
  By making those sowles less, that must adore.

### 520

But to conclude, as moderne tyrannie
Hath not in any kinde established
A state by peace unto prosperitie
Of people, or of honour to the head;
  But rather to the prejudice or shame
  Of both, like torrents, spread abroad ill name;

### 521

So against this, powre absolute should straine
In their estates to settle such a peace,
As people pleasd, Kinges might with pleasure raigne,
By making mens wealth, to their use increase;
  Which so will lincke all members to the head,
  As change shall there finde all her movers dead.

518/4 throne-rights] Thrones rights *1670*          519/5 seemes] seem *1670*

## OF WARR

### Section XII

#### 522

Mans error, havinge fram'de his mynde and sense
So divers, as no reall worcks longe please,
Is justlie scourg'd by that omnipotence,
Which never in it selfe letts vyce finde ease;
   Whence the vicissitudes of peace, and warr,
   Powers punishment, as well as glories arr.

#### 523

Yet since excess in some boundes must subsist,
And warr have grounds from other heads, then might,
Because her torrents els runne where they list,
And in desire, raise tytles infinite;
   Right and defence must therfore be her base,
   Which yet may varied be, to many a case.

#### 524

Amounge which, lett protection be a cheife,
When weake Crownes threatned are to be opprest,
An image of the Deities releife,
Showing that thrones at once can move, and rest;
   And so growe greater, by that ayde they give,
   As in whose pow're, more then their owne states live.

#### 525

Crowne-right againe which natively descends,
Clayminge estates in other Crownes possession,
Must not neglected be in Princes endes,
And yet have curious auditts in progression;
   Wealth, right, occasion from the barr of words,
   In Princes states appealing to their swords.

Section XII *Ed.*: Section 12°: *W*, SECT. XII. *1670*    523/2 grounds]
bounds *1670*   6 to] in *1670*

### 526

In pettie rights therfore proportion'd care
Doth well become the royall state of powre;
But that indeede, by which Crownes honor'd are,
Is care, noe one throne may the rest devoure;
  So that to wayne a growing Empires might.
  Infalliblie is every Princes righte.

### 527

Lastlie, it much more danger will be founde,
Where Princes shall be thought adverse to warr
Out of the harts effeminatish grownd,
Then to be helde, as witt and courage arr,
  Ambitious undertakers, and noe frends
  To any righte, that interrupt their ends.

### 528

For since most Crowns were first established
By warr, can tymes, or fates vicissitudes
So constantlie by man be governed,
As they shall not his idle rests delude,
  And on those monarcks desolation lay,
  That will neglect that base wheron they stay?

### 529

Hence sprange that wisdome, wherbie martiall *Rome*
Did *Janus* temple, in eight hundred yeeres,
Not three tymes shut, but open to the dome
Kepte them of *Mars*, whose force each question cleers,
  And to his banners did one consull fitt,
  As she in Justice made the other sitt.

---

526/2 state] States *1670*    527/6 interrupt] interrupts *1670*    528/2 fates]
States *1670*    4 rests] times *1670*

### 530

Then let not Kinges by their neglect invyte
Aspiringe states, or Princes to doe wronge;
Securitie exposeth wealth and righte
As prays to their ambitions that be stronge;
 Nor is the spoilers hand so soone made free,
 By any thinge as inhabilitie.

### 531

But so provide for unprosperities,
As fate at leaste may qualified succeede,
Framinge for change of tymes such policies,
As no distempers or diseases breed,
 By home broyles to tempte forraine enemies;
 Least wee for them, not for ourselves, prove wise.

### 532

To which end Princes must raise ordinance,
Provide munition, armor, fortifie
Such places, as may best secure mischance,
Seige, or surprise, which conquest trafficks by;
 And such againe as if a tumult growe,
 Wise Princes to them may for refuge goe.

### 533

*Euphrat, Danuby, Rhene* were those old bounds
Of *Rome*, which *Barbars* ventured not to pass,
While many legions kepte their winter grounds;
But chang'd by *Constantine*, when that force was,
 *Gothes, Hunns,* and *Scythians* overspred her face,
 Lyke horses runninge in a champion race.

530/4 As] And *1670*  be] are *1670*  531/3 tymes] time *1670*

### 534

Such bulwarckes modernelie have helde owt *Spaigne*,
From her mixt stiles of righte, and usurpation;
Such have withstood the *Sultans* force againe,
And sav'd the *Germanes* from depopulation;
  Whereas for want of theis, fayre *Albion*
  Hath fyve tymes byn assaild, fowre tymes o'recome.


### 535

Besides stronge Kinges must arme, and exercise
Troopes of their people in securest tymes,
And to the same end ever patronise
Some active speritts, in warrs of forraigne clymes,
  To trayne upp leaders, who before need come,
  May discipline their men for *Mars* his doome.


### 536

*Luctatius*, who the good luck had to end
*Romes* firste greate *Punick* warr, did on the land
By practise teach his seamen, how to mende
That discipline in peace, by which warrs stand:
  As *Philopemen* made *Achaia* spred,
  By lasie peace, yet livelie governed.


### 537

If *Roderigo* that unluckie Kinge,
Over those *Gothes* which did inhabite *Spaigne*,
Had well observ'd theis rules, that savage springe
Of *Saracens* could not have shakte his raigne;
  But still confinde unto their *Affrick* shore,
  Must have remayn'd, and not have sought for more.

537/5 their] the *1670*

### 538

Where he at home affraid of civill warr,
Disarm'd his men; which to boulde *Tariff* was
A signe that active force might venture farr,
And by *Spaignes* weakeness bringe his ends to pass:
    Which showes againe, when frends or foes drawe swords,
    They ever loose, that rest or trust to words.

### 539

Who knowes not that the *Roman* conquering nation,
Least their brave people should degenerate
By peace, to keepe upp speritt and reputation,
Trained their souldiers in each neighboure state,
    And under color of protectinge frends,
    Laid new foundation for her owne new ends.

### 540

Soundinge the witt and force of everie nation,
That when tyme serv'd, they might their masters growe;
Thus helde they upp the *Etolians* reputation,
To conquer *Greece*; and *Asia* overthrowe,
    By frendinge *Eumenes*; *Affrick* is made theirs,
    Color'd by helpe to *Massinissaes* heires.

### 541

Pow're must againe so plante intelligence,
And ballance neighboure Princes by their good,
As in our dangers, they may feele offence,
And hould it fitt, even with their subjects blood,
    In our protection so to worcke out theires,
    That publique powre may warrant publique feares.

538/6 to] in *1670*    540/4 *Greece*; . . . overthrowe,] *Greece*, . . . overthrow:
*1670*    5 *Eumenes*; Ed.: *Eumenes*: W, *Eumenes*, *1670*    *Affrick* is] *Africk*'s
*1670*

### 542

Not lightlie changinge partie, ends, or waye,
But constant keepe their course on beaten grounds,
Urginge, that equallie all Princes may
Abjure incrochinge, rest within their bounds,
   Not stryve by addinge others to their owne,
   To make the worlds devided empire one.

### 543

And as the tymes now stand, unto this end
They must keepe open still that cheife division,
Not peecinge yt for enemie, or frende,
Feare, wante, or any false gloss of misprision,
   For it takes hould uppon the Soveraigne parte,
   Which still by conscience multiplies the harte.

### 544

I meane that many headed separation,
Which irreligious beinge, yet doth beare
Religions name, affects her reputation,
And which (as it is now us'd everie where)
   Becoms the ground of each ambitious thought,
   And shadow of all actions that be nought:

### 545

Her name beinge deerer farr, then peace, and wealth,
Hazerde for her, of freedome, life, or goods
Welcome, as meanes to everlastinge health,
Hope with noe mortall powre to be withstood:
   So much of greater force is conscience,
   Then any lower vision of the sense.

542/1 lightlie] highly *1670*    543/4 gloss *1670*: glass *W*    544/5 of]
for *1670*    545/2 or] and *1670*

### 546

This rupture therfore never must unite,
Nor yet the heate of opposition slake,
Cheifelie, because her *Pope* is infinite,
And to his owne ambition lyves awake;
   Affectinge greatnes by that temporall pow're,
   Which in all els he studies to devoure.

### 547

Deposinge Kinges as heretickes, that leave her,
And peysinge of her owne Kinges in such manner,
As of supremacie none shall bereave her,
But march, as souldiers underneath her banner,
   And all her armies, both for warr and faction,
   Wage at their charge, to serve the Church in action.

### 548

So as to lett their semenaries spred
Within the bowells of a soveraigne state,
Or leave her enemies abandoned,
By force, or secret practise unto fate;
   Were to let frends decrease, and factions growe,
   As still they doe by newters overthrowe.

### 549

Nor let this fallace of her declination
Perswade, that with her strength, her ends be chang'd;
Since pride had never such an elevation,
As when aspiringe superstition ranged;
   Which synne was at the first the Angells fall,
   And in the outward Church, since naturall.

546/2 slake] slack *1670*    547/5 for] of *1670*    548/1 as] that *1670*
their] her *1670*    549/1 fallace] falacy *1670*  2 be] are *1670*

### 550

Wherbie she still unform'd lives, till a head
Supreame she findes, or to her self makes many;
A bodie such as must be governed
Within it selfe, not subject unto any;
  And in each minute of her nature swells,
  Even with that pride, wherwith the whole excells.

### 551

So as this flesh borne Church supremacie,
Whether form'd in monarchall governemente,
Or state *Aristocraticall* it be,
With less then all, can never be content;
  But by the sophistries of witt and will,
  Stryve ever to be head of good and ill.

### 552

Therfore I say, let not this gathering mass
Of superstition (whose true base is feare)
Lurcke, and by false faith, bringe her ends to pass,
Or to the world such threatninge ensignes beare,
  As tyme will shewe are form'd to serve the turne
  Of other Kinges, that in her lust doe burne.

### 553

But let Kinges rather watch this governess,
That by her wisdome, they may fashion theires;
When to be mercifull, where merciles,
Tyme havinge taught her, to use hopes, and feares,
  Power, and witt, that each may helpe her ends,
  Which are to have all slaves, no foes, noe frends.

552/4 threatninge] threatening *1670*    553/3 where] when *1670*

### 554

Therfore when she letts inquisitions raigne,
Pow'rs laws as freelie should their process use;
When by confession she seekes to maintaine
That mapp of secretts, which she doth abuse;
    Then must Kinges by all tryalls gage her neast,
    So as her byrds may neyther hatch, nor rest.

### 555

Nor must wee give her eare, when she propounds
Freedome of Conscience, that yeelds others none;
But worcke against her on the same stricte ground,
Wherbie she would bynde strangers to her owne;
    Suffring no freedome in dispute, or booke,
    But such as her false discipline doth brooke;

### 556

For if she conscience pleade, the like doe wee;
And so in faith the same religious bands;
If she doth therein claime supremacie,
Soveraignitie (which under no pow're stands)
    Pleads that wee may deale so with forraine pow'rs,
    Heere, or abroad, as they shall deale with ours.

### 557

Lastlie when she, and her sword bearers stryve
In peace, warr, practise, league, or combination,
By fall of other Princes states to thrive,
Wee must of force breake that association;
    And if they arme in clowds, then arme so too,
    And countermyne by doinge as they doe.

554/2 Pow'rs laws] Pow'rs, Laws, *1670*          557/2 practise, league, or
combination] League, or any Combination *1670*

### 558

For els she by her contracts without charge,
As well as warr, will still devyde in gayne;
Where Kinges their Crownes, she there her cells enlarge,
And bringe her harvest home with others payne;
   Making poore Princes by her dreams of speritt,
   Lyke slaves, that onlie for their lorde can meritt.

### 559

Trust not their Church with her scope infinite,
As King-shipps in this worlde, more in the other;
Heere to seeme greater then refined righte,
There both of grace and innocence a mother;
   For God, a Pope; for Angells, Cardinalls;
   A Church more overbuilt then Babells walls.

### 560

An owtward Church, that must stand as it grew,
By force, crafte, rapine, and hypocrycie,
An earthlie faith, even every day made new,
Builte on the base of ones supremacie;
   A pride borne of that Angells pride that fell,
   Prisinge for *Peeters* pence, heav'ne, purgatorie, hell.

### 561

Trust not this myter, which forgiveth none,
But damns all sowles, that be not of her creedes;
Makes all Saints Idolls, to adorne her throne,
And reapes vaste wealth from superstitious seeds;
   For must she not with wett, or burnt wings fall,
   Which soares above him, that created all?

558/1 For] Or *1670*          561/5 she not] not she *1670*

### 562

Suffer not men of this divyne profession,
Which should be greate within, religious, true,
As heuallds sent by God to worcke progression
From synne to grace, and make the old man new;
    Let them not by the worlds moralities,
      Thincke to hould upp their doctrine with the wise.

### 563

Let them not fall into those common mouldes
Of fraile humanitie, which skandall give;
From God they must take notyce what they should,
Men watch not what they speake, but how they live:
    Malice soone peirceth pomps mortalitie,
      The sinn derydes her own hypocrysie.

### 564

The Clergies prayse, when they from pulpit come,
Is to keepe that *decorum* in their lives,
Which wall them in, from each unreverend doome
Of libertynes, who to deface them strive:
    For messingers of heav'ne must still appeare,
      As if that heav'ne, not earth, were to them deere.

### 565

From *Abbies* lett them not hope to uphould
Excess, and ryott by the peoples voyce;
Where good and ill alike are chepelie sould,
And fraile mankinde confounded in his choyce:
    Good life and doctrine, are both light and foode,
      To starve the ill, yett do the chosen good.

562/5 by] with *1670*     563/5 Malice] *cancelling* The sinn    564/6 that
*1670*: the *W*

566

Now though this Councell seeme to fitt a Kinge,
And not the steepe excess of Tyrannie;
Yet beames and bodies beinge divers thinges,
Fynelie in shadows may resembled be:
 Whence in the owtward varienge forme of thinges,
 Tyrants may well use rules set downe for Kinges.

567

Let not Kinges therfore on this old foundation
Feare to continewe tax, to hazarde payd;
Since warr and Crownes consist by reputation,
Which must not easilie from their course be swayd,
 Eyther by want of shipp, or sayle, or shrowd,
 Unless Kinges will loose tydes, for everie Clowd.

568

But rather follow *Mars* in forraigne parts,
Who ever frends the undertakinge spiritt,
With honor, hope of spoile, and all those arts,
Which still as treasures are reserv'd for meritt;
 Nor be these helpes in minutes understood,
 Which in the mass, make undertakinge good.

569

Since heere admitt the worst that threatens come,
And causeless fortune, like her selfe should raigne,
How can the assistants yet finde heavie doome,
Whose chance at home is to be cast againe?
 And by their neighbours stumblinge, not their fall,
 Each monarcke taught to have an eye to all.

566/6 set downe] *cancelling* more fitt    567/4 easilie] eas'ly *1670*    568/4
treasures] Treasure *1670*    6 undertakinge] undertakings *1670*    569/3 as-
sistants] assistance *1670*

### 570

Nay graunte theis mutuall succors should at length
Engage our owne estates into a warr;
Yet can they never take us in their strength
Who in their growings interrupted arr;
    And to assaile those pow'rs which wounded come,
    Doth certainelie pronounce them fatall doome.

### 571

Besides it often falls owt in distress,
Where states by want exhausted are, and spent,
That change of vyces give their wounds redress,
And qualifie the common discontent
    In people, who when peace is turnd to warr,
    Finde subsedyes no taxes, but revenewes arr.

### 572

Wherbie disease grows cure unto diseases,
A wisdome proper to humanitie;
Which while in somethinge, she her self orepeases,
Yet stands by equall ballanst vanitie;
    And unto change thinges present sacrificinge,
    Findes from those ashes better tymes arisinge.

### 573

And as wee see in muddie northen ayre,
Wyndes, Thunders, stormes (earths present miserie)
Yet instantlie make fowle horrisons fayre;
So doth the warr, and her impietie
    Purge the impostum'd humors of a peace;
    Which ofte els make good governemente decrease.

572/5 change] Chance *1670*     573/1 as] so *1670*   3 make] makes *1670*
6 make] makes *1670*

### 574

Onlie let Princes that will martiall be,
Reforme that common stayned discipline,
Which is the base of unprosperitie,
Synne against nature, chance, and pow're devyne;
Wherin I feare the *Turck* doth us excell;
They keepinge deedes, wee words of doinge well:

### 575

Againe for those which unto warr are bent,
To right their wronges, revenge themselves, or gaine;
How brave advantageous an instrument
A well fram'de Navie is to intertaine,
Let them be judge, who understand how Sea
For hers, lyke ayre, doth every where make way.

### 576

For whatsoever odds in man or beast
Betweene the *Christian* and the *Turcks* there be;
By delicacie, hardness, industrie, or rest,
Our fatall discord, or their unitie;
Yet wee that thus on disadvantage stand,
Stand fast, because he makes his warrs by land.

### 577

Wheras each man of understandinge spiritt
Knows well, that if this mightie tyrant would
Have chang'd his warr, and so his wayes of meritt,
From lande, and made the wavinge *Ocean* moulde
Of all his expeditions undertaken,
The *Christian* Churches had longe since byn shaken.

575/5 understand *1670*: understands *W*    576/2 *Turcks*] Turk *1670*

578

Nay, in the *Indians* East, and west againe,
What greate thinges men may with Sea forces doe,
Not onlie in surprisinge of the mayne,
But in possessinge land, and Citties too,
    By undertakings of a mayden Queene,
    May, as in modells to the worlde, be seene.

*Queene*
*Elizabeth*

579

So as since Seas be Mothers unto fame,
Whose bravest Fathers martiall actions be;
And mother like, since their breasts nurse that name,
Which they begett with strange prosperitie;
    Let those Kinges seeke the secret of that wombe,
    That will of riches, right, and wronge give doome.

THE EXCELLENCIE OF MONARCHIE,
COMPARED WITH ARISTOCRATIE

Section XIII

580

Now, if the tediousness of mortall dayes,
(Which suffers no man with his state content)
Will seeke a change in all things that displease,
Then can no reall forme be permanent:
    Vayne lust, and noveltie, which never rest,
    Pleasinge diseased natures ever best.

579/2 Fathers] Feathers *1670*    4 with] by *1670*        Section XIII *Ed.*:
Sect. 13°: *W*, SECT. XIII. *1670*        580/2 with] in *1670*    5 which]
will *1670*

### 581

Yet first let these light spirits which love change,
Consider whence, and whither they would goe;
Least while they growe bewitch't with what is strange,
They thinck that happiness which is not soe;
   And by affectinge mortall heavens here,
   Holde onlie those things which they have not, deere.

### 582

Dolefull *Alcyon* had perchance good cause
Both to suspect the fraudes of men, and beasts;
Yet overactinge passion makes ill lawes,
For to avoyde this feare, she built her neast
   Upon the *Oceans* shore, where storme and winde
   Since tyranise both her, and all her kinde.

### 583

From like grounds, doe not thoughts impatient,
Which worcke new-fangledness in peoples mindes,
And have their proper lorde in discontent,
By such dislike of every ayre they finde,
   While they would runne from shaddowes that offend,
   Like rowlinge stones, change place, but never mend?

### 584

For if men will, accordinge to the name,
Conceive th'*Aristocraticall* Estates
Of governement, to be the perfect frame,
And number able to give better rates
   To lavish humors, then a Monarch can;
   What is this but new-fangledness in man?

581/2 whither] whether *1670*    582/4 this] which *1670*    584/4 better]
proper *1670*

### 585

And let not man examine this by booke,
As states stand paynted, or enammeld there;
But rather upon life then pictures looke,
Where practise sees what everie state can beare;
    And where the peoples good, the wealth of Realmes,
    Shew clearelie what formes spread forth sweetest beames.

### 586

Which veiw will prove, how speciouslie soever
These manie heads enter, with gloriouse stile
Of conqueringe worthies; yet that they have never
Longe borne those titles, but within a while
    Bene forc't to change their many heads to one;
    As blest by inequalitie alone.

### 587

For instance of which strange inconstancie,
Take *Rome*, that sublime *Senators* estate;
Did she not first the sonns iniquitie
Plague, in the aged guiltless fathers fate?
    And then her Monarch into *Consulls* throw,
    Under which, yet *Rome* did an Empresse grow?

### 588

Soone after she erects the state of tenne;
And even before th'ungratefull memorie
Of *Appius Claudius* buried was with men,
She still affectinge change of policie,

---

586/3 that] *1670 omits*    6 inequalitie] inequalities *1670*        587/1 strange]
*cancelling* fainte    4 aged] *cancelling* feeble    6 yet *Rome* did an Empresse]
*cancelling* infant *Rome* was lyke to        588/2–5, *before revision*:
        Neither was that ungratefull memorie
        Of *Appius Claudius* buried amongst men,
        But she againe changd formes of policie,
        And left the publique Government in trust

Carelesslie left the Government in trust
For some yeeres, to her Martiall Tribunes lust.

### 589

Lastlie, as if in that unconstant witt
They had concluded to dissolve the frame
Of their Republique, by ofte changinge it;
To such descent of Anarchie they came,
   As in five yeeres they Governors had none,
   But stood upright by happe of time alone.

*Livius*
*lib. 120*

### 590

For had there anie undertakinge state
Assayld them then, this traunce wherin they stood
Twixt life and death, must needs have given fate
To wandringe humors, stain'd with native blood;
   And, by the factiouse Governement of three,
   Have freed her slaves to bringe in Tyrannie.

### 591

Thus sicke, and fullie ripe for cure, or death,
*Rome* did enforce a *Cæsar* of her owne
To loose his honor, or to breake his faith;
Her State alike beinge each way overthrowne:
   Wherin yet he that brought back Monarchie
   Err'd less, then he who sett the people free.

*Vellei Paterc.*
*Lib. 2.*

### 592

For after *Tarquine*, though *Rome* stood entire,
Yet fell shee into manie-headed powre,
By which like straws, light people sett on fire,
Did by confusion, which waites to devoure,
   Yet raise againe that brave Monarchall state,
   As soules well organ'd to be fortunate.

588/5 the] her *1670*      589/6 upright by happe of time] *cancelling* by grace
of happee times    *marginal note lib. 120 Ed.: lib. 2 W, 1670: see note*
590/2 traunce] *France 1670*      591/6 who] that *1670*

### 593

Besides in *Athens*, what were *Codrus* merits,
That after him they would indure no Kinge?
Was it not he that sacrific'd his spirits,
To qualifie *Apollos* threatininge?
   In which worck this captiv'd unthanckfulness,
    Which staynd her fame, soone made her fortune less.

### 594

Againe, what comfort, or true estimation
Can active vertue either take or give,
Where manie heads have power of creation?
Or wherin can these brave intisements live,
   Which rayse exorbitant aspiringe meritt,
    Since many judges never have one spirit?

### 595

Must not lawes there, and ordinances be
Like oracles, meere abstract and ambiguouse;
Fit for discourse, or bookes, not politie?
All practise dull, delayinge, or litigiouse?
   Mans justice seldome cleare, and never wise,
    As seinge right or wronge with chances eyes?

### 596

What symptome is besides so dangerous
To mortall orders, apt to be diseas'd,
As faction? On whose *Crisis* ominouse
Those states depend, where many must be pleas'd;
   And where unequalls are, by governement,
    With equall measure, forc't to be content.

593/2 would] should *1670*    6 fame] *1670 omits*        595/3 politie] policy
*1670*

### 597

For as to make all rulers of Estate
Alike wise, honest, rich, and honorable,
A worcke is hardlie possible to fate:
So (without disproportion) who is able
    True worth, and inequalities ambition,
    To please with equall ballanced condition?

### 598

Out of which swallowed discontentment growes
That monster, which then most the publique spoyles,
When to the world it best pretenccs showes;
And as with faction, emulation, broyles,
    These manie heads ofte Civyll warr invite:
    So against forraine force they worse unite.

### 599

Under three leaders did not *Athens* wayne
Her right at *Samos*, and her reputation?
As she before at *Siracuse* did stayne
Her glorie, and lett fall her estimation,
    Under the guide of *Alcibiades*,
    Joynd with sterne *Nicias*, faint *Demosthenes*.

*Charo*
*Timotheus*
*Iphicrates*
*Æmil. Probus*
*in Vita*
*Timothei*

*Justin li: 4⁰*

### 600

Whence the *Athenian* Orator aver'd,
That their State never prospered in warr,
But when all power was upon one confer'd.
And when againe was *Rome* ingag'd so farr,
    As under *Cannas* many headed flight,
    Where chance, and mischance had power infinite?

*Isocrates in*
*Nicocles*

*Terentius*
*Varro*
*Paulus*
*Æmilius*
*Livius*

599/2 at] to *1670*          600/6 had power] *cancelling* power have

### 601

Besides, as milde streames in an Ocean Sea
Loose both their current, sweetness, and their name;
So here the best men must be sent away
By *Ostracisme*, to qualifie their fame;
   As for this state too greate, which feareth worth,
   Knowinge that it still Monarchie bringes forth.

### 602

For is it not with them of banishment
Sufficient ground, to be reputed just?
What other cause was there of discontent
Gainst *Aristides*, but his worths mistrust?
   Howe us'd they him that conquered *Marathon*?
   Or him who *Xerxes* host had overthrowne?

### 603

*Rome* shew'd her greatness, when she did subdue
*Africke* and *Carthage*; yet who will observe
How little she thought to the *Scipios* due,
Or from *Camillus* how soone she did swerve,
   Shall see, in *Aristocraties* the fate
   Of noble actions is the peoples hate.

### 604

Besides where this name *Publique* shall have powre
To binde reward, with wreath'd frugalitie;
Where sad-stil'd justice shall mankinde devoure,
Thorough a bloudie sterne severitie;
   Must not those glorious stiles of common weale,
   Wound even that worth wherwith it should deale?

602/1 with] to *1670*    604/5 those] these *1670*

### 605

Faction againe is ever soonest made,
Where manie heads have parte; and councells knowne
There soonest are, where men with manie trade;
Besides alliance here bindes not her owne,
   Nor adds unto the publique anie might:
    Which makes their leagues, their love, their malice slight.


### 606

Lastlie, our finite natures doe not love
That infinite of multiplicitie;
Our hopes, affections, feares, which ever move,
Can neither fix'd, nor yet well governd be,
   Where idle busie rulers, with a breath,
    Give doome of Honor, grace, shame, life, or death.


### 607

Thus is mankinde, in numerouse estates,
Wantonlie discontent with libertie;
Where equalls give and take unequall rates,
Mouldinge for good and badd one destinie:
   Whence *Athens*, swayinge to *Democratie*,
    For ever changinge her *Archontes* bee.


### 608

And as ill lucke makes man in man dispayre,
And thence appeale a supreame Soveraigne:
So growes adversitie the peoples stayre,
Wherbie they climbe to Monarchie againe.
   What wants *Dictator* but the name of Kinge,
    Beinge as Soveraigne else in everie thinge?

608/1 in] of *1670*

### 609

So as if *Aristocraties* will claime
To be the best of humane Government,
Why doe they from their Magistrates disclaime,
As in extremities still impotent?
　Since who in stormes the fittest pilotts be,
　Are ablest sure to guide prosperitie.


## THE EXCELLENCIE OF MONARCHIE
## COMPARED WITH DEMOCRATIE

### Section XIV

### 610

Nowe if the best, and choycest Governement
Of manie heads, be in her nature this;
How can the *Democraticall* content,
Where that blinde multitude cheife Master is?
　And where besides all theis forespoken fates,
　The most, and worst sorte governe all Estates?

### 611

Since, as those persons usually do haunt
The market places, which at home have least:
So here those spiritts most intrude and vaunt
To doe the business of this common beast,
　That have no other meanes to vent their ill,
　Then by transforminge reall thinges to will.

### 612

Besides, this equall stil'd *Democratie*
Lets fall mens mindes, and makes their manners base;
Learninge, and all arts of Civilitie,
Which adde both unto nature, and to place,
　It doth ecclipse; as death to that Estate,
　Wherin not worth, but idle wealth gives fate:

Section XIV *Ed.*: Sect. 14°. *W*, SECT. XIV. *1670*

### 613

Nay where religion, God, and humane lawes
No other use, or honor can expect,
Then to serve idle liberties applause,
As painted toyes, which multitudes affect:
    Who judginge all thinges, while they nothing knowe,
    Lawlesse, and Godless are, and would live so.

### 614

Therfore if anie, to protect this State,
Alleadge Emperiall *Rome* grew greate by it:
And *Athens* likewise farr more fortunate,
As raysinge types up both of worth and witt;
    Such as no Monarchie can parrallell,
    In the rare wayes of greatness doinge well:

### 615

Or if againe, to make good this position,
Anie averre that *Romes* first Monarchie,
For lack of courage, soone changd her condition
Of Union, to multiplicitie;
    Whence *Germans* over *France*, and *Goths* in *Spaine*,
    In *Africke Saracens*, *Turcks* in *Asia* raigne:

### 616

I answer first, that those subduinge prides
(Wherof the People boast) were to their hand
Form'd, by the three precedinge Monarch tides;
And what succeeded (if exactlie scand)
    But imitation was of their brave deedes,
    Who, but their owne worth, no example needes.

615/2 Anie averre that *Romes*] *cancelling* He would averr that their    4 to]
into *1670*   6 *Asia*] *cancelling Europe*    616/2 their] the *1670*

617

For did not their *Tarquinius*, ere he fell,
Conquer the *Latine*, and the *Sabine* Nation;
Makinge their Martiall discipline excell,
And so increase their strength by reputation?
    Out of which active Legionarie worth,
    That Cittie brought her after Conquests forth.


618

But be this as it may be: I denie
Either the Empires growth or consummation
To be the worcke of *Romes Democratie*;
Since betweene her first *Cæsars* domination,
    And *Tarquine*, her Soveraignitie was mixt
    Of one, fewe, manie; wavinge, never fixt;


619

As Consulls, Senate, or the Peoples might;
The first a power which *Rome* did Conquer by,
The second sett her publique Councells right,
The last approve, encrease, or qualifie
    Paine, and rewards of good or evill deedes;
    Two beames of justice, waighinge owt good speed.


620

Whence you may easilie pregnant reasons drawe,
To attribute the glorie of olde *Rome*
Unto the Monarch part, which helde in awe
The conquered world; and not the peoples doome,
    Proportion from the greate worlde to the small
    Shewinge, with manie limmes, one head rules all.

### 621

What but the peoples mutinouse conventions
Under their factiouse Tribunes, scattered
*Romes* publique patrimonie? And with dissentions
Her wise opposinge Senate threatened,
  By their *Agrarian* lawes, engines of wronge,
  Dispersinge lands which to the State belonge?

*Cic. de lege
Agraria:
contra
Rullum*

### 622

Besides, as who at home ill husbands be,
Seldome make daintie to stretch out their hand
Into their neighbors harmeless treasurie:
So did it with this banckrupt people stand;
  Who sent their Armies out by force, or stealth,
  To bringe them home the Kinge of *Cyprus* wealth.

*Ptolmæus
Florus lib. 3*

### 623

Allur'd by no pretence of wronge or right,
But onlie that he must not be their frende
Whose wealth was reckoned so indefinite;
Not caringe how they get, or what they spend:
  But makinge good their ill by confidence,
  A worth of more use there, then innocence.

### 624

Lastlie, where they had manie tymes proclaim'd
Against the *Mamertines* their just offence;
Yet came they to their succor, and disclaim'd
With *Carthage* their longe-livd intelligence:
  Whence the first *Punick* quarrell did proceed,
  And had the fates bene just, with farr worse speed.

*Polybius
lib. 1*

/2 their] the *1670*  6 lands] laws *1670*  *marginal note Rullum*] *Rutilium*
*1670*    622/4 this] these *1670*  5 or] and *1670*

### 625

Wherin the *Senate* noblie did oppose
This headie Peoples incivilitie;
As besides faith, in wisdome loth to lose
The rich returnes of that affinitie:
   Publique respect, and shame wrought in the one,
   Who saw that ill deedes seldome pass alone.

### 626

Whereas the People, which no notyce take
Of these small minutes in humanitie,
But wayes above theis thinne-lin'd duties make,
Thinckinge they rule not, that restrayned be;
   With raveninge and irregular excess,
   Staine good and ill to serve their wantonness.

### 627

Now for the Empires finall overthrowe,
Falsely imputed to the Monarchie;
Who doth not by the course of nature knowe,
That periods in the growth of all States be
   Ordain'd? Which no republique can exceed;
   Fate makinge each forme selfe diseases breed.

### 628

Or if too abstract this replie appeares,
Forgett not how the *Monarchie* preserv'd
*Rome*, for a thousand and seaven hundred yeeres;
Part of her glorie her first Kinges deserv'd,
   The rest by *Cæsars* in successive raigne,
   Till *Mahomet* the second made her wayne.

*245 yeeres
He tooke Con-
stantinople
Anno 1453*

626/2 in] of *1670*    627/6 Fate] For *1670*    628/1 Or] *cancelling* But

### 629

Where on the other side, *Democratie*
Did in few ages rise, and fall againe;
There beinge but fowre hundred sixtie three
Yeeres, betweene *Cæsars*, and *Tarquinius* raigne:
  In which time *Rome* corrupted her selfe so,
  As change she must, or suffer overthrowe.

### 630

But that indeed which brake this Empires frame
Was flotinge swarmes, and mightie inundations
Of rude Barbarians, which from *Scythia* came,
To traffique vices with all civile Nations:
  Nor can that be peculier staine to *Rome*,
  Which of all other Empires was the doome.

### 631

*Attila, Alaricke, Omar, Tamerlan,*
Beinge in Martiall worth rays'd up as high
As he that most unto the Empire wanne,
And against whom old *Romes Democratie*,
  Even in her pride, must have made such retreat,
  As would have shew'd, at home she was not greate.

### 632

Such as she did at *Allia* of olde,
When naked *Galls* both tooke and burnt their towne:    *Livius lib. 5*
Or *Italie* from *Spartacus* the bolde,                 *Plutarch in*
When by a slave their Eagles were throwne downe:           *Camillo*
  So that the Monarch fell by outward fate,
  Whereas the peoples owne faults shak't their state.

630/1 this] the *1670*        632/2 their] the *1670*          *marginal note in*
*Camillo*] *in vita Camilli 1670*
811710                    O

### 633

Neither doe I doubt, but the Roman frame
Of Monarchie might have out lasted all
The Governments of whatsoever name;
But that excess did make her olde age fall
    Into a gulf, whose two streames soone devoure
    The rights and Majestie of reall powre.

### 634

The first was, their tumultuouse election
Of *Cæsars*, which did manie times make way
To Civile broyles, disorder, and defection;
Whence she became to Foraigners a pray:
    This powre of choice makinge the souldiers knowe,
    Their head above had yet his head belowe.

### 635

The second was their lacke of Crowne demaine;
By which their Emperors still forced were
In publique, and self indigence to straine
Lawes, by mens voices; men, by hope and feare;
    Who sawe their wealth and freedome, both in one,
    By this course of exactions overthrowne.

### 636

And yet, in this disease of Monarches State,
I dare avowe their breed of home-borne spirits
To have bene active, worthie, fortunate,
Above *Democraties* in everie meritt:
    For instance, whom can that State parallell
    With *Trajan* in the powre of doeinge well?

633/1 Neither . . . the] Nor . . . that the *1670*        634/6 his] a *1670*
635/2 their] the *1670*    5 wealth] wealths *1670*

### 637

Whom with *Augustus* in felicitie?
With *Constantine* in true magnificence?
With *Marcus* can in wisdome ballanc't be?
Or with good *Antonine* in innocence?
    *Julian* in learninge; *Julius* in worth,
    That ever yet *Democratie* brought forth?

*It was a pro-*
*verbe amongst*
*them Felicior*
*Augusto,*
*melior*
*Trajano.*
*Julian in*
*Cæs[aribus]*

### 638

For Tribunes be the Champions they can boast,
An heteroclite Magistrate, devis'd
Without rule, to have all rules by him lost;
Religion scorn'd, lawes, dutie tyranniz'd:
    A fierie sparcke, which lackinge forraigne stuffe,
    At home findes fewell to make blaze enoughe.

### 639

So as if *Chilo* trulie calld those States
The best, which most unto their lawes did give,
And kept their *Demagogues* at humblest rates,
Then this conclusion ratified must live:
    *Democraties* are most unnaturall,
    Where reall things with humors rise and fall.

### 640

Whence I conclude that since *Democratie*
In her craz'd mouldes greate Empires cannot cast;
Of force, theis frayle confused policies,
Which cannot breed States, can make no State last:
    But as the Viper doth, must teare the wombe
    Of Monarchie, whence her foundations come.

637/1 Whom] Who *1670*    4 *Antonine*] Anthony *1670*    Marginal note *Julian*
*in Cæs[aribus]*] *1670* omits        639/2 did] do *1670*

## THE EXCELLENCIE OF MONARCHIE
## COMPARED WITH ARISTOCRATIE AND
## DEMOCRATIE JOYNTLIE

### Section XV

### 641

Now though I knowe our bookes be fill'd with praise
Of good mens vertues, freedomes popular;
Yet he that will not auditt wordes, but wayes,
And overlooke the dreames of time with care,
    In smart succession; he shall cleerlie finde
    No longe liv'd state hath bene of either kinde.

### 642

For whatsoever stile these men affect
Of *Optimats*, or of *Democratie*;
Their Councells basely practise, and effect
A servile *Oligarchall* Tyranie:
    As well in lawes, as in establishmente,
    Like ill mixt humors, never well content.

### 643

So that such onlie have escap'd mischance,
As luckilie, by publique opposition,
To ballance *Consulls*, *Tribunes* did advance,
Or by a more refined composition,
    Have rais'd (like *Venice*) some well-bounded *Duke*,
    Their selfe-growne *Senators* to overlooke.

Section XV *Ed.*: Sect. 15. *W*, SECT. XV. *1670*    641/1 be] are *1670*
642/3 Councells] courses *1670*

### 644

So managinge the whole in everie parte,
As these vast bodies, valetudinarie,
May, in the native feavers of the harte,
Yet some degrees of good complexion carie:
　　And while they keepe their forraigne foes at rest,
　　Winne time, their home confusions to disgest.


### 645

Besides, if either of theise States doe choose
Their Magistrates, or officers by lott,
And chance instead of worth or knowledge use:
What strange confusions then begett they not?
　　So that no wise man will himself commit,
　　Much less wise States, to be disposed by it.


### 646

Againe if they by suffrages elect,
Then what scope that doth unto practise give,
The old *Comitia*, and the new erect
*Conclave* of *Rome* pregnant examples lyve;
　　To shew worth there must be abandoned
　　Where reall grounds are passion governed.


### 647

Nay more, let us consider if it be
Easie at once of good men to finde manie;
Since we with odds of birth, and breedinge see,
Even amonge Kinges, how rarely time yeelds anie
　　That owt of conscience, or for Countries sake,
　　Will hazard, care, restraine, or undertake?

644/6 home confusions] own confusion *1670*          645/3 or] and *1670*
6 States] State *1670*          646/1 suffrages] *cancelling* suffrings          6 are passion
governed] *cancelling* by spleene are governed

648

But graunt such may be found, yet States thus peaz'd
Must of necessitie (as fortune bounde)
Eyther by Princes have their ballance rays'd,
Or loose to undertakinge Princes ground:
    In which the thanckes they offer to a Crowne
    Is often thanckless mines, to pull it downe,

649

And foolishlie; since union containes
All native strengthes of Soveraignitie,
As bearinge over nature meekest raynes:
Wherby all other formes of politie
    Must either freelie yeeld to her subjection,
    Or at the least crave under it protection.

650

Whence to conclude; since in this abstract veiwe
Of these Estates, the multiplicitie
Proves apt to over-wrest, or loose their dewe,
As onelie true frends to extremitie;
    Can mankinde under anie Soveraigne
    Hope to finde rest, but in the Monarchs raigne?

651

Out of which ground, the poet makinge fates,
Hath registred three thousand dieties,
The least of whose powers governd manie states,
And yet acknowledg'd *Joves* Supremacie,
    A worcke of supernaturall succession,
    Derivd from Godheads of the first impression.

648/1 such may be found] *cancelling* they stand upright   3 their] the *1670*
649/4 politie] Policy *1670*  6 the] *1670 omits*   650/5 under] *cancelling*
then under   6 the] a *1670*

### 652

Againe, who lookes downe from these *Christall* Spheres,
To veiwe the *Ocean*, where *Joves* brother raignes,
Shall he not finde the water *Nereids* there,
In office subalterne, not Soveraigne?
   Yet us'd to stirre, or calme the *Oceans* race,
   As royalties of his three-forcked mace.


### 653

Whence if theis lively Images prove true,
It must be 'alike true, that the best times pris'd
That old Monarchall forme, before these new
Confused moulds, by error since devis'd:
   For els their types of rulinge providence
   Absurdlie, will seeme farr excell'd by sense.


### 654

Let man then waigh, whether this strange excesse
Followe the nature of each mortall frame,
As time-borne, with her to growe more or lesse;
And like her, never to remaine the same?
   Or whether this relax, or overbent,
   Springe from the Subject, or the Government?


### 655

And he shall finde the ground of Change to be
A wandringe, and unmeasured affection
Of power to binde, and people to be free;
Not in the lawes, Church rites, or their connexion;
   But practise meerlie, to raise or keepe downe
   Crownes by the people, people by the Crowne.

653/2 be 'alike *1670*: be as *W*    3 these] the *1670*        655/2 wandringe]
wandering *1670*.

### 656

In which misprision, while each doth suppress
That true relation, by which states subsist,
They first loose names, then make their natures less,
Growinge deform'd, by forminge what they list:
    For they that still cast old foundations newe,
    Make manie shapes, but never anie true.

### 657

And as we doe in humane bodies see,
Where reason raignes in cheife, not the affection,
Order is greate, not wanton libertie,
Man to himself, and others a direction;
    Where if too much abstracted or let fall,
    The tares of passion there runne over all:

### 658

So when men fall away from *Monarchie*,
Whether it be to States of few, or more,
Change leades them nearer unto *Anarchie*
By divers minutes, then they were before;
    Since unitie divided into manie
    Begetts confusion, never frende to anie.

### 659

For in each kinde of humane government,
Where custome, lawes, or antient constitutions
Serve as true scales, to waigh out powers intent,
Honor and wealth there finde no diminutions:
    But where will raignes, and overleapes those bounds,
    What can establish, but that which confounds?

### 660

Therfore to end this point, if any one
(Accordinge to our natures) fond of newe,
Into more Rulers would translate a Throne,
Let him at home this paradoxe finde true:
  Or els yeeld that, unfitt for publique states
  Which in his private everie creature hates.

### 661

Thus have we veiwd the spirit of Governement,
Shewd both her ends, and errors in some kindes,
And by comparinge, yet made excellent
This brave Emperiall Monarchie of mindes:
  Not makinge Tyrants Gods, to unmake Kinges
  With flatteringe ayre for oversoaringe winges.

### 662

And though the wayes of witt be infinite,
Not to be cast in anie mould or art;
Like shaddowes, changinge shape with everie light,
Ever and never, still the same in part:
  Yet by this Modell, wiser men may see,
  That there is choice even in the vanitie;

### 663

And formes establisht, which must be obay'd,
As levells for the world to guide her owne,
Foundations against Anarchie well layd,
Whose beinge is but beings overthrowne;
  Where Thrones (as mortall shrynes) with mortall feare
  Must be ador'd, and worship everie where.

663/2 for] *cancelling* from

## 664

Therfore I thus conclude this fruitlesse dreame,
That if the bodie have imperfect features,
Or swimme (like *Æsops* wife) against the streame,
Each age must adde to all the worckes of creatures,
   And perfect thinges unperfectlie begunne,
   For else in vaine sure I have rowld this Tonne.

664/6 For] Or *1670*

# A TREATISE OF RELIGION

### 1

What makes these manie lawes, these reynes of Power,
Wherwith mankind thus fettered is and bound?
These diverse worships which mens soules deflowre,
Nature, and God, with noveltie confound?
   Tis ignorance, sinne, infidelitie,
   By which we falne from our Creation be.

### 2

What is the chaine which drawes us backe againe,
And lifts man up unto his first Creation?
Nothinge in him his owne hart can restraine,
His reason lives a captive to temptation,
   Example is corrupt, precepts are mixt:
   All fleshlie knowledge frayle, and never fixt.

### 3

It is a light, a guifte, a grace inspired,
A sparcke of power, a goodnesse of the good,
Desire in him, that never it desired,
An unitie where desolation stood;
   In us, not of us; a spirit not of earth,
   Fashioninge the mortall to immortall birth.

### 4

His Image that first made us in perfection,
From Angells differinge most in time and place;
They fell by pride, and we by their infection,
Their doome is past, we yet stande under grace:
   They would be Gods, we would their evill knowe;
   Man findes a *Christ*, these Angells doe not so.

A TREATISE OF RELIGION *1670*: OF RELIGION *W*, *1670 adds By*
*Sir* FULK GREVILL, *Lord* BROOK.   1/1 makes] make *1670*   3/3 it]
is *1670*   4/6 doe] did *1670*

### 5

Sense of this God by feare the sensuall have,
Distressed nature cryinge unto grace;
For Soveraigne reason then becomes a slave,
And yeilds to servile sense her Soveraigne place,
   When more, or other she affects to be,
   Then seate or shrine of this Eternitie.

### 6

Yea, Prince of earth let man assume to be,
Nay more, of man let man himselfe be God,
Yet, without God, a slave of slaves is he;
To others, wonder; to himselfe a rod:
   Restlesse despayre, desire, and desolation,
   The more secure, the more abhomination.

### 7

Then by affectinge powre we cannot knowe him,
By knowinge all thinges else we knowe him lesse;
Nature containes him not, Art cannot showe him,
Opinions, idolles, and not God expresse:
   Without, in power, we see him everie where;
   Within, we rest not, till we finde him there.

### 8

Then seeke we must, that course is naturall
For owned soules, to finde their owner out;
Our free remorses, when our natures fall,
When we doe well, our harts made free from doubt,
   Prove service due to one Omnipotence,
   And Nature, of Religion to have sense.

8/2 out;] out, *1670*    3 fall,] fall; *1670*

### 9

Questions againe which in our harts arise
(Sinne lovinge knowledge, not humilitie)
Though they be curiouse, Godlesse, and unwise,
Yet prove our nature feeles a Deitie:
    For if these strifes rose out of other grounds,
    Man were to God, as deafnesse is to soundes.

### 10

Religion thus we naturallie professe,
Knowledge of God is likewise universall,
Which diverse Nations diverslie expresse:
For truth, power, goodnesse men doe worship all.
    Duties to parent, child, men, time, and place,
    All knowe by nature, and observe by grace.

### 11

And that these are no positive, made lawes,
Appeares in this, since no consent of Nations,
No custome, time, or anie other cause,
Can unto vice give vertues estimation;
    Or root out those impressions from our harts,
    Which God, by Nature, unto man imparts.

### 12

Yea, these impressions are so firmlie fixt
In understandinge, and the conscience too,
That if our nature were not strangelie mixt,
But what it knewe, it could as easilie doe;
    Men should (even by this spirit) in fleshe and blood,
    Growe happilie adorers of the good.

9/2 Sinne] Since *1670*       10/5 men, time] Time, Men *1670*    6 knowe]
*cancelling* knowne: known *1670*   observe] observ'd *1670*    12/1 firmlie]
finely *1670*   4 it knewe] we knew *1670*

### 13

But there remaines such naturall corruption
In all our powers, even from our parents seed,
As to the good gives native interruption;
Sense staines affection; that, will; and will, deed:
  So as what's good in us, and others too
  We praise; but what is evill, that we doe.


### 14

Our knowledge, thus corrupted in our lives,
Serves to convince our consciences within;
Which sentence of record with selfe love strives,
Leads us for rest, and remedie of sinne,
  To seeke God, and Religion from without,
  And free this condemnation, which we doubt.


### 15

Yet in this strife, this naturall remorse,
If we could bend the force of power and witte
To worcke upon the hart, and make divorce
There, from the evill which perverteth it;
  In judgment of the truth we should not doubt
  Good life would finde a good Religion out.


### 16

But our infirmitie, which cannot brooke
This stronge, intestine, and rebelliouse warre,
In witte and our affections makes us looke
For such Religions as there imag'd are:
  Hence growe these manie worships, Gods, and sects,
  Wherewith mans error all the world infects.

13/5 as] that *1670*

### 17

For when the Conscience thus Religion fashions
In blinde affections, there it straight begetts
Grosse superstition; when in wittie passions
It moulded is, a lustre there it setts
    On harts prophane, by politique pretense;
    Both buying shadowes with the soules expence.

### 18

For they Gods true Religion (which a state,
And beinge is, not taken on, but in)
To bottomlesse hypocrisie translate;
The superstitiouse doth with feare beginne,
And so deceiv'd, deceives; and underrates
His God, and makes an idoll of his sinne:
    The politique with craft enthralles mankinde,
    And makes his bodee sacrifice his minde.

### 19

Both, in our selves make us seeke out a God,
Both take selfe love and feare, for scale and measure,
They both become their owne, and others rodd;
The one takes care, the other wronge, for pleasure:
    As manie mindes, as manie Gods they make;
    Men easlie change all what they easlie take.

### 20

This superstitiouse ignorance and feare
Is false Religion; offeringe sacred thinges
Either to whom it should not, or else where;
The maner to the Godhead scandall bringes:
    It feares sea, earth, skie, silence, darcknesse, light,
    And in the weake soules still hath greatest might.

17/1 thus] this *1670*    6 buying *1670*: bindinge *W*    18/5 underrates]
*cancelling* undertakes    19/6 Men easily change all they easily take *1670*
20/2 offeringe] offring *1670*    6 soules] soul *1670*

21

Which naturall disease of mortall witte
Begetts our Magicke, and our Starr-Divines,
Wizards, Impostors, Visions stand by it:
For what feare comprehends not, it inclines
    To make a God, whose nature it beleeves
    Much more inclinde to punishe, then releeve.


22

The reason is, when feares dimme eyes looke in,
They guilt discerne; when upward, justice there
Reflects self-horror backe upon the sinne,
Where outward dangers threaten everie where:
    Fleshe the foundation is, fancie the worcke,
    Where rak'd up, and unquencht the evills lurcke.


23

For feare, whose motion still it selfe improves,
Hopes not for grace, but prayes to shunne the rod;
Not to doe ill, more then doe well it loves;
Fashions God unto man, not man to God:
    And to that Deitie gives all without,
    Of which within it lives and dies in doubt.


24

The other branch is meere hypocrisie,
The worlds Religion, borne of wit and lust;
All which, like hunters, followe thinges that flie,
And still beyond thinges found, finde somethinge must:
    As God is boundlesse, endlesse, infinite,
    So seeme these Idolls to the hypocrite.

### 25

Witte there is preist, who sacrifice doth make
Of all in heaven or earth to this desire;
For from this witte, God and Religion take
As manie shapes, as manie strange attires,
  As there be in the world degrees of change,
  Which upon humors, time, occasion range.

### 26

This teacheth all ambitiouse Magistrates,
On sinnes unquiet humors, howe to build
Idolls of power to alter Natures rates;
And by false feares and hopes, make people yeild
  Their harts for temples unto Tyrants lawes,
  Which zeale divine to humane homage drawes.

### 27

And when our spirituall lights, which truth expound
Once to this traffique of mans will descend,
With chaines of truth mankinde no more is bound,
Wherby their harts should up to heaven ascend;
  But vaynlie linckt unto their tongues, which drawe
  Religion to a fleshlie, outward awe.

### 28

And though they beare a holienesse in showe,
Such as no eye of man can peirce the vayle;
Yet least Gods houshold to contempt should growe,
Or this hypocrisie not still prevayle,
  To raise them reverence above their worth,
  Blood, inquisition, question they bringe forth.

25/2 or earth to this] and Earth to his _1670_          27/1 our] _1670 omits_
2 this] the _1670_          3 mankinde no more] _cancelling_ no more mankinde
28/1 they beare] this Fear _1670_          3 Yet] But _1670_

### 29

They drawe the sword of power against her owne,
Or else stirre people up to warre their Kinges;
Both must be theirs, or both be overthrowne:
They binde man unto wordes, God bindes to things:
    For these false heades of holie mother see,
    Scepters to Miters there inferior be.


### 30

Amonge our selves besides there manie be,
That make Religion nothinge else but Art
To master others of their owne degree,
Enthrall the simple well-beleivinge hart:
    These hate opposers, scorne obedient fooles,
    Affectinge raigne by educations tooles.


### 31

And though they serve ambitiouse Princes use,
While they protecte them, like a nursinge father;
And while this common traffique of abuse
Mutuallie helpeth either side to gather:
    Yet marcke the end of false combined trust;
    It will divide, and smart the people must.

### 32

For in all these kindes of hypocrisie,
No bodies yet are found of constant beinge;
No uniforme, no stable mysterie,
No inward nature, but an outward seeminge;
    No solid truth, no vertue, holienesse:
    But types of these, which time makes more or lesse.

30/1 besides] likewise *1670*   5 hate] have *1670*      32/1 in all these] sure
in all *1670*

### 33

And from these springes strange inundations flowe,
To drowne the sea-marckes of humanitie,
With massacres, conspiracie, treason, woe,
By sect and schisme prophaninge Deitie;
    Besides with furies, feends, earth, ayre and hell
    They fill, and teach confusion to rebell.

### 34

But as there lives a true God in the heaven,
So is there true Religion here on earth:
By nature? no, by grace; not gotte, but given;
Inspir'd, not taught; from God a second birth.
    God dwelleth neare about us, even within,
    Worckinge the goodnesse, censuringe the sinne.

### 35

Such as we are to him, to us is he;
Without God there was no man ever good:
Divine the Author, and the matter be,
Where goodnesse must be wrought in flesh and blood:
    Religion standes not in corrupted thinges,
    But vertues, that descend with heavenly winges.

### 36

Not heathen vertue, which they doe define
To be a state of minde, by custome wrought,
Where sublime reason seemeth to refine
Affection, perturbation, everie thought
    Unto a *Mens adepta*, which worck spent
    Halfe of the dayes to humane *Hermes* lent.

33/4 sect and schisme] Sects and Schisms *1670*    5 furies, feends, *1670*:
furies feends *W*   6 fill] fit *1670*    35/6 vertues,] vertues *1670*   with]
have *1670*    36/3 reason seemeth] Religion seems *1670*

### 37

For in this worcke man still rests slave to fame,
To inward caution, outward forme, and pride;
With curiouse watch to guard a rotten frame
Safe, undiscovered from the peircinge-eyd;
   Assiduouse caution tyrannisinge there,
   To make frayle thoughts seeme other then they were.

### 38

Under this maske besides no vice is dead,
But passion with her counterpassion peas'd;
The evill with it selfe both starv'd and fedde,
And in her woes with her vayne glories eas'd:
   The worcke and tooles alike, vayne flesh and blood,
   The labor great, the harvest never good.

### 39

For in this painted tombe, let mans owne spirits
Reallie judge what that estate can be,
Which he begettinge in himselfe, inherits,
Other then deserts of hypocrisie,
   Within the darckninge shadowes of his witte
   Hidinge his staines from all the world, but it.

### 40

And if the habits of hypocrisie
With such attention must be kepte, and wrought;
If to maske vice be such a mysterie,
As must with her captivitie be sought;
If to be nothinge, and yet seeme to be,
So nicely be contreiv'd, and dearlie bought
   As vanitie must in a *Phenix* fire
   Smother herselfe, to hatch her false desire:

37/1 this] his *1670*   4 undiscovered] undiscovet'd *1670*   6 were] are *1670*
39/1 spirits] spirit *1670*   4 deserts] DESERTS *1670*

### 41

Then judge pore man! Gods Image once, 'tis true,
Though nowe the Devills, by thine owne defection,
Judge man, I say, to make this Image newe,
And clense thy fleshe from this deepe-dy'de infection,
What miracles must needes be wrought in you,
That thus stand lost in all thinges but Election?
  What livinge death, what strange illumination
  Must be inspir'd to this regeneration?


### 42

Must not the grace be supernaturall,
Which in forgivinge gives sanctification;
And from this second *Chaos* of his fall
Formes in mans litle world a newe Creation?
  And must not then this twice-borne child of heaven
  Bringe forth in life this newe perfection given?


### 43

Then man! pray, and obtaine; beleeve, and have;
Omnipotence and goodnesse readie be
To rayse us with our Saviour from the grave,
Whence *Enoch* and *Elias* lived free:
  He made all good, yet suffered sinne and death
  To raigne, and be exil'd againe by faith.


### 44

Then till thou feele this heavenlie change in thee
Of pride, to meeknesse; Atheisme, to zeale;
Lust, unto continence; anger, to charitie;
Thou feelst of thine Election no true seale:

41/2 by] be *1670*    3 man, I say,] man (I say) *1670*    43/5 suffered]
suffred *1670*    44/1 feele] find *1670*    3 unto] to *1670*    4 thine] thy
*1670*

But knowledge onlie, that pore infancie
Of this newe creature, which must thence appeale
   Unto the father for obedience,
   Judginge his hopes, or condemnation thence.

### 45

For what else is Religion in mankinde,
But raysinge of Gods Image there decaid?
No habit, but a hallowed state of minde,
Worckinge in us that he may be obayd.
   As God by it with us communicates,
   So we by duties must with all estates.

### 46

With our Creator, by sincere devotion;
With creatures, by observance and affection;
Superiors, by respect of their promotion;
Inferiors, with the nature of protection;
   With all, by usinge all thinges of our owne
   To others good; not to our selves alone.

### 47

And even this sacred band, this heavenlie breath,
In man his understandinge, knowledge is;
Obedience, in his will; in conscience, faith;
Affections, love; in death it selfe, a blisse;
   In bodie, temperance; in life, humilitie;
   Pledge to the mortall of eternitie.

44/8 condemnation] *cancelling* contemplation   46/6 To others] For others
*1670*     47/5 in life] life *1670*

### 48

Pure, onely where God makes the spirits pure;
It perfect growes, as imperfections die;
Built on the rocke of truth, that shall endure;
A spirit of God, that needs must multiplie:
  He showes his glorie clearlie to the best,
  Appeares in clowdes and horror to the rest.

### 49

Such was the soule in our first sires creation,
When man knewe God, and goodnesse, not the evill:
Farre greater in the Godheads incarnation
Where truth subdued the sinne that made the Devill:
  She still is Gods, and God for ever one;
  Both unbeleiv'd in fleshe, and both unknowne.

### 50

Then man! learne by thy fall, to judge of neither;
Our fleshe cannot this spirit comprehend;
Death, and newe birth, in us must joyne together,
Before our nature where it was ascend:
  Where man presumes on more then he obayes,
  There straight Religion to opinion strayes.

### 51

Then since 'tis true, we onlie here possesse
These treasures but in vessels made of slime;
Religion we by consequence confesse
Here to be mixt of base thoughts and sublime;
  Of native evill, supernaturall good;
  Truth borne of God, and error of our blood.

48/2 imperfections die] imperfection dies *1670*          51/4 thoughts] things
*1670*

### 52

Yet gould we have, though much allayd with drosse,
Refininge, never perfect in this life;
Still in our journie meetinge gaine and losse,
Rest in our deathes, and untill then a strife:
    And as our dayes are want, temptation, error,
      So is our zeale warre, prayer, remorse and terror.


### 53

Such is the state of infants in newe birth,
Fedde first with milke, too weak for stronger foode,
Who learne at once to knowe, and doe in earth,
(Both enemie, and impotent to good)
    Must feele that our *Christ* can of his loose none,
      Which unto us makes grace and merit one.


### 54

These be true antidotes against dispayre,
Cradles for weaknesse, stories for corruption
To reade, howe faith beginnes to make her fayre,
By cleansinge sensuall sinckes of interruption;
    Wherby the throwes of manie thoughts bringe forth
      Light, onlie showinge man is nothinge worth.


### 55

For this word *Faith*, implies a state of minde,
Is both our wooinge, and our mariage ringe;
The fyrst we meet, and last, but *Love*, we finde;
A given hand that feeleth heavenlie thinges:
    And who beleive indeed God, heaven, and hell,
      Have past, in that, cheife lets of doeinge well.

52/6 prayer] Prayers *1670*     53/4 to] in *1670*     55/3 *Love*, we
finde;] Love we find *1670*

## 56

Then let not man too rashlie judge this light,
Nor censure God by his owne imperfection;
What can give limit to the infinite,
When he by worckes will witnesse our Election?
Degrees I graunt there be of will and might,
    Some to begett, some onlie to inherit,
    Yet still the conscience must obay the spirit.

## 57

Yea, though God call his Labourers everie houre,
And pay the last and first with heavenlie gaine;
Though he give faith beyond the Lawe, and power;
Yet is Gods nature, where he is, to raigne:
    His word is life, the letter all mens fall,
    That it without the spirit measure shall.

## 58

This sacred word is that eternall glasse,
Where all mens soules behold the face they bringe;
Each sees as much as life hath brought to passe,
The letter can showe fleshe no other thinge:
    The harts grace worckes to knowe what they obay;
    All else prophane God, and the world betray.

## 59

This worcke is Gods, even his that worckes all wonder,
His arme not shortned, and his goodnesse one;
Whose presence breakes sinnes middle wall in sunder,
And doth in fleshe deface the evilles throne:
    He is all, gives all, hath all where he is,
    And in his absence never soule found blisse.

56/2 imperfection] imperfections *1670*    58/4 fleshe] Life *1670*    59/2
shortned] shorned *1670*   6 found] finds *1670*

60

His *Egypt* wonders here he doth exceed;
For there he mixt with windes, rayne, natures Line;
Nowe by his spirit he doth blast our weedes,
Immediate grace, true miracle Divine:
   Guides not by fires and Meteors, night and day,
   His wandringe people, howe to move or stay;

61

But to the harts of sinne, shaddowes of death,
The savinge light of truth he doth inspire;
Filleth our humane Lunges with heavenly breath,
Our mortall natures with immortall fire:
   He drawes the Cammell through the needles eye,
   And makes the chosen fleshe die, ere they die.

62

Yet keepes one course with *Israel*, and us;
The fleshe still knewe his power, but not his grace:
All outward Churches ever knowe him thus,
They beare his name, but never runne his race:
   They knowe enough for their selfe condemnation,
   His, doeinge knowe him, to their owne salvation.

63

His Church invisible are fewe, and good;
The visible erroniouse, evill, manie:
Of his the life and letter understood,
Of these nor life, nor letter, dwell in anie:
   These make his word sect, schisme, philosophie;
   And those, from fishers call'd, Apostles be.

60/4 miracle] miracles *1670*   61/1 to the harts of sinne] into sinners
hearts *1670*  3 Filleth] Fitteth *1670*   63/4 nor life, nor letter, dwell
*1670*: nor letter, or not life *W*

### 64

These doe in prayinge, and still pray in doeinge;
Faith, and obedience are theyr contemplation;
Like lovers, still admiringe, ever woeinge
Their God, that gives this heavenlie constellation:
   They warre that finite infinite of sinne,
   All arts and pompes the error wanders in.

### 65

God is their strength; in him, his are not weake;
That spirit Divine which life, power, wisdome is,
Workes in these new-borne babes a life to speake
Things, which the world still understandes amisse;
   The lie hath manie tongues, truth onlie one,
   And who sees blindnesse, till the sinne be gone?

### 66

Fooles to the world these seeme, and yet obay
Princes oppressions, wherat fooles repine;
They knowe these Crownes, these theaters of clay
Derive their earthlie power from power Divine:
   Their suffringes are like all thinges else they doe,
   Conscience to God, with men a wisdome too.

### 67

Booke-learninge, Artes, yea Schoole Divinitie,
Newe types of old Law-munginge Pharisies
(Which curst in bondage of the letter be)
They knowe, they pittie, and would faine advise:
   The goodnesse moves them, yet the wisdome stayes
   From sowinge heavenlie seed in stonie wayes.

64/1 These] *cancelling* They: They *1670*     65/3 life] *cancelling* power
66/5 suffringes] sufferings *1670*

### 68

To you they crie: O you that hold the shrine,
As sent from God, yet preists of chance and gaine!
Your charge is to distribute thinges Divine,
O doe not lie for God, and sinne in vayne!
  Reveile his word, his mysteries expound;
  Else what he worckes, you travayle to confound.

### 69

You should be keyes to let his will passe out,
Binde sinne, and free repentance by his word,
Seare those that scorne, and comfort them that doubt;
What drowned *Pharaoh*, still is *Israels* ford:
  Wisdome above the truth was *Adams* sinne;
  That vayle which *Christ* rent of, will you walke in?

### 70

Observe faithes nature in these hallowed shrines,
Both of the old, and perfect testament;
Worckes be her fruits, her nature is Divine,
Infus'd by him that is Omnipotent.
  Doe we beleive on him, on whom we stay not?
  Can we beleive in him, whom we obay not?

### 71

His penne lefte two examples, it is true;
First of his chosen, howe he grosslie fell,
Then of the theefe borne instantlie anewe;
Vice rays'd to heaven, perfection fal'n to hell:
  And of each nature therfore lefte not manie,
  Least hope or feare should over-worke in anie.

68/2 from] by *1670*    6 travayle] travel *1670*    69/3 Seare] Fear *1670*
70/6 in] on *1670*

### 72

Is it not then by warrant from above,
That who gives faith, gives true obedience?
What other *Medium* hath our fleshe to prove,
That sinne with God keepes no intelligence?
  Takes this from man the fruict of *Christ* his death?
  No; it translates him into it, by faith.

### 73

For though God gave such measure of his grace
As might in fleshe fullfill the second table;
Yet sinne against the first, did first deface
Gods Image, and to rayse that who is able?
  Betweene the fleshe, and grace that spirituall fight
  Needs father, sonne, and their proceedinge might.

### 74

Nay let us graunt, God would enable man
After his callinge to accomplishe all:
From *Adams* sinne yet who redeeme him can,
Or *Paules* transgression cleare before his Call,
  But *Christ*? that comes to none of Gods in vayne;
  The justest need him, for the weake hee's slaine.

### 75

His life he makes example, where he please
To give his spirit; which is, to forgive:
But can the fleshe assume it selfe in these,
Since reason dies, before this faith can live?
  Who knowes Gods power but where he sinne removes?
  What should restraine th'almightie, where he loves?

72/5 fruict] fruits *1670*        73/3 first deface] quite deface *1670*        74/3 yet
who] who yet *1670*    6 weake hee's] worst he is *1670*          75/4 this] his
*1670*    5 he *1670*: the *W*      6 th'almightie] the Almighty *1670*

### 76

Besides, who marcks Gods course, from our Creation
Downe unto *Christ*, shall by succession see
Blisse of the goodnesse, evills condemnation
Establisht by unchanginge destinie:
The word is cleare, and needs no explanation,
Onlie the councell is a mysterie;
    Why God commanded more then man could doo,
    Beinge all things that he will, and wisdome too?

### 77

Why came our Saviour, if fleshe could fullfill
The Lawe enjoynd? Or if it must transgresse,
Whence tooke that justice this unequall will,
To binde them more, to whom he giveth lesse?
    Here power indeed to wisdome must direct,
    Else light saves fewe, and manie doth detect.

### 78

Strive not then wit corrupt, and disobayinge,
To fetch from Popes, Schooles, powers commandinge Thrones,
Doctrines of might, that suffer no denieinge,
Yet diverse, as earthes tempers in her zones:
    Since *Christs* owne heard him, sawe him live and die,
    Yet till he rose, knewe not the mysterie.

### 79

Pray then; and thincke, fayth hath her mediation,
Aske for thy selfe, that spirit which may judge;
Wayte the degrees of thy regeneration;
Count not without thy God; nor doe thou grudge
Limits or bounds of thine illumination:
    But give accompt of that which God hath given;
    Since grace, not merit, with the Lawe makes even.

78/2 Popes, Schooles] Popes stools *1670*    79/5 or] and *1670*

## 80

And if thou seekst more light to cleare the minde,
Search not Gods councells in himselfe contracted;
But search his written word, where thou shalt finde
That *Adams* fall was breach of Lawe enacted;
  By which in stayned wombe the chosen seed
  Together with the reprobate did breed.

## 81

The one shewd forth the light which he receiv'd,
Fashiond within him, by the Infinite;
The other serv'd the evill, was deceiv'd;
And in that which condemn'd him tooke delight:
  Both states partakers of Eternitie
  In life or death, as good and evill be.

## 82

Both had one Schoole, one forme, one education;
Each knewe one God, but onely one obayd;
Wherin the oddes was spirituall adoration,
And outward rites, which ever have betray'd:
  *Abel* sought God alone, *Caine* would have more;
  Which pride was in the Angells judg'd before.

## 83

Thus when Creation was a freshe tradition,
And miracle the proper ground of faith,
Guidinge the sinne unto her true physition;
Yet then (we see) sinne multiplied death:
  For him that made them, Men would not obay;
  Idolls, and sects had never other way.

80/1 the] thy *1670*    81/6 or death] *cancelling* and death    and evill be] or
ill they be *1670*    82/1 one education] and Education *1670*    83/5 Men]
*cancelling* sinne   6 had never other way] n'er had any other way *1670*

## 84

Men would be Gods, or earthlie Giants rather;
Number their strength, and strength their wisdome is;
Their doctrine, sinne; which as it spreades, doth gather
This present world: fleshe seekes no other blisse.
  As God by goodnesse saves those soules he chooseth,
  So hell condemnes those wicked soules it useth.


## 85

Nowe while both Churches lived thus together,
Parted by grace, by myracles united,
The outward worship common was to either,
And both alike by benefits invited:
  Yet murmur and obedience prov'd them two;
  For while both knewe, yet onely one could doe.


## 86

Thus though by life the spirit spirits trieth,
So as Gods goodnesse is by his exprest,
Which goodnesse in the Divells ever dieth;
Yet God hath here more latitude imprest:
  For unto those who onlie bare his name
  He gave such Gentiles as denied the same.


## 87

But when with Idolles they prophan'd that land,
Which he gave them for seeminge to adore him;
When they that held by forme, even brake that band,
And *Israel* in th'outward fail'd before him:
  Then came captivitie, that earthlie hell,
  Plantinge the Gentiles where his owne did dwell.

---

84/2 wisdome] number *1670*        85/6 could] would *1670*        86/4 hath
*1670*: did *W*    5 bare] bear *1670*            87/1 that] the *1670*    6 owne]
*1670 omits*

### 88

In this times wombe, this uttermost defection
Of fleshlie *Israel*, came the Virgins seed,
That righteousnesse which wrought Gods owne Election,
And in the fleshe fullfilld the Lawe indeed:
   When doctrine, miracles, benefits prov'd vayne,
   Then was this Lambe ordained to be slayne.

### 89

Thus, by defection from obedience,
Successively both sinne, and sects have growne;
Religion is a miracle to sense;
The newe man of the old is never knowne:
   And to those harts, where grosse sinnes doe not die,
   Gods Testaments are meere philosophie.

### 90

What latitude this to the world allowes,
Those soules, in whom Gods Image was decayd,
Then knowe, when they performe such spirituall vowes,
As underneath our Saviors crosse are layd:
   They that receive his wages, beare his armes,
   Knowe onlie what avayles us, and what harmes.

### 91

Wherin, to take Thrones first, as cheife in might,
*Davids* we wishe, of *Salomons* finde some,
Not in those wisdomes of the Infinite,
But in the rest, which bide more doubtfull doome:
   Thrones are the worldes; howe they stand well with heaven,
   Those powers can judge, to whom that grace is given.

88/3 righteousnesse] rightfulness *1670*          91/6 that] such *1670*

92

Next that high preisthode, which the spirit-falne *Jewe*
So prised, and erroniouslie maintayned,
Ceased in him, whose sacrifice was due
To all the world, by her defections stained:
    Small scope this gives to our Cathedrall chayres,
    The spirit onlie choosinge spirituall heyres.


93

Againe, for such as strive to undermine
The vanitie of *Romes* o're-built foundation,
With sinnes ambition, under wordes divine,
Hopinge to raise sects from her declination:
    O let them knowe! God is to both alike;
    The one he hath, the other he will strike.


94

And in the world, where Power confirmes opinion,
Advantage, disadvantage, as they stande;
*Rome* hathe the oddes in age and in dominion,
By which the Devills all thinges understand:
    The superstition is too worne a wombe,
    To rayse a newe Church nowe to equall *Rome*.


95

Last for our selves, who of that Church would be,
Which (though invisible) yet was, is, shall
For ever be the state and treasurie
Of Gods elect, which cannot from him fall;
    Arckes nowe wee looke for none, nor signes to part
    *Egypt* from *Israel*; all rests in the hart.

92/5 scope] hopes *1670*    95/1 who] which *1670*    6 rests] *cancelling*
lies

### 96

Our three-crown'd Miters, are but worckes of Spirit;
Faith, key and sceptre; our ambition, Love:
Built upon grace we are, and thence inherit
Temptation, which in us doth purge, doth prove,
   Mortifie, regenerate, sanctifie, and raise
   The old falne *Adam*, to newe *Adams* wayes.

### 97

This word of life then let not fleshlie man
Corrupt, and unregenerate expound;
As well the mortall judge th'immortall can,
Or deafnesse finde the discordes out of sound,
   Or creatures their Creator comprehende;
   Which they presume, that judge before they mende.

### 98

Mixe not in functions God, and earth together;
The wisdome of the world, and his, are two;
One latitude can well agree to neither;
In each, men have their beinges, as they doe:
   The world doth build without, our God within;
   He traffiques goodnesse, and she traffiques sinne.

### 99

Schooles have their limits, wherin man prescribes;
What credit hopes truth there, which contradicts?
States have their Lawes, all Churches have their tribes,
Where sinne is ever strongest, and inflicts;
   For man is judge, and force still wisdome there;
   Howe can God thence expect a spirituall heire?

96/4 doth prove] and prove *1670*   6 The] Our *1670*   97/3 th'immor-
tall] the immortal *1670*

### 100

But Gods elect still humblie passe by these,
Make Love their Schoole, and skale of righteousnesse,
Which Infinite those harts desire to please,
While to the world they leave her wickednesse:
   Sect and division cannot here arise,
   Where everie man in God is onlie wise.

### 101

Can it then be a doctrine of despayre,
To use the wordes or councells of our God,
As they stand in him? Though they seeme severe,
Health of the chosen is the lost childs rod.
   Though fleshe cannot beleive, yet God is true;
   And onlie knowne where he creates anewe.

### 102

Things possible with man are not in question:
Gods power, guifts, will here faithes true *Basis* be;
All *Mediums* else are but the sinnes suggestion,
The mover onlie makes our nature free:
   Faith, and obedience, he that asketh gives;
   And without these Gods spirit never lives.

### 103

Againe, in this strange warre, this wildernesse,
These *Egypt* brick-killes, from our strawe depriv'd,
God liveliest ever doth himselfe expresse,
Helpe beinge here from heavenlie power deriv'd:
   Affliction of the spirit made mans true glasse,
   To showe him, God brings what he will to passe.

102/1 not] yet *1670*    2 *Basis*] Bases *1670*    103/3 liveliest ever] ever
liveliest *1670*

104

Nowe in this fight, wherin the man despayres
Betwene the sinne, and his regeneration;
Fayth upon credit never takes her heires,
Gods wonder in us worcks her adoration;
    Who from the heaven sends his graces downe,
    To worcke the same obedience he will crowne.


105

This leades us to our Savior, who no more
Doth aske, then he enables us to doe;
The rest he frees, and takes upon his score;
Faith and Obedience only bindes us to:
    All other latitudes are fleshe and Devill,
    To staine our knowledge, and enlarge our evill.


106

Offer these truthes to Power, will she obay?
It prunes her pompe, perchance plowes up that roote;
It pride of Tyrants humors doth allay,
Makes God their Lord, and casts them at his foote:
    This truth they cannot wave, yet will not doe,
    And feare to knowe, because that bindes them too.


107

Showe these to Arts; those riddles of the sinne
Which error first creates, and then inherits;
This light consumes those mists they florishe in,
At once deprives their glorie, and their merits:
    Those mortall formes, moulded in humane error,
    Dissolve themselves by lookinge in this mirror.

106/2 plowes] *cancelling* pulls   that] the *1670*    107/4 merits] Merit *1670*
5 in] of *1670*

### 108

Showe it to Lawes; Gods Lawe, their true foundation,
Proves howe they build up earth, and lose the heaven,
Give thinges eternall mortall limitation,
Ore-rulinge him, from whom their rules were given:
 Gods Lawes are right, just, wise; and so would make us:
 Mans captiouse, diverse, false; and so they take us.

### 109

Showe it the outward Church; strange speculation
For that hypocrisie to see the life;
They that sell God for earthlie estimation,
Are here divorc'd from that adulterouse wife:
 For this truth teacheth mankinde to despise them,
 While God more justlie for his owne denies them.

### 110

Offer these truthes to fleshe in generall;
God in his power, and truth they doe confesse,
But want of faith, that venome of their fall,
Despayres to undergoe his righteousnesse:
 They thincke God good, and so his mercie trust;
 Yet hold good life impossible to dust.

### 111

Only that litle flocke, Gods owne elect,
(Who livinge in the world, yet of it are not)
God is the wealth, will, Empire they affect;
His Lawe their wisdome, for the rest they care not:
 Amonge all flouds this Arck is still preserved,
 Stormes of the world are for her owne reserved.

---

108/1 their] the *1670*    4 rules] *cancelling* lawes: Laws *1670*    111/2 *1670*
*omits brackets*    5 preserved] preserv'd *1670*    6 reserved] reserv'd *1670*

## 112

For their sakes, God doth give restraininge grace
To his seene Church, and to the heathen too;
Sets sinne her latitudes of time, and place,
That onlie she her owne may still undoe:
    And where the sinne is free to all, as one,
    He bindes temptation, to preserve his owne.


## 113

So as though still in wildernesse they live,
And gone from *Egypt*, suffer *Israels* care,
Yet foode and clothes that weare not out he gives,
Of them that hate them they preserved are:
    This grace restraininge, bounds those hypocrites,
    Whose ravine else might spoile the world of lights.


## 114

Then man! Rest on this feelinge from above,
Plant thou thy faith on this celestiall way.
The world is made for use; God is for Love;
Sorrowe for sinne; knowledge, but to obay;
Feare and temptation, to refine and prove;
The heaven, for joyes; Desire that it may
    Finde peace in endlesse, boundlesse, heavenly things;
    Place it else where, it desolation bringes.

112/1 sakes] sake *1670*     3 latitudes] Latitude *1670*         113/2 And] As
*1670*     2 care] *cancelling* thrall    5 those] the *1670*        114/6 joyes] Joy
*1670*     Desire] desire thou *1670*

# COMMENTARY

ANY full commentary on Greville's treatises, where the involutions of syntax call for the analysis of alternative interpretations in stanza after stanza, would prove more extensive than the poems themselves—and might seem to inflate their worth. In the scope of this edition it has seemed more practical to indicate the drift of the argument by providing summaries phase by phase, discussing certain vexed passages, and adding notes on the historical and mythological illustrations through which—especially in *A Treatise of Monarchy*—the argument is developed. For these annotations I have kept as far as possible to sources which an Elizabethan would have used; the authorities Greville specifically acknowledges are Plutarch, Polybius, Isocrates, Livy, Florus, Cicero, Justinus, Velleius Paterculus, and Aemilius Probus (as author of a work really by Cornelius Nepos).

Any references to classical authors in other than sixteenth- or seventeenth-century texts are to the Loeb editions.

### An Advertisement

*the . . . Families of* Nevil, Beauchamp, *and* Willoughby *Lord* Brooke: Greville's mother was Anne Nevill, daughter of the Earl of Westmorland, and through his paternal grandmother, Elizabeth Willoughby, and her mother, Elizabeth Beauchamp, he was connected with the families of Beauchamp of Powick and Willoughby de Broke.

## A TREATISE OF MONARCHY

### Section I · *Of the Beginning of Monarchy*

Section I establishes that monarchy, as it now exists, is a product of the fallen state of the earth. In the golden age—'when nature raign'd, in stead of lawes or artes'—kings lived in an ideal harmony with their people, and were worshipped as gods after death (1–10). Heroes like Hercules and Jason were their subalterns, their exploits serving the good of all (11–16). But as the golden age declined, the gods withdrew from the earth, inflicting tempests and earthquakes to punish 'mans corrupting errors'. Left to the mercy of their own frailty, men raised kings from among themselves (17–24). Subjects therefore should not complain of the power of kings, as it is founded in their own depravity; kings in turn should not pretend to an authority 'more absolute then God himself requires'. Subjects and rulers share alike in the corruption of mankind (25–31).

Monarchy has a surer foundation in the fact of 'degree' and in the benefits issuing from it (32–34). To impose an absolute rule, however, kings have tried to exploit religion, laying claim to infinite power. Such pretensions are exposed in 'true religions cleare beames', which show that power is not infinite, but bounded with wrong and right—principles flouted under the tyrant's rule (35–42). Where tyranny has prevailed it has served to keep men from the disorder to which their natures are prone, but the ideal to be preferred is a 'mutuall confidence', restraining both sides from excess (43–45).

1/1. *There was a tyme before the tymes of story*: cf. the account of the golden age in *Met.* i. 89–112, and *Caelica*, xliv, 'The *Golden-Age* was when the world was yong'.

4/5. *allay'd*: alloyed (cf. 231/5, 357/2, 400/3). Greville also uses 'allay' in the sense of 'assuage', as at 148/1 and 293/3.

11/1. Euristeus, *that brave Prince of* Greece: the king to whom Hercules was subjected during the performance of his labours.

11/2. *Noe* Pallas, *noe* Narcissus: freedmen of the emperor Claudius, who as his favourites amassed riches for themselves.

12/2. *having freed* Greece *from home-tyrannie*: Hercules' deliverance of Thebes from Erginus of Orchomenos.

12/3. *to meritt*: to deserve well of (for services performed), as 126/3 (*O.E.D.* merit, *v.* 3).

12/5–6. Hercules (seen as typical of the 'Kinges creatures' of the golden age) purged Egypt of Busiris, who offered strangers entering his kingdom as human sacrifices; captured the mares of Diomedes, which fed on human flesh; destroyed Cacus, the robber giant who plundered the Italian countryside; and overcame the monster Geryon and took his oxen. Cf. Diodorus Siculus, iv. 15, 17, 18.

13/1. *a Goddess spite*: Juno's persecution of Hercules in revenge for the infidelity of Zeus with his mother, Alcmena.

13/2. *spetious*: used in the primary sense of 'fair or pleasing to the eye' (cf. 93/2, 340/1, 586/1).

13/4. *One God appeasing other Godds offences*: i.e. the divine assistance given to Hercules (his helmet from Minerva, his sword from Mercury, his bow and arrows from Apollo) compensated for Juno's enmity ('other Godds' = another god's).

15/1. Jason . . . *undertaking passages unknowen*. It was not uncommon for the Elizabethans to regard the voyage of the Argonauts as historical (cf. 377/6). In his *History of the World* (1614), Ralegh observed 'that which is most probable . . . is that the Storie of such a passage was true, and that *Jason* with the rest went to robbe *Colchos*, to which they might arrive by boate' (II. xiii. 6).

17–18. The withdrawal of the gods from the earth, and the assault of the giants on heaven, is described in *Met.* i. 149–63.

19/6. *curiouse*: studious (cf. 128/1, *R.* 37/3).

24/3. *privation*: used (as at 27/3) with the implication of severance from good (cf. *Caelica*, cii, ll. 9, 43).

25/3–6. *To whome God did foretell, on humane winges* . . .: Samuel's attempt to dissuade the Israelites from monarchy, by predicting their lot under kings (1 Samuel viii. 4–22).

28/3. *tuch*: blemish or taint.

32/3–6. *Not peasing these* . . .: not judging these things by criteria from religion (ll. 3–4) or philosophy (ll. 5–6).

35/6. *like beasts, left noe rights but in sence.* A contrast is implied (as again at 37/5) between 'sense' (the level of existence of the beasts) and 'reason' (proper to man). Greville consistently regards the tyrant's rule as degrading man to the level of brutes, denying his rational nature (cf. *Life*, pp. 116, 194).

38/1. *by optick repercussions.* The metaphor might have been clearer to a contemporary familiar with the account of reflections and rainbows in Aristotle's *Meteorologica*, iii. iv. The sense seems to be: When power claims a religious sanction the human is falsely exalted to the divine (st. 37). For as by an optical illusion the 'light with shadowes mixt' can make the smaller object seem the larger (as Castor, not himself immortal, was raised to partake of the divinity of Pollux); and as the rainbow, itself a shadow, 'formes another to our seeing': so these pretensions to divine power ('these visions' referring back to 37/3) cast 'second reflections', which represent the false accommodation of divine and human in laws and government—revealing to men that 'thrones may seeme, but are not infinite'. Cf. 313/5–6.

## Section II · *Declination of Monarchy to Violence*

With the earth's lapse from perfection the 'auntient forming pow'rs' gave place to others, which by preserving deceptive appearances, and exploiting the distraction and inconstancy of men, betray them into complete subjection (46–52). This is the emergence of the tyrant state, where men are but 'blankes where pow'r doth write her lust', and religion, honour, and nature's laws are perverted and debased (53–57). So Mahomet made religion an instrument of conquest, Cambyses and Caracalla set their will above the law: the tradition is carried on by the Pope, in inciting subjects to assassination and revolt under 'pretence divine' (58–62). Effective tyranny requires constant surveillance and manipulation (63–65), but the more it prospers, the more it is liable to endanger itself by overreaching (66–69). Excessive despotism alienates former supporters (e.g. Brutus and Cassius), and stirs up internal discontents that make the state vulnerable to an aggressor, or give occasion to aspirers within (70–74). Tyranny escaping these hazards receives judgement from heaven—a truth reflected in the fables of Lycaon, Tereus, and the Furies (75–79).

**46/1.** *the world on these excentricks*: i.e. with its axis displaced from the centre.

**50/1–6.** The 'webbs of authority' in which the people become more and more entangled, as they seek to 'redeeme that state they had before' (49/6), are really spun from their own substance; monarchy arose in the first place (24–25) from the people voluntarily yielding their power to kings.

**56/2.** *a giant creature*: the tyrant who abuses religion to magnify his power (cf. 'these Monsters', 57/3).

**56/4.** *that*: i.e. worth.

**58/5.** *the sacred dove*: the pigeon Mahomet was reputed to have taught to pick wheat from his ear, claiming that it was a messenger from the Holy Ghost. Cf. 'Machomet the fals prophete' in Lydgate's *Fall of Princes*, ix. 92–98.

**59/1–3.** Cambyses . . . *mariage with his sister*: seen as an instance of the tyrant placing his will above the law (cf. Herodotus, iii. 31), as a parallel (ll. 5–6) to the incest of Caracalla with his stepmother Julia Domna, who assured him *Si libet, licet. an nescis te imperatorem esse et leges dare, non accipere?* (*Historia Augusta*, ii. 27).

**60/1.** *our great* Capitolian *Lord*: the Pope, represented as another tyrant who (like Mahomet, st. 58) exploits religion for imperialist ends.

**60/4.** *assassinate*: obsolete form of 'assassination' (cf. 73/5).

**61/3.** Phœbus *and* Sybilla *raign'd*: the heathen oracles to whom the Pope is the successor, the pronouncements from his 'tripode' (the three-legged stool on which the medium sat when possessed by the spirit) claiming the authority of the Godhead.

**74/2.** *If* Nero *lack a forreigne enemy*: Nero's fall was caused by the revolt of one of his subordinates, Vindex Julius, the governor of Gaul; Caligula was murdered by a tribune of the praetorian cohort; Otho committed suicide when the armies of Vitellius marched against him.

**77/1.** *Lycaon*: turned into a wolf by Jove for serving a meal of human flesh (*Met.* i. 198–244).

**77/6.** Upupas *fowle-feeding dust*. The metamorphosis of Tereus into a hoopoe (for his assault on Philomela) was considered 'a fit transformation, that the filthinesse of inordinate lust, in which *Tereus* delighted, might be represented by the filthinesse of the dung in which the Lapwing takes pleasure' (Alexander Ross, *Mystagogus Poeticus*, 1649, 'Tereus').

78/1. Megera *and her sisters*: the Furies, as agents of divine vengeance.

78/5–6. Pentheus: attacked and dismembered by the Bacchanals (led by his mother) for scorning their worship and spying on their rites.

## Section III · *Of Weake Minded Tyrants*

Section III (a preliminary to the section following) is on the theme of vicissitude. The decay, in the course of time, of the majesty of Olympus, and the rise and fall of the empires of the past, show monarchy as subject to 'the naturall variety of frailties, raigning since the world began' (80–86). So weak rulers succeed the strong, relaxing the authority of their predecessors, but bringing the people only another form of misrule (87–89). Lacking judgement, the weak ruler is timorous, and prone to inaction: he becomes (like Galba and Claudius) the thrall of favourites, whose undisciplined humours disrupt the proper government of the state and bring it into disrepute (90–98). But again vice is seen 'against her own estate become transgressor'. Those who have shrewdly appropriated power, becoming complacent and tyrannical in the exercise of it, find it undergoing subtraction (as Austria lost control of Switzerland, and Spain of Holland). Vices prosper and wane as part of *vicissitudo rerum*, showing that 'pow'r hath noe longe beinge, but in worth' (99–105).

81/1. *A worke of* Saturne: Saturn in his role as god of time, which fits awkwardly into this context, as he was also ruler of the golden age and patron of agriculture.

87/3. *imping*: the grafting of feathers in the wings of birds to make good any deficiencies (falconry).

88/2. *a doinge lust*: a desire to act.

88/5. *which o're wound*: i.e. which were o're wound.

91/1. *might*: although 'Right' (*1670*) is possible (cf. 'right, witt, and heart' in 120/3), the *W* reading continues the train of thought from 'power absolute' in st. 90.

92/1–6. *Whence from inferiors, visions fitted be.* Under the influence of subordinates weak kings are deceived into thinking that ease is synonymous with greatness ('Resting as God, whoe yet distributes fate'), that to depute responsibility is dispensing freedom, and that to withdraw from affairs is political astuteness.

95/1. *Thus did old* Galba *raigne in pupillage*: the subjection of Galba and Claudius to their favourites is treated at length in the *Lives* by Suetonius and Plutarch.

102/1. *The pride of such inferiors.* The Swiss confederacy, as a departure from monarchic rule, cannot have Greville's approbation. Cf. his account of 'the *Switzers* swolne with equality; divided at home; enemies, yet servants to Monarchies . . .' (*Life*, p. 85).

102/3-6. *the* Belgians . . . *new* Republique. Grosart (i. 1) took this as an allusion to the truce between Spain and Holland concluded in 1608—an indication of when this section of the treatise may have been written. However, the mention of Alva suggests an earlier period in the history of the Dutch Republic, and the reference to the Belgians being forced to release a new state points to the separation of the northern provinces at the Treaty of Utrecht in 1579: 'Belgium' then came to refer to the Spanish Netherlands, as distinct from the United Provinces of the north. Alva, the most effective enemy of Dutch aspirations, had been recalled in 1573.

### Section IV · *Cautions Against These Weake Extremities*

Though some of the diseases of monarchy seem beyond human remedy, an attitude of stoic resignation cannot be commended. The need is for perseverance; vicissitude itself remains under the sway of 'powres divine' (106-14). Kings should realize that if perfection is unattainable, yet some imperfections are open to cure—to live by 'rules' makes for the security of kings and subjects alike (115-16). The people should learn to expect little, reconciling themselves to what is beyond their competence to reform; weak kings should refrain from excesses that might imperil their estate, and contrive to gain 'subjects strength' to support the crown (117-24). Their best help lies in the prudent choice of subordinates, taking fame as a guide (125-30); in shrewdly delegating and reserving authority (131-3); and in so balancing one faction against another that the royal power remains unimpaired (134-9). Weak kings may derive support from 'all moulds of their forefathers', such as exchequers, courts, and parliaments; though to attempt to add to their prerogatives would be imprudent (140-2). If these cautions fail to check frailty in its course, weak rulers must submit to being engulfed (143-5).

109/1. *Whoe then can wary Seneca reprove?* Seneca, who had been tutor and adviser to Nero, sought to retire from his service in A.D. 62, when the poisoning of Britannicus and the murder of Agrippina were followed by other excesses.

111/4. *Soe* Priscus *pass'd* Domitians *torride clymes.* Neratius Priscus, who served as *consul suffectus* under Domitian, became a noted jurist in the age of Trajan and Hadrian.

112/2-3. Cato *soe impatient of his owne life.* Cato committed suicide to escape the tyranny of Caesar, after Pompey's defeat and murder.

117. As st. 115-16 had been addressed to the king, this and the stanza following are directed to the people. Ideal relationships between ruler and ruled cannot be expected where so much is at the mercy of the ruler's temperament; when rulers are weak and shed no good influence, to make demand upon them is to risk total ruin.

118/5. *as of old, curst with confused speech*: the tower of Babel (cf. *Caelica*, lxxxviii, l. 9).

122/1. *as when birdes and beastes would have a kinge.* I have not been able to trace this fable.

124/3–4. The two ways of regarding royal wisdom—as a 'quintessence of abstract trueth', and as 'sweet sympathie or counterpease Of humours'—are formulated in terms of the opposition of the Paracelsian doctrine that each thing is preserved in health by its quintessence and the Galenist theory that health is a balance of the humours. But the construction 'Nor is . . . More then' is probably meant to reconcile the two, presenting 'Crowne wisdome' as both theoretical and practical. In the *Life*, similarly, Greville praises his ideal monarch, Queen Elizabeth, for her skill in managing her great subjects ('she well understanding the humours of both, temper'd them so equally one with another', p. 202), and again as a ruler possessing 'a quintessence of abilities, gathered out of those blessed, and blessing mixtures of Nature, Education, and Practice' (p. 192—cf. p. 176).

125/3. *discretely*: an alternative spelling of 'discreetly' at this time.

126/2–4. Alexander . . . *by help of Councell uncorrupt.* M. Aurelius Alexander Severus (A.D. 222–35), becoming emperor in his seventeenth year, placed himself under the tutelage of his mother, Julia Mammaea, in the early years of his reign, and reformed abuses in the state.

127/5. *kinlesse fame helpes weakenes what to judge.* As the choice of 'underministers' (125/2) is difficult for weak rulers (who lacking experience are subject to chance), they may take good or ill report as a guide. Greville gives a more extended treatment of fame in *An Inquisition upon Fame and Honour*; the scope is limited here to its uses to a weak prince, as an impartial 'echo' of worthiness or unworthiness (cf. 317–19).

128/2. *easily represent*: i.e. may easily represent.

129/1–5. *fame . . . on her winges*: possibly a recollection of the description of *Fama* in *Aeneid*, iv. 184–8 (to which Greville refers in *Fame and Honour*, st. 53), though Fame as a winged figure was also familiar as an emblem (as in the *Iconologia* of Caesar Ripa).

134/3. *The whole is by an* equilibrium *sway'd*: i.e. when the disease is distributed through the whole body it cannot gain enough strength in any one part to bring death to the whole; similarly in a weak kingdom (st. 135) a variety of factions, none able to gain the advantage, allows the king to keep the 'tottering ballance upp by art'.

136/2. *When* Galienus *buried was in lust.* Greville follows tradition in representing the emperor Gallienus (A.D. 253–68) as cruel and profligate, his incompetence exposing Rome to the barbarian hordes.

136/5. *the thirty, ryvalls to each other*: the *tyranni triginta* (so styled in the *Historia Augusta*, on the analogy of the Thirty Tyrants of Athens), the pretenders who arose in the provinces during the reign of Gallienus, and resisted the invaders.

## Section V · *Stronge Tyrants*

The 'tyrant' here is not only the despot (146–7), but also (in a familiar Elizabethan usage) the 'strong ruler'. Most political theorists seem to have allowed this use, observing (like Thomas Smith in *De Republica Anglorum*) that the Greeks used *tyrannos* as equivalent to 'king'. This section offers advice on how such rulers may be restrained from excesses that bring monarchy into hazard (148).

As history shows, there are some vices that tyrants have safely indulged, as not prejudicing their estate, but binding people to the throne (149–52). Vices to be shunned are rather those that publish a monarch's weakness to the world, or allow subordinates to gain influence over him (153–8). As authority is enhanced by fame and reputation, kings should avoid courses that detract from these—cruelty and extortion, headstrong counsels (159–63), and above all faithlessness in leagues and contracts (164–75). They must preserve their supremacy over all that govern under them, not committing themselves to one party rather than another (176–8); suppress faction before it can gather strength (179–84); and learn from 'practicke wisdome' how to heal dissension and subdue all to the throne—remembering, as a curb to inordinate ambition, that their actions remain open to public view (185–8). Kings should not court public regard, but win respect by 'reservednes'. If excess occurs, people have no choice but to submit to it (189–91).

146/1. *the setting of this evening starr*: the weak king, now giving way to the strong ('that morning planetts influence'), who will surpass the kind of reign that can be no more than momentarily effective ('Cometts of stronge powre in feeble sence').

150/1–2. Vitellius . . . *by a gluttons familiaritie*: the affability of Vitellius secured the goodwill of the army he commanded on the Rhine at the time of Otho's accession, so that he marched against Otho and gained the throne. After his feasting and prodigality had lost favour with the populace Vitellius was deposed by Vespasian.

151/1–2. Pertinax . . . *in whome predominant Fewe vyces were.* The reforms proposed by Pertinax incurred the hostility of the court retainers and praetorians, and led to his death after a reign of less than three months.

154. *the* Macedonians . . . *greate kinge.* Among the weaknesses that appeared in the character of Alexander the Great in his later career, the older historians (e.g. Arrian, Plutarch, Quintus Curtius) stress the extravagance of his grief at the death of Hephaestion, and the command

that he should be deified, and sacrifices offered to him. Greville seems to combine this (in st. 155) with the tradition of the superstitious heed paid by Alexander to soothsayers and priests interpreting signs.

156/3. *vents*: opportunities for sale, marts (*O.E.D.* vent, *sb.*³ 2, 3— from *vendere*).

163/1. *Rehoboham*: Solomon's son, who forsook the counsel of the old men for the counsel of the young, with the consequence that the Israelites revolted from him (1 Kings xii).

165. *that great* Charles *the fifte . . . mis-letterd writts*. Roger Ascham, in *A Report . . . of the affaires and state of Germany* (1570?), tells how Philip, Landgrave of Hesse, in 1547 surrendered himself to Charles V on condition that he should not be held in any prison—but was nevertheless imprisoned by the emperor. The manner of the deception was explained by Duke Frederick's preacher, who (Ascham relates)

tooke his penne and wrote in my booke the very wordes wherein the very controversie stode, Duke *Maurice* sayd it was
       *Nicht in einig gefengknes*. Not in any prison.
The Imperials sayd no, but thus
       *Nicht in ewig gefengknes*. Not in everlasting prison.
And how soone *einig* may be turned into *ewig*, not with scrape of knife, but with the least dash of a pen so that it shall never be perceived, a man that will prove, may easely see (H2ᵛ).

166/1. *The precept of* Lysander: that 'children should be deceived with the play of kayles [skittles], and men with othes of men' (Plutarch's *Lives*, in Tudor Translations, iii. 232).

166/5–6. *that perjury noe synne, Which by equivocation enters in.* Lysander is represented as the instructor of the Jesuits, whose doctrine of equivocation permitted a witness to swear certain statements to be true, while making mental reservations that made them false. As this sense of the word 'equivocation' does not seem to have been current in England until the early years of the seventeenth century (the *O.E.D.* has no instance earlier than *Macbeth*, v. v. 43, the passage thought to have been influenced by the trial of Garnet for the Gunpowder Plot) this may be another indication of when Greville was at work on the treatise. See further H. N. Paul, 'Garnet's Doctrine of Equivocation', in *The Royal Play of Macbeth* (New York, 1950).

167. Tiberius . . . *the law beguil'd*. Suetonius, discussing Tiberius' manipulations of the law to serve his cruelties, observes 'as for young girles and maidens of unripe yeares, because by auncient custome and tradition, unlawfull it was to strangle Virgins, first deflowred they were by the hang-man and afterwards strangled' (Tudor Translations, i. 279).

168/2. *sacred oath of* Stygian *lake*. To swear by the waters of the Styx was for the gods to swear an inviolable oath. Of the various explanations of the punishment of Tantalus in hell, Greville adopts the story (st. 169) that he abused the hospitality of the gods, to whose society he had been admitted, by divulging their secrets.

169/3. *Battus*: the shepherd of Pylos who saw Mercury steal the flocks of Admetus, and promised not to betray him—'That stone will tell of your thefts sooner than I.' Breaking his oath, he was turned into a pumice-stone (*Met.* ii. 676–707).

169. The line missing from this stanza is marked by a space left in *W* and by dashes in some copies of *1670*.

172/5. *peece*: make peace (*O.E.D.* pease, *v.* 1b).

173/2. *wronge prescribes not Crownes*: 'prescribe' is used with the force of 'give entitlement to' (cf. 496/2), although the *O.E.D.* records no sense exactly corresponding to this.

178. Princes must so unite all parties that none are ruined by exactions of public life or withdraw from it for private ends; but make only such demands on their greatest subjects as will not discontent them though the prince lives beyond his own means. The ruin of estates through the high cost of a career at court is a well-known feature of the period.

187/1. *stirrage*: obsolete form of 'steerage'.

## Section VI · *Of Church*

Defects in a king's nature may be increased by their diffusion through the various spheres of his government (192–5). But these spheres—Church, law, commerce—also provide a common ground for kings and people, tempering the extremes to which each is liable, and contributing to the stability of the realm (196–201).

The Church is the most important of the branches of government. The power of religion may be gauged from her shadow superstition (as in the conquests of Islam), and kings must take care how they manage 'this cheif strength of tirranny' (202–7). The Church's arms are 'teares and prayer', not the sword; people should honour the king and reverence their priests, but by keeping 'the better part to God alone', shun the tyranny of the theocrat; kings must resist any encroachment on the sceptre by the mitre—the Papal domination is an ever-present warning (208–17).

The crown should curb such practices as simony, which cast scandal on doctrine and bring ancient establishments to ruin—to the discredit of Church and state alike (218–21). No 'new, or irreligious sects', making for disaffection and controversy, can be tolerated: those who will not cease from dispute should be banished to the schools, so that from the pulpit may be heard 'nothing, but that which seemes mans life to mend' (222–5). Bishops should be 'antient', and preferably celibate; a discipline should be observed that consists not merely in compliance with outward law (as under a tyrant), but seeks 'from within man, to worke out the right' (226–32). The Church should contribute to the harmony of the state, not (as in the hands of the Pope) dividing subjects from kings, or usurping the authority that is God's alone. Were there any truth in the pretensions of the 'superstitious spheare', tyrants would depend on conscience alone as the base of their authority—whereas they 'enwall themselves with lawes of terror' (233–8).

192/6. *Jubilees*: used with something of the original sense (Lev. xxv. 9–13) of emancipation from restraint, as in the *Life*, p. 194.

197. I can make sense of this stanza only by taking 'Church, lawes, Commerce' as in apposition with 'lower orbes', and taking 'rights' as a verb—a reading supported by 'this well ballancinge of might' (198/1).

199/1–2. Theopompus . . . *rays'd upp a plebean magistrate*. By establishing the ephors in Sparta, Theopompus surrendered part of the royal prerogative. To the complaint that he must thereby bequeath less power to his successors, he answered:

Not lesse but more, for that it shall continue lenger, and with a more suertie. For in losing thus their too absolute power, that wrought them great envie and hatred among their cittizens, they dyd escape the daunger and mischief that their neighbours . . . dyd feele: who would not geve over the soveraine authoritie which they had gotten once. (Plutarch, *Lives*, Tudor Translations, i. 127.)

200/6. *woeing*: wooing, as at *R.* 64/3.

203/3–4. Mydas . . . *shedd Seedes of this ceremony*. On succeeding Gordius as king of Phrygia, Midas, 'beinge traded up by *Orpheus* in manye superstitious ceremonies, filled all the realme full of sectes of religion, by the whyche he lived more in safegarde all hys lyfe, then by his chivalrye' (Justinus, *Histories*, tr. Golding, 1570, H5ᵛ).

210/5. *Cannons*: Church decrees.

211/4. *superstition bound*: bound by superstition.

212/3–4. *the* Druides . . . *Gott goodes from them that tooke their words*. Applying the Druid doctrine of immortality, the Gauls took loans from the living, promising to repay them in the next world. Cf. Valerius Maximus, *Facta et dicta* (1559, F6ᵛ), and Pompeius Mela, *The Situation of the World* (tr. Golding, 1585), III. ii.

213/6. *that double frame*: the Papacy (and by implication Spain) as an organization 'mixing the temporall, and spirituall sword' (*Life*, p. 83), the alliance of priest and king which Greville condemns (st. 209).

214/5. *And was not* Venice *excommunicate*. The conflict of the Venetian republic with Paul V led to the excommunication of the Doge and Senate in 1606.

214/6. *such false purchasers*: 'purchaser' is used in the obsolete sense of one who acquires possessions by unscrupulous means.

227/1. *The* Romane *lawes for magistrates*: candidates for the consulate were required to be forty-three years of age.

228/3. *doth well deserve*: is meritorious.

230/1. *Censure*: judicial sentence or punishment (*O.E.D.* censure, *sb.* 1a, b). These views of godly discipline recall Calvin (cf. *Institutes*, IV. xii), though Greville diverges from him (st. 229) in upholding celibacy.

234/1. *sophistication*: sophistry.

235/2. *as to their* Muftie Turkes *lyv'd under*. Busbecq, in his *Epistolae quatuor* (Frankfurt, 1595), in the course of relating the story of Mustapha, describes the Mufti as *apud Turcas sacerdotum supremus; ut apud nos Romanus pontifex* (C5r).

235–6. Salmoneus of Elis, wishing to be regarded as a god, drove his chariot over a brazen bridge to imitate the thunder, flinging torches on every side to counterfeit lightning. For his impiety he was struck by a thunderbolt. Cf. *Aeneid*, vi. 585 ff.

238/1. *pretends*: puts forward as a cover.

## Section VII · *Of Lawes*

The first lawgivers were the gods, whose laws were engraved in man's understanding, and enforced by his conscience. With the withdrawal of the gods from the earth came man's laws, 'which but corrupt reason be'. The human lawgivers—Solon, Lycurgus, Zaleucus, Zoroaster, Numa —brought bondage and division upon men, giving power an instrument for securing their obedience (239–45). Yet as 'Church rites' alone cannot guard all the branches of government, monarchs must avail themselves of laws also. At first sight a restriction of sovereignty, laws may be enlisted to support absolute power (246–50); they prevent subjects from interfering in crown affairs by offering scope for dissension among themselves (251–3).

The most effective laws are not those framed for a particular occasion, but those which bear a 'universall face', paying heed to both 'the groundes of nature' and the laws of God (254–7). While laws can never reach the 'inward cause' of man's corruption, they help to make men wiser, and more competent in state affairs (258–60). Summaries of the law should be published in simple language, and not kept as a preserve of the initiate, as in ancient Rome (261–7). The respective rights of kings and people should be clearly stated: any uncertainty has the effect of 'makinge Judges, and not Princes greate', raising the courts above the crown (268–70). Kings must superintend the administration of justice, prohibiting the sale of offices, curtailing the length and variety of trials, curbing the delays and malpractices of advocates, and setting up provincial courts to carry justice to all (271–81).

Kings should not encroach on the legal rights of subjects, whose obedience can be secured by the rule of equals over equals: craft is no foundation for good government, and broken pledges destroy reputation. Tyranny beyond all law reduces men to slavery (282–6). No challenge can come from prerogatives granted to 'speritts inferior', whose very elevation exposes them to hazard. Assemblies of state are to be valued as a mirror of the condition of the realm (287–91), as a safe indulgence of the stirrings of liberty and conscience felt by the people (292–5), and as a concession returning the king far more power than he yields (296–302). Thus Rome found it politic to consult the *comitia tributa*, as the Greek states frequented their *synedrion*: avoiding the ways of despotism, sovereignty is best maintained and extended by ruling the people with their own concurrence, as a power supreme rather than absolute (303–14). The choice of the administrators necessary to good government may be guided by birth, education, and fame (315–19). These directions for laws serve the king and the tyrant alike: let the reader distinguish them as he may choose (320–1).

242/2. *banisht mylde* Astrea: Astraea, goddess of justice, was the last of the immortals to be driven from the earth by the wickedness of men, at the close of the golden age. Cf. *Met.* i. 150; Thomas Cooper, *Dictionarium Historicum & Poeticum* (1584).

243–4. The human lawgivers were not typically regarded as enslaving mankind, although Zaleucus (the lawgiver of the Italian Locri, *c.* 650 B.C.) was like Solon noted for his severity, and Zoroaster (reputed king of Bactria before the Trojan War) was regarded as a magician as much as a lawgiver. Greville so presents them in contrast to the divine lawgivers (cf. *Caelica*, lxxvii), and as authors of the laws 'which bynde mans birth to thrones' (312/1).

248/5. *the lawes of wounded majestie*: the tyranny of the successors of Augustus, expressed in the form of law—as st. 249–50 explain.

251/2. *intend*: fix attention on.

252/1. *that apple fatallie cast downe*: the apple of discord, the occasion of the contest of beauty between Juno, Venus, and Minerva, submitted to the judgement of the shepherd Paris. (Greville sees the dissension amongst them as freeing Jove of their interference.) I can find no authority for connecting Momus with this; Eris (Discordia) is normally represented as responsible.

253/3. Appius *brought from* Athens *rules of life*. Envoys were sent to Athens in 454 B.C. to copy the laws of Solon, and the new code was framed by the decemvirs, led by Appius Claudius (Livy, III. xxi–xxiv). Greville seems to attribute to this (ll. 5–6) the political eclipse, by the decemvirs, of plebs and patricians alike (Livy, III. xxxvi–xli).

263/5. Flavius *revealed this snaringe mysterie*: Gnaeus Flavius, who published a formulary of the substance and procedures of Roman civil law, previously kept secret by the pontiffs and patricians (Livy, IX. xlvi).

264/1–2. *the craftie preisthood . . . by their intercalation.* The control which the pontiffs exercised over the intercalary system allowed them to shorten or extend the year, abridging an official's term of office or— 'sellinge the tyme to publicans more deere'—increasing the revenue of the tax-gatherer. Cf. Censorinus, 'De Annis Romanis', in *De Die Natali.*

267/3. *The forraine accents . . . multiplienge dowbte.* It was usual for law reports at this time to be written in Old French (cf. W. S. Holdsworth, *History of English Law,* v. 356–63). There had been complaints against this jargon since the time of Henry VIII, when in *A Dialogue between Reginald Pole and Thomas Lupset* (ed. K. M. Burton, 1948), Thomas Starkey had advocated the displacement of 'this barbarous language' by laws 'written . . . in our mother tongue, or else put into the Latin' (p. 174—cf. pp. 117, 129).

268/1. *lawes ordered must be.* Arguments for the codification of the law, removing confusion and uncertainty (st. 269–70) and abbreviating processes (st. 273), also go back to the early sixteenth century (Starkey, op. cit., pp. 172–4). Bacon carried on the movement for reform, stating his proposals in *The Amendment of the Law* and in the *De Augmentis,* viii. 3.

270/2. *dowbtfull sences*: preferred to 'double sences' (*1670*), as recalling 'dowbtfull sence' in the stanza preceding.

272/1. *these lawless marts of place*: perhaps an allusion to the *paulette* (cf. 441/5–6, and note).

276/1–2. Lacedemon *suffered not . . . any advocate.* I can find no specific authority for this, though it may be inferential from the decree of Lycurgus that none of his laws should be written down.

276/4. *partie*: the accuser or the accused in the action, who had to present his case directly to the judge.

279/4. *lyve by rote*: by custom and routine merely (*O.E.D.* rote, *sb.*[2] 1 and 2) instead of by law. The sense of 'roster' or 'rotation' (*O.E.D.* rota, 2) does not seem to have arisen until the late seventeenth century. Greville could possibly be referring to the court called the rote or rota, the main tribunal for judging cases brought before the Holy See. The stanza is concerned with the remoteness of the people from the seat of justice ('charge of cares farr fetched right').

280/1. *those seaven sinews misticall.* The seven *parlements* of France date roughly from the fifteenth century: Toulouse had been created in 1443, Grenoble in 1453, Bordeaux in 1462, Dijon in 1477, Rouen in 1499 (as the Exchequer of Normandy, taking the style of *parlement* in 1515), and Aix in 1501. Greville's omission of Rennes (Brittany) may indicate that this part of the treatise was written early, for while the *parlement* of Rennes had been created in 1560, Henry IV did not gain control of Brittany until the treaty of Ponts de Cé in 1598. Rennes is numbered among the *parlements* of France in Pierre d'Avity's *The Estates, Empires, & Principallities of the World* (1614, tr. Grimestone, 1615). The functions of the *parlement* at this time are described by La Roche Flavin, *Treize livres des Parlemens de France* (1621).

**285/1.** *your othes of coronation*: i.e. the oath taken by the king not to alter the laws of the land.

**297/2.** *Shreeves us'd noe selfe art in their County dayes*. As head of the county, the sheriff was responsible for conducting the elections, and was able to manipulate the proceedings (cf. Sir John Neale, *The Eliza-bethan House of Commons*, 1949, pp. 77 ff.). As Sheriff of Warwickshire, Sir Thomas Lucy had tried to unseat Greville by illegally postponing the election in 1601. He was rebuked by the Privy Council for seeking to 'dyvert the choice and election from some person who both in respect of his bloud and quality, his sufficiency to do service to the State and estymacion in her Majesty's gratious opynion deserveth to be preferred before others' (*Acts of the Privy Council, 1601–1604*, xxxii. 248, cit. Neale, pp. 52–53).

**297/3.** *shrapes*: snares (for catching birds or game).

**304/5.** *fyve and thirtie trybes*: the tribes of the *comitia plebis tributa*, which met on the field of Mars to vote on such matters as the election of the lower magistrates (st. 305).

**306/5–6.** *a martiall mutinous election Of Emperors*: a feature of the decline of the *comitia tributa* under the empire; it eventually became a political nullity (cf. *Caelica*, xxx, ll. 1–8).

**309/3.** *Their auntient* Amphiction *Synodie*. The tribes of the Amphictionic League (supposedly founded by Amphiction, son of Deucalion) twice a year sent representatives to a *synedrion* to vote on issues of concern to all states.

**313/1.** *stylde*: distilled (*O.E.D.* still, *v.*²).

## Section VIII · *Of Nobilitie*

The principle of degree, reflected in the diverse natures of men as in the constellations in the heavens, furnishes power with more 'paternes of creating art'—and harmony imposed on discordant elements magnifies the single authority that rules over them all (322–31). The power of kings to confer nobility adds to their prestige, as the reward of merit gives worthy examples to the people (332–3). Yet the crown must not be impaired by these creations: the award of honorific titles (in the Roman fashion) is a prudent way of signalizing worth; no honours should be indiscriminately or frivolously granted (334–9). The nobility should neither gain an oppressive power over the people (as in Poland), nor usurp the king's authority: the disorders of 'peere-greatness' are plain in the history of England (the Barons' Wars), of Naples, and of Scotland (340–9). The role of the nobility is to keep the people in check, and reinforce the power of the king, who remains supreme (350–4). A state once brought to order must be guarded from 'devidinge humorous discontent', especially from the private feuds that allow the subject to exceed his place, and threaten turmoil to the realm (355–60).

**322/1.** Prometheus *had his fine clay drest.* There was a tradition that Prometheus created man out of earth and water (Apollodorus, I. vii. 1; Hyginus, *Fabulae,* cxliii) and, in doing so, added an ingredient drawn from each of the animals (Horace, *Odes,* I. xvi).

**326/1.** *that* Hercules *high priz'd*: that set a high value on Hercules (cf. 336/1 and *O.E.D.* prize, *v.*¹ 2).

**326–8.** The argument is that the places of honour among the stars are held by heroes deified for noble actions: Hercules is ranked above Cassiopea (mother of Andromeda, and so 'onlie canoniz'd For Perseus sake'); Castor and Pollux, the guardians of mariners, above Erigone (set among the stars for pity, after she had hanged herself for grief at her father's death); and Orion above Arcturus, who pursuing his mother (transformed into a she-bear) in the chase, was saved by Zeus from killing her by being placed in the sky as the constellation Bootes. Orion is an unsatisfactory example, as he was normally held to have been chased from the earth by a scorpion for trying to assault Diana.

**332/3.** *as the stampe gives bullion valuation*: bullion had to be taken to the mint for stamping (Greville extends the figure in *A Treatie of Humane Learning,* st. 124).

**336/3–4.** *titles . . . Costles, and yet of force to quicken speritts.* Scipio was given the title 'Africanus' for his conquest of Hannibal at Zama; his brother won the surname 'Asiaticus' for defeating Antiochus, king of Syria. The capture of Perseus of Macedonia gave Aemilius Paulus the title 'Macedonicus'; the consul Q. Caecilius Metellus was surnamed 'Numidicus' for prosecuting the war against Jugurtha.

**339.** Nero's fraternizing with musicians and actors, and the preferment he gave them, are described by Suetonius, ch. 20–23, 30.

**339/4.** *statuas*: obsolete form of 'statues' (cf. 479/5).

**342.** The abject state of the Polish peasantry is described in d'Avity's *The Estates, Empires, & Principallities of the World* (tr. Grimestone, 1615): 'The people are miserable, and held in great captivitie, for that great men when they passe through the countrie accompanied with many footmen, enter into Peasants houses, and take away what they please, yea and many times beat them cruelly' (3H6ʳ).

**343/4.** Poland *and* Germanie *are ballanc't so.* The limitations on the sovereignty of the king of Poland are described in Grimestone's *Estates* (1615):

> He may not undertake any war without the advice of the Senat, nor treat any alliance or accord, nor impose subsidies, or taxes, nor alienat any thing of his demeanes, nor do any thing of importance which belongs to the commonweale; for the nobilitie hath great authoritie in Diets and Councells. They chuse the king, and give him what authoritie they please: and the power of the nobilitie doth dailie increase. (3I3ʳ)

The weakness of imperial power in Germany ('scepters glorie is in both those lost') was due to the succession being elective instead of hereditary. The emperor, bound to confirm all the privileges and immunities of the subordinate princes as a condition of his election, could make no league or contract with foreign powers without their consent, nor undertake any war, nor summon the Diet or impose taxes (Grimestone, *Estates*, 1615, 3F3ᵛ–6ᵛ).

345. George Sandys gives a similar account of the instability of Naples, in *A Relation of a Journey begun An: Dom: 1610* (1615):

> The so many innovations that have happened to this unhappie kingdome, have proceeded partly from the overmuch power, and factions of the Nobilitie: but chiefly in that the election of their Kings depended on the Popes, who deposed and crowned according to their spleenes and affections. (Z3ʳ)

346/1–2. *this waving course . . . Under a greate Lorde wrought their servitude.* Cf. Sandys on the Spanish domination:

> But the *Spaniard* hath secured his estate by the prevention of these disturbances: taking all power and greatnesse, more then titular, from the Nobilitie: suppressing the popular, and indeed the whole country by the forraine souldiery garrisoned amongst them: who may obay perhaps with as much love, as gally-slaves obay those that have deprived them of their fortunes and libertie. (Z3ʳ)

348/1. *hereditarie sheriffes.* The practice was well developed by the sixteenth century of making Scottish feudal lords the hereditary sheriffs of the districts in which they held large possessions, as a method of maintaining order. See I. F. Grant, *The Social and Economic Development of Scotland before 1603* (1930), pp. 181–6.

354/4. *Phœbus . . . did his banishmente deserve.* Phoebus was banished from heaven for killing the Cyclops, by whose thunderbolts his son Aesculapius had been slain.

## Section IX · *Of Commerce*

The gods, joining nature with art, first taught handicrafts to men, and by making one clime needful of another, encouraged commerce and trade (361–72). Power should foster these activities, providing occupation for all—Venice shows the prosperity to be won by trade—for flourishing commerce adds strength to the crown (373–9). Princes must direct trade in the nation's interest, check the growth of unfair advantage (like that held by the Hanseatic League), and curb any abuse, fraud, or disproportion that threatens prosperity (380–9). A judicious policy would aim at 'buyeinge for toyes the wealth of other landes', taxing luxuries rather than food and cloth, and at so distributing trade that no one town becomes 'the gulf of all' (390–401). Princes should regulate trade with foreign countries, fix staples to draw foreign markets into their own ports, strengthen the navy (Holland shows the prosperity possible in a maritime state), and control exchange (402–18). Wealth, not poverty, will be found the best means of keeping the masses subordinate and content (419–25).

363/4. *veyne*: practice.

366/4. *theis movinge bridges*: Pallas was credited with building the first ship.

367/2. Castor *and* Pollux, *as two savinge lights*. Besides being the guardians of mariners, the Gemini were associated with the lights appearing at the masts of ships during storms (the phenomenon of St. Elmo's fire). According to *Batman uppon Bartholome* (1582), 'ther are two lights which do often settle on ships called *Castor* and *Pollux*, which if they ascend is a token of fair weather, and if they fal on the seas a shew of tempest' (Book VIII, ch. 12).

370/1–2. *slye* Mercurie . . . *his goulden tounge*: Mercury as the god of eloquence, and so author of the arts of persuasion.

383/1. *Thus did the* Hanses *sometimes tyrranise.* The Hanseatic League, which had held trading concessions in England from medieval times, found their privileges assailed under Elizabeth by the Merchant Adventurers, and were forced to evacuate the Steelyard in 1598. A contemporary account of the dispute ('theis Contracts wonne by stealth') is given in John Wheeler's *A Treatise of Commerce* (1601).

394/1–2. *the* Sabeans . . . *venting incense unto everie nation.* Sabaea was the city in Arabia Felix famous for its traffic in spices (cf. Diodorus Siculus, iii. 46–47).

394/4. Syria *gott* by Balsam *estimation.* Greville follows the habit at this time of taking Syria to include Palestine. Balsam from Gilead and the Jordan valley near Jericho was a valuable trading commodity (Diodorus Siculus, ii. 48), and the Jordan plantations later became a lucrative source of Roman imperial revenue—'wealth kepte for him, that their state overthrewe' (394/6). Cf. *The excellent and pleasant worke* of Julius Solinus Polyhistor (tr. Golding, 1587), ch. xlvii.

395/1–2. *the* Hollander . . . *toyes for the vanitie of us.* The 'toyes' from the Low Countries were the despair of contemporaries anxious about the import of luxury goods. The analysis of the traffic in T. S. Willan's *Studies in Elizabethan Foreign Trade* (Manchester, 1959) shows the imports to include brushes, combs, dolls, shoe buckles, tennis balls, candlesticks, gloves, and purses. See also the list in Wheeler's *Treatise of Commerce* (1601), E2$^v$.

395/5. *synne*: probably an alternative spelling of 'seen' ('standerd' being used in the sense of 'flag', as at 407/3); but to adopt the *1670* spelling would be to suppress the possibility that 'sin' might conceivably be intended. In *W* 'synne' is a consistent spelling of 'sin', and is nowhere used as an equivalent of 'seen'.

397/4. *any towne the gulf of all be made*: the provincial ports constantly complained (cf. st. 401) that London engrossed all the trade.

399/1. *Admitt againe the* Holland *industrie*: i.e. 'Granting that Holland taxes victual, yet this is no ground . . .' (the same construction is used in the *Life*, p. 106). Fynes Moryson complained of the 'huge impositions' in his *Itinerary* (ed. MacLehose, 1907–8), iv. 61.

402/1–2. Power must fix and marshal foreign commerce with her own.

402/6. *Which double customes bringe*: the duty on the cargo, and the levy on the bottom.

403/1. *Noe monopolies suffred in the lande*: not presumably the monopolies granted to companies to the trade of a given region (see note following), but patents from the crown giving individuals the exclusive rights to deal in certain commodities. Greville's own accounts for 1609 mention income from a 'patent of wines' (*Hist. MSS. Earl Cowper*, i. 69–70).

403/2. *All interlopinge practises withstood.* An interloper infringed the monopoly of a trading company by trading independently in the area covered by its privileges (cf. 'Interlopers and the Staple', in T. S. Willan's *Studies in Elizabethan Foreign Trade*). Greville sat on a Privy Council Committee on interloping in 1617.

406/2–3. *that staple wealth Of the* Moscovian *Empire*. Although the Russia Company had been incorporated in 1555, and its monopoly confirmed by Elizabeth in 1566, it did not gain exclusive control of the Russian trade, or fix a staple in England. The traffic must have languished in the early seventeenth century, from the testimony of Robert Kayll in *The Trades Increase* (1615):

I have not named *Muscovie*, because we have in a manner lost that trade, the troubles of that kingdome, and our desire of security having deprived us thereof . . . there repairing not thither above two shippes English in stead of seventeene of great burden for the company formerly. (B2$^{r-v}$).

410/1. *moving*: 'wavinge' (*W*) is possible, but unlikely in the face of Greville's habit of using it pejoratively (cf. 113/2, 346/1, 618/6). A 'safe, yet wavinge [unstable] policie' would to him be a contradiction in terms.

410/4–6. The defeat of the Persian fleet at Salamis (480 B.C.) led Xerxes to retreat from the invasion of Greece; the Turkish fleet was defeated by the forces of the Holy League at Lepanto in 1571.

414–16. These stanzas reflect the account of Netherlands commerce in the *Life*, pp. 142–3, where Greville purports to be giving Sidney's views. The prominence of the Dutch in the carrying trade at the turn of the century is attested by L. R. Miller, 'New Evidence on the Shipping and Imports of London, 1601–1602', *Quarterly Journal of Economics*, xli (1926–7), 740–60.

417/2. *that much us'd unknowne mysterie*: the confused Elizabethan theories of exchange are analysed by Raymond de Roover in *Gresham on Foreign Exchange* (Cambridge, Mass., 1949).

420/2. The readings 'forrain straynes of tyrannie' (*1670*) and 'over straynes' (*W*) suggest a genuine discrepancy between the two texts. As neither could be explained as a copyist's error, and as there could be no motive for any interposing hand to change 'forrain' to 'over' or vice versa, it would appear that Greville wrote 'over' on one occasion and 'forrain' on another. Either yields good sense, but 'forrain' is more consonant with the warnings against 'vitious formes of forraine tyrranie' (458/6) that Greville makes throughout the treatise (cf. 214, 307–8, 441).

425/5. *mutine*: obsolete form of 'mutiny' (vb.) (cf. 497/6).

## Section X · *Of Croune Revenue*

The variety of natural resources in the world gives each country native riches, which kings should exploit by industry and art (426–32): a prudent administration may then make government secure (433–6). The crown should itself rely on the traditional income from its estates and privileges, and on the parliamentary subsidy: kings must eschew such 'bleedinge taxes' as are levied in France, which invite disorder (437–45), and such straining of prerogatives and such deceptions as were practised in ancient Rome (446–50). Coin is better squandered at home than in sending agents to gather intelligence abroad, in imitation of the Papal practice (451–60). In expenditure kings should not exceed their means, giving priority to works that 'multiplie obedience, and regarde' (461–6).

426/1. *The antient sages*: Thales and his successors, Anaximander and Anaximenes, who held that the basis of the universe was some single eternal and imperishable substance (as they considered water or air to be) undergoing modifications. See the account of Diogenes Laertius, *Lives of Eminent Philosophers*.

427/6. *Pales*: goddess of pastures and sheepfolds. *Pomona*: goddess of gardens and orchards.

430/1–2. France . . . *her late fowrth Henries policie*. As Henry IV was assassinated in 1610, this is one of the less equivocal indications of the date of the treatise. Greville qualifies this account of the state of France during Henry's reign in st. 441.

432/3. Phœbus *throne*: the elaborately decorated throne of Apollo at Amyclae, described by Pausanias (III. xviii. 9–16).

436/5. *high rais'd* Athens, *and* Pireum *port*. The difference in 'manners' and 'lawes' between Athens and the Piraeus would be due to the larger population of 'metics' in the port. These were aliens, generally of the artisan or mercantile class, who were allowed the right of residence, but denied the full privileges of citizens. It also seems to have been a commonplace of classical political theory to regard maritime communities as a special case (Cicero, *De Re Publica*, ii. 3–5).

441/2. *Crowne demeasne*: the king's revenue from his hereditary privileges and estates (as described in st. 437).

441/3. *bleedinge taxes*: strongly resented imposts like the *taille* (based on the value of the peasant's land and dwelling) and the *gabelle* (an arbitrary tax on salt).

441/5. *forcing them to sell tribunall seates*: a practice (the *paulette*) introduced by Henry IV in 1604, when the royal domains were heavily pledged and the revenues alienated to meet the expense of his wars. For the payment of an annual sum judges were confirmed in the ownership of their offices and had the right to sell and bequeath them.

442. Cf. the account of Louis XI in *An Epitome of All the Lives of the Kings of France* (tr. R. B. in 1639, from an original attributed to Philip de Comines): 'The Realme of *France* he said was a meddow which he did cut every yeere, and as often as he listed' (T2ʳ).

443/5. *as, but myters, few by stewes doe gett*. One of the charges made by Protestant controversialists against the Church at Rome was that it tolerated 'baudery', receiving income from taxing harlots (cf. Bishop Jewel's *Apologie*, 1562, sig. G1ʳ, and Thomas Harding's *Confutation*, 1565, sig, 2R4ᵛ–2S3ʳ). In his *Anatomie of Abuses* (in the second of the two editions of 1583) Philip Stubbes made the same complaint of the Church in England. He deplored the practice of allowing offenders to exculpate themselves by paying fines: 'Is not this a maintenance of the Stewes? . . . not onely a maintenaunce, but also a stirring of them up to commit whoredome, when for a little money they may be discharged of all gilte' (H6ʳ ᵛ).

443/6. *who, but* Negars, *tax on breathing sett*. I cannot arrive at a satisfactory explanation of this. As 'Negar' is a variant spelling of 'Negro', it may refer to the tribute paid to their rulers by African tribes. In Leo Africanus' *A Geographical Historie of Africa* (tr. John Pory, 1600), some of the tribes are described as 'continually burthened with grievous exactions, so that they have scarce any thing remaining to live upon' (2C1ᵛ). But as Greville is giving instances of taxes levied by despotic kings, *Negars* may be intended as a plural of *Negus*, the title of the king of Ethiopia, and a byword for absolutism in the Renaissance (cf. *The French Academie*, 1586, 2S4ᵛ). The despotism of the Negus, and the tribute exacted from his subjects, are described in *Purchas his Pilgrims* (vii. 49–50 in the Hakluyt Society text) as part of the narrative of Alvarez.

444/4. *the dyinge farmer*. The story of the farmer's children who dug his land for the treasure buried there, and found their reward instead in the crops that followed, is fable xvii of Book V of Caxton's *Aesop* (1484). Other allusions by Greville to Aesop's fables occur in st. 664, in *Caelica*, xxi, xxxvii, lxxviii, and *Fame and Honour*, st. 65.

446/2. *prise*: estimate, reckon (*O.E.D.* prise, *v.*¹ 1).

446/5–6. Infancy is the state of being under guardianship and without full control of one's own property. Kings should not multiply their prerogatives to the prejudice of their subjects who gave them only some privileges, intending to keep others for themselves.

448/5. Caligula . . . *by quirckes of law*: Caligula's habits of declaring wills void in order to make himself the beneficiary, and of abusing the law to enrich himself from fines (Suetonius, ch. 38).

449/3. *When they with* Carthage *did capitulate*. When the Carthaginians sought terms of surrender in 149 B.C., the Senate, on condition that its commands were obeyed, 'granted them freedom and their laws, besides their whole territory and all other possessions both public and private' (Polybius, xxxvi. 4–6). With this assurance the Carthaginians yielded 300 hostages, and their arms and engines of war. When they were next ordered to leave Carthage, to live under their own laws at a place of their choosing 10 miles from the coast, it became apparent that the ambiguous terms of surrender ('freedom and their laws') did not preserve the inviolability of the city. 'We considered *you* to be Carthage,' they were told, 'not the ground where you live' (Appian, *Roman History*, VIII. xii). The city was then razed to the ground.

455/2. *that longe breath'd incrochinge Courte of* Rome: cf. the account of 'that creeping Monarchie of *Rome*', and her 'Arch-instruments the Jesuits', in the *Life*, pp. 81–82.

## Section XI · *Of Peace*

Peace is 'the most perfect state of governemente', giving monarchs scope for large enterprises: building bridges, cleansing harbours (not undertaking any work of vanity), and founding schools (467–74)—in this last imitating the Romans, who honoured Mars and the Muses equally (475–83). All sciences should be framed not to contemplation, but to use: former ages flourished through their men of 'actyve worth', who also proved the best chroniclers of their deeds (484–90). From this foundation kings will strive to unite in the throne all aspects of government and all

degrees of men (prevailing not 'by transcendencie' but 'by applause'),
and consolidate this union by settling 'all wandringe titles of succession'
(491–8). Such a government might proceed to the planting of colonies
in foreign parts, mindful of how Rome established order wherever her
armies conquered, until the whole world was 'lincked with her in
traffick, league, and law' (499–506). Modern princes err in directing
their colonial ventures to harassing and despoiling their enemies
(507–10), and in seeking (like the Turk) rather to impose a tyrannical
rule on subject provinces than to win their loyalty by good government
(511–16). Power should be provident and ubiquitous (not absolute and
remote in the Turkish fashion), aimed at establishing a peace where
'people pleasd, Kinges might with pleasure raigne' (517–21).

470/1. *the clensinge of the* Egyptian *sluces*: the enterprise of clearing the
silt from the canals into which the Nile overflowed, to increase the
supply of grain from the province (Suetonius, ch. 18).

471/4. *Through* Athos *who yet sailes.* The canal which Xerxes cut across
the promontory of Mt. Athos, when invading Greece in 483–481 B.C.,
shows the vanity of works designed to alter the natural order of things.

471/5. *Is* Corinths Isthmus *from the mayne land torne?* Nero tried
unsuccessfully to cut across the isthmus of Corinth and join the two
seas.

472/4. *over* Ister Trajans *bridge did goe.* Trajan's bridge over the
Danube (described in detail by Dio Cassius, lxviii. 13) is an instance
of 'Natures producements' made more fruitful by 'arte'.

472/5–6. Amasis *and* Cheops . . . *in their useless* Pyramids. Although
Amasis is noted as a builder of pyramids in Diodorus Siculus (i. 64. 4),
the irony of his burial was rather that his corpse was later disinterred
and insulted by Cambyses (Herodotus, iii. 10, 16).

474/2–3. Lacedemon . . . *pedagogies meete.* The compulsory state education in Sparta was closer to military training, and Sparta was notorious
rather for its disdain of learning. Cf. Greville's *Treatie*, st. 42:

> *Learning* hath found distaste
> In Governments, of great, and glorious fame;
> In *Lacedemon* scorned, and disgrac'd,
> As idle, vaine, effeminate, and lame.

477/5. Hercules *for* . . . *defence*: the Roman worship of Hercules gave
him, like Apollo (st. 478), the function of protector of the Muses.

479/3. *that of* Fulvius *well deserv'd the prise.* M. Fulvius Nobilior, as
consul in 189 B.C., brought home statues and paintings from his conquest of Aetolia.

489/1. *the birth*: the *W* reading 'birth right' hardly fits the context.
The epoch recalled in st. 486–8, when those who performed heroic
deeds were also those who recorded them, cannot be described as

anyone's 'birth right'. Having described those times, Greville then says summarily

> This was the forme, the birth, the education
> And art of that age ...

using 'birth' and 'education' in a natural sequence.

492/1. *attone*: bring into concord, unite in harmony.

492/6. *Which union is all els but combination*. 'Combination' (the state described in st. 493) is used with an implication common at this time (*O.E.D.*, sense 4), as applying to a league formed for wrongful and self-seeking purposes (cf. 557/2, *Caelica*, cix, l. 4, or the *Life*, p. 107).

496/2. *where men prescribe*: cf. 173/2, and note.

496/3. The order of corrections here is hard to discern. Apparently the scribe in *W* first wrote 'commonly Kinges', then struck out 'ly Kinges' and wrote 'likinge' above it. The reading 'things' (in the hand of scribe *d*) was then sandwiched in between 'likinge' and the original reading, and then crossed out.

504. The omitted line is marked by a gap in *W* and by dashes in *1670*.

511/5–6. *that* Sultans *worde*. Richard Knolles, in *The Generall Historie of the Turkes* (1603), records as a common saying: 'That wheresoever the Grand signior his horse setteth his foot, the grass will there no more grow: meaning, the destruction that their great armies bring in all places where they come' (5F2ᵛ).

512/1–2. *the holie prophet spake . . . of fowre monarchies*. Cf. Daniel vii. 17–23. In John Sleidan's *A briefe Chronicle of the foure principall Empyres* (tr. Stephen Wythers, 1563), the vision is interpreted as referring to the empires of Assyria (Babylon), Persia, Greece (under Alexander), and Rome (2C4ᵛ–2D1ʳ). These four kingdoms Greville approves of, on the dubious ground that they did not enslave the peoples they conquered: the contrast he has in mind (cf. Sleidan, 2D1ʳ) is the empire of the Turk. Other references to the four monarchies occur in *Mustapha*, I. i. 20, and *A Treatie of Warres*, st. 32.

## Section XII · *Of Warr*

While war exists in the world as a scourge for man's depravity it is also necessary to kings for protection, and for the enforcement of their legal claims (522–6): a known aversion to war may encourage an aggressor (527–31). Princes must raise ordnance and erect fortifications; arm and train their troops in time of peace (imitating Luctatius rather than Roderic the Goth); encourage 'neighbour Princes' to identify our interests with their own (532–42)—and remain implacably opposed to the power of Rome in all its guises (543–65). Since 'warr and Crownes consist by reputation', kings must be ready to venture in foreign parts (566–70); war can cure other diseases in the state (571–3). Such martial princes must reform discipline, and keep a strong navy—the main advantage held by the Christians over the Turks—to spread their power abroad (574–9).

529/2. *in eight hundred yeeres, Not three tymes shut*: the interval between Numa and Augustus, when the temple of Janus was closed only twice (Livy, I. xix), as an indication that the Romans were at peace.

529/4–6. Mars . . . *to his banners did one consull fitt . . . in Justice made the other sitt.* It was the practice in the early years of the consulate for one consul to remain in Rome while the other went to the wars (Livy, III. iv. 7, xxii. 3–4; VII. xxxviii. 8–9).

533/1–2. *those old bounds Of* Rome. Augustus had secured the frontiers of the empire by stationing the legions there, instead of sending them into winter quarters. Disbanding the legions, Constantine sought to stabilize the frontiers by entrusting the Rhine to the Franks, the Danube to the Goths, and the Euphrates to the Armenians, giving lands to them—a policy censured by earlier writers as opening the gates to the barbarian invasions (cf. the chapter 'Of Peace, and of Warre' in *The French Academie*, 1586, 3C1$^r$).

534/1. *Such bulwarckes modernelie have held owt* Spaigne. In the light of Greville's discussion of the Spanish menace in the *Life*, this would refer to the successful military resistance made by Protestant leaders in the Netherlands and France, in wars Elizabeth had supported.

534/6. *fyve tymes byn assaild*: by the Romans, Saxons, Danes, Normans, and Spaniards.

536/1–3. Luctatius . . . *did on the land . . . teach his seamen.* The naval victory by which C. Luctatius Catulus put an end to the First Punic War was made possible by the rigorous training given his sailors; the Carthaginian crews were by contrast raw and awkward.

536/5. *Philopemen*: the general of the Achaean League who owed much of his military success to army reforms. During the later Roman ascendancy he used his diplomacy to gain advantages for the Achaeans without resort to war.

537/1. Roderigo *that unluckie Kinge*: the last of the Visigoth kings of Spain, overcome by the Muslims in A.D. 711. In Curio's *Notable Historie of the Saracens* (tr. Thomas Newton, 1575), his defeat (538/1–2) is attributed partly to the circumstance that the Spanish forces were 'withoute harnysse armour or habilimentes meete for the warres: because *Vitiza, Roderike* his Predecessour, a most cruell and bloudie Tyraunt, had caused all weapons to be taken away from the people and to bee broken' (K3$^v$). Tarif had led the expedition of 710, preliminary to this final Saracen attack.

540/3. *Thus helde they upp the* Etolians *reputation*: through their hostility to Macedonia the Aetolians became Rome's first allies within Greece; they were conquered and made subject allies in 189 B.C.

540/4–5. Asia *overthrowe, By frendinge* Eumenes: the Roman alliance with Eumenes II, king of Pergamus, led his grandson to make the Romans heirs to his kingdom in 133 B.C.: the resulting dispute was the occasion of the Roman conquest of much of Asia Minor.

540/5. Affrick *is made theirs*: Rome's power in Africa was extended through Massinissa, the Numidian king, who befriended her against Carthage. He bequeathed his kingdom to the care of Scipio Aemilianus, who was to divide it among Massinissa's heirs.

543/2. *that cheife division.* This long excursus (543–65), with its repeated injunctions against any slackening of opposition to Rome, is one of several passages in the treatise that read like a criticism of the policies of James—though this can be no more than conjecture.

543/3. *peecinge*: mending or joining (*O.E.D.* piece, *v.* 1 and 2).

543/4. *any false gloss of misprision.* The *O.E.D.* gives no sense of 'glass' (the *W* reading) of particular force in this context. The sense required seems to be gloss, *sb.*[1] ('Often used in a sinister sense: A sophistical or disingenuous interpretation') or *sb.*[2] 1b ('a deceptive appearance, fair semblance, plausible pretext').

546/2. *slake*: decrease in intensity, abate—one of the senses of 'slake' in which it has been replaced by 'slack' (*1670*).

549/1. *fallace*: obsolete form of 'fallacy'.

560/6. *Prisinge for* Peeters *pence, heav'ne, purgatorie, hell.* 'Prisinge' is probably used in the sense of 'reckoning the value of' (*O.E.D.* prize, *v.*[1], 1 and 2): '*Peeters* pence' was the tax levied, before the Reformation, on each householder with land of a certain value, as tribute to the Holy See. 'Prisinge' in the sense of 'seizing' (prize, *v.*[2]) would also fit the context, though this is not so typical of Greville's use of the word (cf. 326/1, 336/1, 446/2).

570/1. *theis mutuall succors*: possibly an allusion to the English practice of soldiering in the Low Countries, in aid of the Protestant cause (cf. 535/3–6).

### Section XIII · *The Excellencie of Monarchie, Compared with Aristocratie*

Though it is inherent in man to be discontented with his state, the possible alternatives to monarchy are apt to prove worse (580–4). The imperfection of aristocracy, the rule of 'manie heads', is apparent from the history of Rome: kings were banished in favour of consuls, then came the decemvirs, next the tribunes, then the anarchy of the triumvirate—until monarchy was restored by the emperors (585–93). Where authority is distributed, merit is uncertain of its reward, justice is imperilled, faction and dissension are promoted—weakening the state in war (594–600). Worthy men are liable to ostracism, through the jealousy or suspicion of their fellows, and the diffusion of power causes disorder and instability (601–7). From such conditions aristocratic governments tend to revert to the single rule again—a sufficient proof of their inadequacy (608–9).

582/1. *Dolefull* Alcyon. Greville argues that by nesting on the seashore to escape 'the fraudes of men, and beasts', Alcyon (who had been transformed into a kingfisher after the drowning of her husband Ceyx) exposed herself to hazards even greater. I have not found any precedent for this view of the fable, though Ovid's embellished account (*Met.* xi. 415–43) stresses Alcyon's fearfulness; most authorities emphasize rather that the seas subside and the winds abate for seven days in winter while she hatches her young (Hyginus, *Fabulae*, lxv; Lucian, *Halcyon*; Ovid, *Met.* xi. 744–8).

587/3–4. *the sonns iniquitie . . . in the aged guiltless fathers fate*: Tarquinius Superbus was expelled from Rome for the crime of his son Sextus against Lucrece.

588/1. *the state of tenne*: the decemvirate, during which Appius Claudius acquired such power; he was overthrown after his attempt to dishonour Virginia (Livy, III. xxxiii, lvi–lvii).

588/6. *her Martiall Tribunes*: instituted in 444 B.C. (Livy, IV. vii).

589/5. *in five yeeres they Governors had none*. The triumvirate of Octavius, Lepidus, and Antony ('the factiouse Governement of three', st. 590) was formed to administer the Republic for five years. This is recorded in Livy, *lib. 120* (of which only the summary survives), not *lib. 2* (as in *W* and *1670*).

591/2–3. *enforce a* Cæsar . . . *to breake his faith*. The restoration of the monarchy by Augustus was a breach of faith on his part, but (in Greville's view) one forced upon him by the disorders of the state; Velleius Paterculus is referred to as an encomiast of Augustus and of the benefits of his rule (*Roman History*, Book II).

592/1–5. The sense appears to be: After Tarquin, Rome fell into a demagogy by which the people, set on fire like straws, by confusion (which waits to devour such states) raised up the monarchy again.

592/6. *well organ'd to be fortunate*: so fashioned or disposed as to deserve good fortune. This reflects Greville's notion (44/5–6) that chance must favour the properly constituted state.

593/1. *what were* Codrus *merits*. Codrus was king of Athens at the time of the Dorian invasion, when the oracle had predicted victory for the Dorians, provided the Athenian king did not lose his life. Disguising himself as a beggar, Codrus entered the enemy camp, and was slain: on the discovery of his identity, the Dorians relinquished the invasion (Justinus, *Histories*, Book II). The Athenians then supposedly abandoned the institution of kingship, convinced that so selfless a ruler could not be replaced.

599/1–2. *Under three leaders . . . at* Samos. Timotheus, Iphicrates, and Chares (given as 'Charo' by Greville) were joint commanders of the Athenian fleet sent to Samos in the Social War of 357–355 B.C. When Timotheus and Iphicrates anchored to avoid a storm, Chares ventured alone and was badly defeated.

*Æmil. Probus in Vita Timothei*: the *Vita Timothei* is ch. xiii of *De Excelentibus Ducibus Exterarum Gentium*, the largest surviving portion of the *De Viris Illustribus* of Cornelius Nepos, formerly attributed (as by Greville) to Aemilius Probus.

599/3–6. *As she before at* Siracuse *did stayne Her glorie . . .* The Athenian forces under the multiple leadership of Alcibiades (recalled to Athens before the fighting), Nicias, and Demosthenes had been crushingly defeated at Syracuse in 413 B.C.

*Justin li: 4⁰*: the widely read abridgement of the histories of Trogus Pompeius, made by Marcus Justinus (tr. Golding, 1570).

600/1. *the* Athenian *Orator*: Isocrates praises monarchy in *Nicocles*, 14–26.

600/5. Cannas *many headed flight*: the dissension of the consuls Terentius Varro and Paulus Aemilius contributed to the Roman defeat at Cannae (Livy, XXII. xl–xli).

602/4. *Aristides*: Aristides 'the Just', ostracized in 483–482 B.C.; he figures in a similar list of the victims of fickleness and ingratitude (with Themistocles, Scipio, and Camillus) in *Fame and Honour*, st. 46.

602/5. *him that conquered* Marathon: Miltiades, accused and brought to trial by Xantippus in 493 B.C., and subsequently condemned.

602/6. *him who* Xerxes *host had overthrowne*: Themistocles, who was ostracized and retired to Argos in *c.* 470 B.C.

603/3. *How little she thought to the* Scipios *due*: Scipio Africanus, after his services to the state, retired from Rome to avoid the malevolence of his enemies; Scipio Asiaticus was accused and fined on a charge of appropriating funds from Antiochus; Africanus the Younger, when he died in 129 B.C., was thought to have been assassinated by his political enemies.

603/4. *from* Camillus *how soone she did swerve.* Plutarch's *Vita Camilli* (to which Greville refers in st. 632) develops the tradition that after his victory at Veii, Camillus was banished over the issue of the 'tenth of the spoils', as a victim of the malice of those he had served.

607/5–6. Athens . . . *ever changinge her* Archontes: at first three in number, then nine, the archons were the supreme magistrates in Athens. Some conception of the vicissitudes of the system may be gathered from Aristotle's account in *The Athenian Constitution*.

### Section XIV · *The Excellencie of Monarchie Compared with Democratie*

Under democracy the 'blinde multitude' is master, offering scope to the ill-disposed, debasing all values to serve 'idle liberties applause' (610–13). That the greatness of Rome or Athens sprang from this system could not be maintained: the growth of Rome during the Republic came from imitating the martial example of the Tarquins, and from varying popular sovereignty by the rule of consuls and Senate (614–20). The people themselves (under the tribunes) squandered Rome's patrimony, and brought dishonour by their spoliation of Cyprus and their perfidy to Carthage (621–6). The empire's final overthrow was due not to the weakness of the monarchy, but to *vicissitudo rerum*: the rule of kings and emperors, having preserved Rome for a far longer span than her democracy, succumbed at last to the barbarian hordes that were the doom of all empires—and that republican Rome would have been less capable of withstanding (627–32). Even in the decay caused by the 'tumultuouse election' of emperors and by the exactions to which they were forced, Rome boasted men of greater worth than her democratic ages could afford (633–8): in democracy there is neither order nor permanence (639–40).

621/5. *their* Agrarian *lawes*: the laws proposed by the tribune P. Servilius Rullus in 64 B.C., giving the decemvirs power to sell certain public lands. Cicero's three orations *De Lege Agraria* attacked the influence of the decemvirs and deplored the dispersal of public property.

622–3. *the Kinge of* Cyprus *wealth*: in 59 B.C., at the urging of Publius Clodius, a tribune of the people, the Romans confiscated the property of King Ptolemy of Cyprus. The marginal note refers to the account in the *Epitome* of Florus, III. ix (I. xliv in modern editions).

624/2–5. *the* Mamertines . . . *Whence the first* Punick *quarrell did proceed*. The 'offence' of the Mamertines against Rome had been their act of treachery in taking Messana. When the Carthaginians made war and occupied the city, however, Rome found it expedient to give assistance to the Mamertines, and so provoked the First Punic War (Polybius, I. x–xi). The Roman Senate, declining to sanction this assistance, was overruled by the plebs (st. 625–6).

628. *245 yeeres*: the duration of the reign of the kings (to the expulsion of Tarquin). The 'thousand and seaven hundred yeeres' for which monarchy preserved Rome is the sum of the reign of the kings and the reign of the emperors (omitting the republican period).

632/1. *at* Allia *of olde*: the Roman humiliation at Allia is given as an instance of the vulnerability of democratic Rome to barbarian inroads. As the defeat was blamed by Livy (v. xxxvii–xxxviii) on the mismanagement of the tribunes, 'the peoples owne faults shak't their state', whereas the fall of the empire is ascribed to 'fate'.

632/3. Spartacus *the bolde*: the gladiator who in 73 B.C. collected an army of escaped slaves and led marauding expeditions in southern Italy (Florus, II. viii).

634/1–2. *tumultuouse election of* Cæsars: part of the decline of the *comitia tributa* (cf. 304–6, and note).

635/1. *lacke of Crowne demaine*: see st. 441, and note.

636/7. *Felicior Augusto, melior Trajano*: the proverb is recorded in the chapter on Trajan in the *De Gestis Romanorum* of Eutropius, and repeated in the *Historia Augusta* (Venice, 1490, P4$^r$).

637/5. Julian *in learninge*: the emperor Julian was noted for his study and admiration of the Greek philosophers. The marginal note *Julian in Cæs[aribus]* (presumably the *Caesares*, where Julian holds the emperors up to ridicule) is puzzling, and it is omitted in 1670. It might possibly be read as *Julian in Cæs: 6*—a reference I cannot explain.

639/1–2. *if* Chilo *trulie calld those States The best*: in Plutarch's 'Septem Sapientium Convivium' Chilon asserts that 'the best government is that which gives greatest heed to the laws and least to those who talk about them' (*Moralia*, ii. 397). The currency of his precept is shown by its appearance in *The French Academie* (1586), 2Q4$^r$.

Section XV · *The Excellencie of Monarchie Compared with Aristocratie and Democratie Joyntlie*

No democratic or aristocratic state has long endured—except by alteration from itself (641–4). Rulers cannot properly be chosen by lot or suffrage; where (in monarchies) a good prince is hard to find, it will be harder (under the other systems) to find the number of rulers required; states so constituted tend to revert to monarchy, as to the natural order (645–53). Deviations from this order spring from the 'unmeasured affection' of power to bind, and people to be free: the consequence is anarchy, as when reason is deposed by will (654–60). Monarchy remains the only safeguard against disorder (661–4).

646/3. *The old* Comitia: see st. 304–6, 634, and notes.

646/3–4. *the new erect* Conclave *of* Rome: Greville frequently refers to the conclave (the assembly of the cardinals at Rome) in the *Life* as being manipulated by Spain, through various cardinals in her pay (pp. 82–83, 85–86).

664/3. Æsops *wife*: *Uxor contraria*, so perverse that when she fell into the river the master commanded the servants to look for her not downstream, but against the current. Not included in Caxton's *Aesop*, the fable is no. 682 in B. E. Perry's *Aesopica* (Urbana, Illinois, 1952).

### A TREATISE OF RELIGION

The oppression of mankind, and the 'diverse worships' that afflict them, are tokens of the fall: powerless to help himself, man can be restored only by grace (1–4). All men have some sense of God, and feel impelled to seek him: hence 'diverse Nations' are found honouring truth and goodness, and observing duties to kindred (5–11). Though these impressions are firmly fixed in man's understanding and conscience, they are kept from fulfilment by the 'naturall corruption' in his powers. To evade the reproach of conscience, men then seek God and religion from without, searching the wit and the affections for the religions imaged there (12–16). The religion fashioned from the affections is superstition, and from the 'wittie passions' a religion of craft, hypocrisy, and 'politique pretense'. Superstition—appealing to 'weake soules', and strengthened by 'our Magicke, and our Starr-Divines'—is expressed in fear of natural phenomena (sea, sky, darkness) which seem to man to threaten punishment—an indication of his sense of guilt (17–23). The other false cult ('meere hypocrisie') is a means of enslaving men and an instrument of political ambition—as with Rome, or with those among ourselves who 'serve ambitiouse Princes use', causing division and upheaval (24–33).

Yet there remains a true religion on earth, not to be won by human effort (like the ideal of the stoic, 36–39), but given through supernatural grace (34–42). Through grace comes complete regeneration, restoring man to his true relationship with God and with all estates, and recovering the purity of his first creation (43–50). As in the world perfection is not possible, we must regard life as a pilgrimage, persevering in faith (51–55). For man must not 'censure God by his owne imperfection', trusting the letter rather than the spirit: God moves ineluctably to conquer sin and work the miracle of regeneration (56–61). The outward Church knows his power, but not his grace: the members of his 'Church invisible' devote themselves to prayer and obedience, submit to the oppression of princes, and look compassionately on 'Booke-learninge' and 'Schoole Divinitie' (62–67).

The 'preists of chance and gaine' profess God, but in their works do not obey him: the nature of true faith is that it issues in obedience (68–72). Christ's mediacy is still needed, to raise in man God's image there decayed, and redeem him from Adam's sin: man unaided by God (as scripture shows, paradoxically) cannot fulfil even the law God himself has given him. In humility we must await our regeneration, knowing that 'grace, not merit, with the Lawe makes even' (73–79).

Since Adam's fall, good and evil (like the Church invisible and the outward Church) have shared the world—Abel seeking God alone, Cain desiring more; the Israelites first prevailing over the Gentiles, then for their idolatry being delivered into their power—until the law could be satisfied only by the coming of Christ, and his death. By such 'defection from obedience' the false sects have grown (80–89).

How then are the values of the world to be regarded? How thrones stand with heaven must be left to those competent to judge; the Church hierarchy found its condemnation when the person of Christ replaced the 'high preisthode' of the 'spirit-falne *Jewe*'; the effort to 'rayse a newe Church nowe to equall *Rome*' is likewise vain (90–94).

For the elect, the Church invisible, 'all rests in the hart'. They make faith their key and sceptre, and love their ambition, persevering with faith in the redeeming power of Christ (95–105). Tried by these standards, in turn power, arts, laws, the outward Church, and 'fleshe in generall' are exposed in their pretension and inadequacy (106–10)— only the small company of the elect remain (111–14).

8/3. *Our free remorses*: i.e. the fits of remorse (*O.E.D.* remorse, *sb.* 2b) we cannot avoid when we do ill, and the freedom of heart we feel when we do well, alike prove 'service due to one Omnipotence'.

11/1. *no positive, made lawes*: the distinction between 'positive' (formally imposed) law and 'natural' law was common in Renaissance political theory. Cf. John Poynet, *A Shorte Treatise of politike power* (1556), C2ʳ–C7ᵛ, and the distinction of 'civil' (i.e. positive) laws from the laws of God and the laws of nature in Bodin's *Six Bookes of a Commonweale* (tr. Knolles, 1606), I. viii.

14/3. *sentence of record*: a legal expression for evidence accepted as not open to dispute (*O.E.D.* record, *sb.* 1).

17/6. *buying shadowes with the soules expence*. The sense demands the reading of *1670* ('buying') rather than of *W* ('bindinge'). As in the stanza following the scribe has corrected 'undertakes' to 'underrates' in the MS., 'bindinge' is probably a similar error that was not picked up.

18/1–3. *Gods true Religion . . . To bottomlesse hypocrisie translate*. The second of the two false religions Greville variously describes as 'hypocrisie', the 'worlds Religion', a cult of 'craft' and 'politique pretense'. These are the terms he uses to denote religion in its political guise— above all the Church of Rome, with the armies of Spain as its instrument. The false religion of 'hypocrisie' acquires more of the attributes of Rome ('inquisition', 'false heades of holie mother see') as his account of it proceeds (st. 25–29).

36/1. *Not heathen vertue*: a repudiation of the stoic ideal on which Greville had patterned his hero in *Mustapha*, and which he himself had commended in *A Letter to an Honorable Lady*. *Mens adepta* is used here, as in the *Letter*, to refer to the state of stoic resolution achieved. It is seen now, however, as no more than 'passion with her counterpassion peas'd' (38/1–2), like a mask over sin.

36/6. *humane* Hermes. The association of Hermes Trismegistus with stoicism was not unnatural at this time: for a summary of the Renaissance conception of him, see Baldwin's *A Treatice of Morall Philosophy* (1575), Book I, ch. xxv. The 'sayings' of Hermes are cited freely in *florilegia* like Baldwin's under such headings as 'Patience', 'Wrath', 'Wisdom' and 'Sorrow'.

41/6. *That thus stand lost in all thinges but Election.* Greville's theory of 'the elect', like his view of 'hypocrisie', has to be understood from his own definition of it in this treatise, and from his allusions elsewhere (*A Treatie of Warres*, st. 59–60; *Humane Learning*, st. 64, 128–31). His view of mankind as 'lost in all thinges but Election' indicates that he did not take the Calvinist view of man as predestined to eternal salvation or reprobation: the elect are rather those who choose to accept God's calling (43/1–2), who are regenerated through his grace (44/1–4), and persevere in faith and works (45–46, 56). They constitute the 'Church invisible' (63–67), as distinct from the 'outward Church'.

56/2. *censure*: judge, estimate.

59/3. *sinnes middle wall*: recalling the epistle to the Ephesians, formerly 'aliens from the common wealth of Israel', now 'made nigh' by Christ: 'For hee is our peace, who hath made both one, and hath broken downe the middle wall of partition betweene us' (Eph. ii. 12–14).

60/1. *his* Egypt *wonders here he doth exceed*: i.e. by acting directly on the heart, and not through other agents.

61/1. *to the harts of sinne*: the *1670* variant ('into sinners hearts') is one of those yielding an equivalent sense, but phrased in a more obvious way (cf. 51/4, 74/6).

73/6. *their proceedinge might*: i.e. the might that 'proceeds' from them.

75/3. *But can the flesh assume it selfe in these*: i.e. can the flesh take these things (imitation of Christ and his forgiveness) upon itself (*O.E.D.* assume, 5b)? Compare the argument of *Caelica*, lxxxix, ll. 7–18 ('The flesh is dead before grace can be borne').

76/7. *Why God commanded more then man could doo.* This recalls, at some distance, the dilemma felt in the Chorus Sacerdotum in *Mustapha*:

> Is it the marke, or Majesty of Power
> To make offences that it may forgive?
> Nature herselfe, doth her owne selfe defloure,
> To hate those errors she her selfe doth give.

Now the outcome of the discussion is a warning against presumption.

81/6. *as good and evill be.* For this view of good and evil as 'partakers of Eternitie', cf. *Humane Learning* st. 103 and *A Letter to an Honorable Lady* (Grosart, iv. 291). The *1670* reading ('as good or ill they be') is a misguided effort to improve the sense.

92/5. *our Cathedrall chayres.* This attack on the episcopate, with the censure of the Church in st. 30–31, 68–69, helps to explain the suppression of the treatise in 1633.

# INDEX OF NAMES

PRINTED IN GREAT BRITAIN
AT THE UNIVERSITY PRESS, OXFORD
BY VIVIAN RIDLER
PRINTER TO THE UNIVERSITY